The Art of Drawing Anatomy

DRAWING CLASS

The Art of Drawing Anatomy

Project and Publication by
PARRAMÓN EDICIONES, S.A.

Editorial Director
MARÍA FERNANDA CANAL

Editor
TOMÀS UBACH

Editorial Assistant and Picture Archivist
M. CARMEN RAMOS

Text
DAVID SANMIGUEL

Drawings and Exercises
MERCEDES GASPAR
ÓSCAR SANCHÍS
DAVID SANMIGUEL

Series Design
JOSEP GUASCH

Design and Layout
ESTUDI GUASCH, S.L.

Photography
NOS & SOTO

Production Director
RAFAEL MARFIL

Production
MANEL SÁNCHEZ

Prepress
PACMER, S.A.

Translated from Spanish by
MICHAEL BRUNELLE AND BEATRIZ CORTABARRIA

Library of Congress Cataloging-in-Publication Data Available

10 9 8 7 6 5 4 3 2 1

Published in 2008 by Sterling Publishing Co., Inc.
387 Park Avenue South, New York, NY 10016

A company of Grupo Editorial Norma de América Latina www.parramon.com
Published originally in Spanish under the title *Dibujo de Anatomía Artística*.

Distributed in Canada by Sterling Publishing
c/o Canadian Manda Group, 165 Dufferin Street
Toronto, Ontario, Canada M6K 3H6
Distributed in the United Kingdom by GMC Distribution Services
Castle Place, 166 High Street, Lewes, East Sussex, England BN7 1XU
Distributed in Australia by Capricorn Link (Australia) Pty. Ltd.
P.O. Box 704, Windsor, NSW 2756, Australia

Sterling ISBN-13: 978-1-4027-5517-0
ISBN-10: 1-4027-5517-1

For information about custom editions, special sales, premium and corporate purchases, please contact Sterling Special Sales Department at 800-805-5489 or specialsales@sterlingpub.com.

The Art of Drawing Anatomy

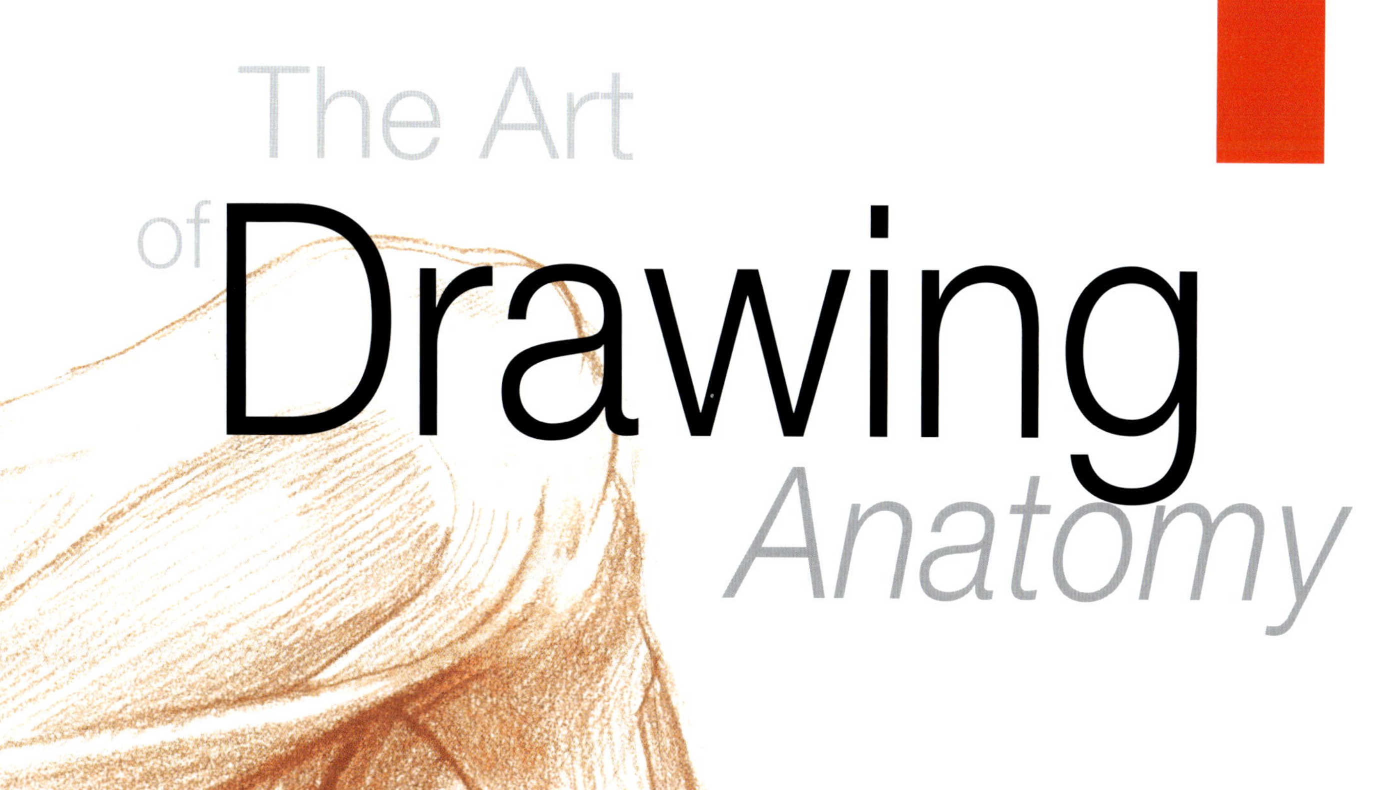

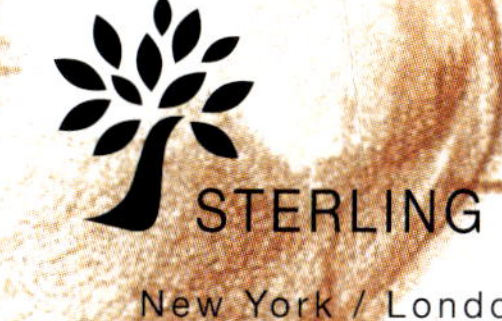

New York / London
www.sterlingpublishing.com

Con-tents

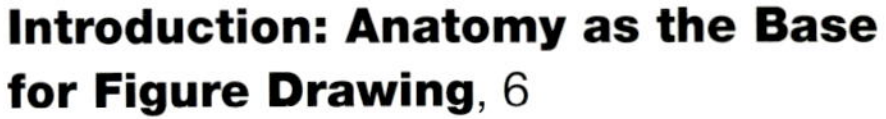

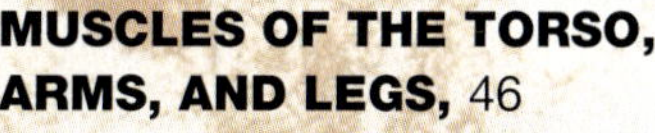

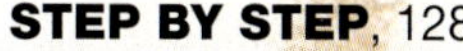

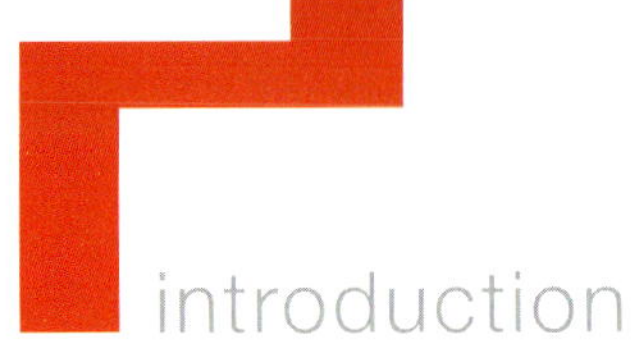

Anatomy as the Base for Figure Drawing

Art and science follow different paths, but there was a time when the problems of both fields came together in one common area and science and art collaborated in the great advances of learning. During the Renaissance, the consensus was that any idea, no matter how sublime, could be represented with the nude figure. Humanists showed artists the secrets of the body's proportions and anatomy: Science, art, and technique were intertwined. Nowadays, there is little common area left between art and science; however, the human figure is still at the center of any creative activity, and anatomy constitutes the most effective method for understanding the structure and the movement of the body's limbs. And although the artist cannot make a beautiful drawing solely with the knowledge of anatomy, it must always be present in his or her mind because, in the end, it is necessary.

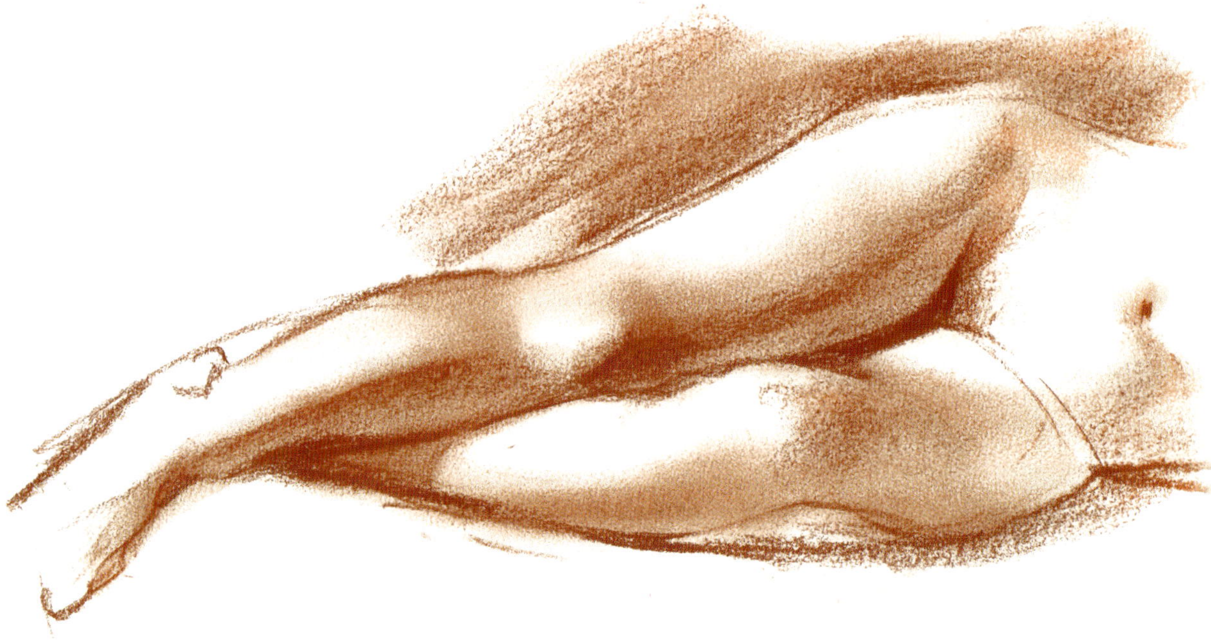

Figure drawing combines the objective knowledge of bones and muscles with the particular skills of the act of drawing.

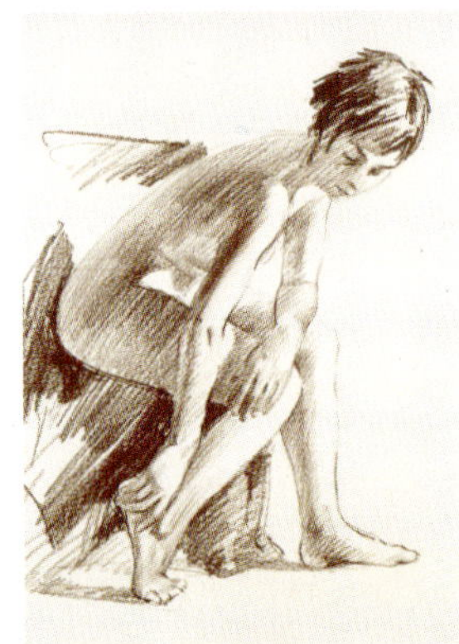

This book clearly and precisely presents the knowledge and steps required for correctly representing a nude figure. All the anatomical explanations are illustrated in detail, and each concept is put into practice through sequences of drawings studied step by step. In this book, the reader will see each aspect of anatomy put into practice immediately as examples in many works of art.

These are the best testimony of how art fully profits from the science of the human body.

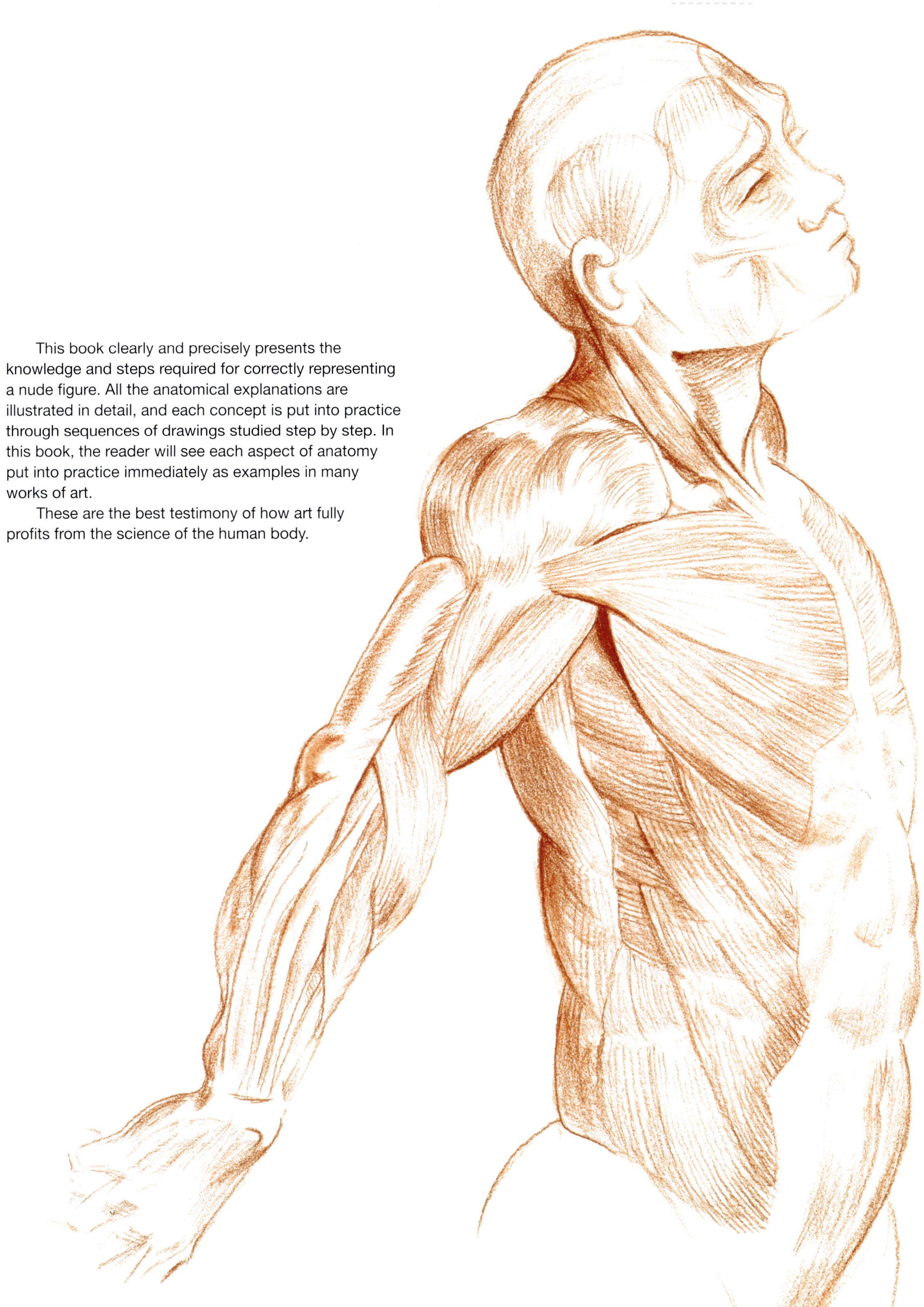

Drawing the Nude and Drawing Anat-omy

"MICHELANGELO USED TO DRAW FIGURES THAT WERE NINE, TEN, AND TWELVE HEADS TALL. LOOKING FOR A HARMONY THAT IS NOT FOUND IN NATURE HE USED TO SAY THAT ONE SHOULD HAVE THE MEASURE IN THE GAZE AND NOT IN THE HAND."
Giorgio Vasari (1511-1574)

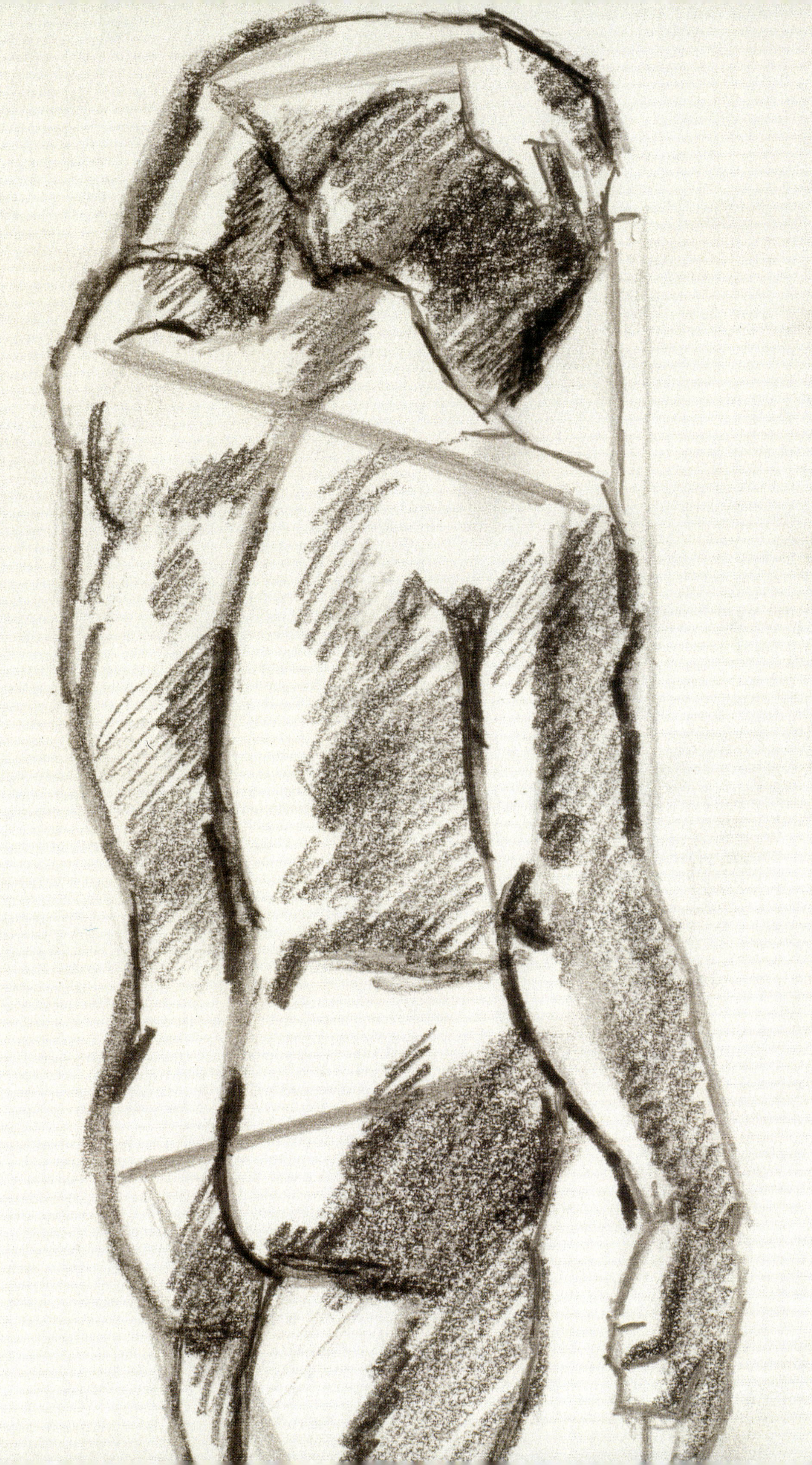

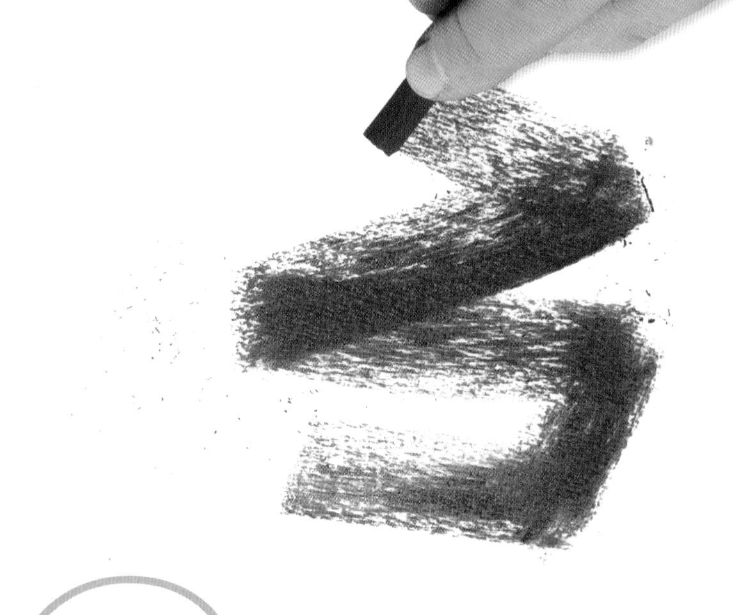

General Concepts

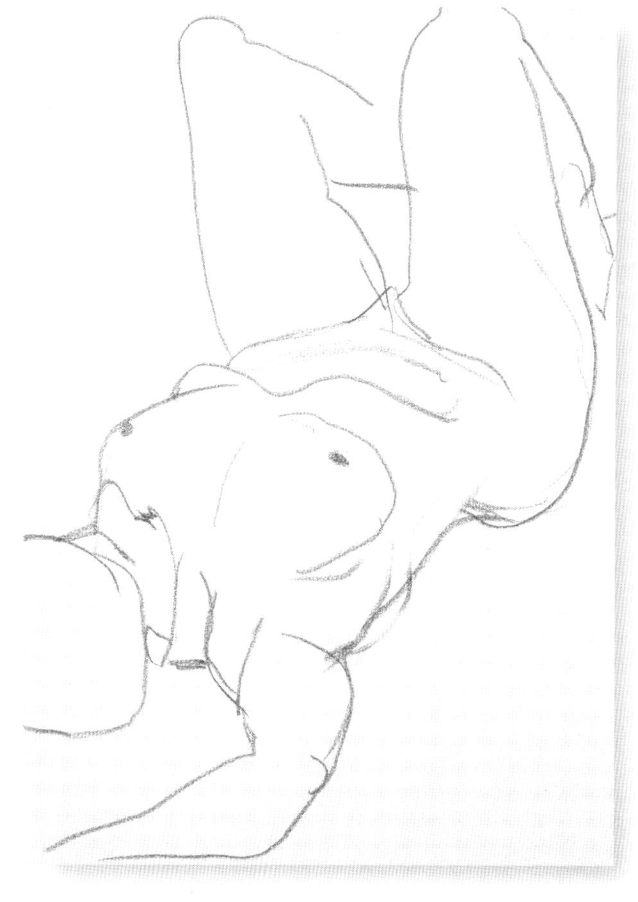

DAVID SANMIGUEL. MODEL RECLINING, 2003.
PENCIL ON PAPER

# of Anatomy.

Anatomy and the proportion of the human body are two factors that are always interrelated.

Detailed knowledge of anatomy is related more to science than to art, but it is only when knowledge about anatomy comes into play with true artistic expression that we can begin talking about figure drawing. However, knowledge of human proportions alone without taking concepts of anatomy into account inevitably causes errors and mistakes in the execution of the piece. In this first part of the book, we will study the factors that pertain to the proportionate distribution of the body's masses.

Elements for Drawing Anatomy

For artists, knowledge of anatomy must always go hand in hand with the constant practice of figure drawing. This practice can be carried out with very different models, two-dimensional or three-dimensional. The most immediate and accessible are pictures of nude or dressed figures, but there are many others that are even more useful.

PRINTS AND PHOTOGRAPHS

Books about drawing anatomy have many useful models that artists can carefully reproduce. This practice is vital, because the drawing of a model offers many more keypoints for copying than a photograph or a real model can. Drawings always highlight the important factors and clearly show the graphic solutions.

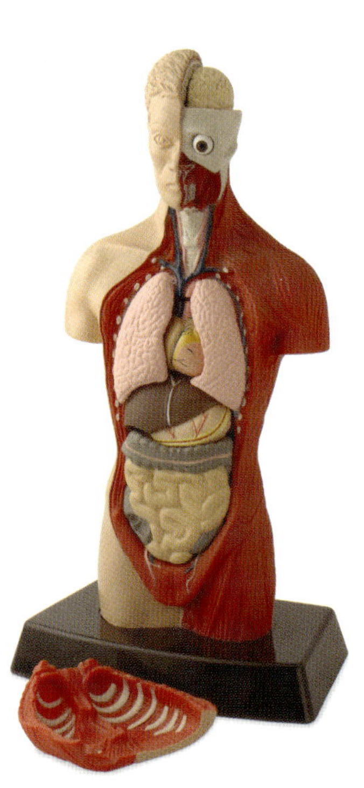

Three-dimensional models of anatomy are easier to understand. They constitute a primary and useful aid in certain cases.

Articulated skeletons make the complete and detailed study of the distribution of the bones possible; the downside is that they tend to be quite expensive and bulky.

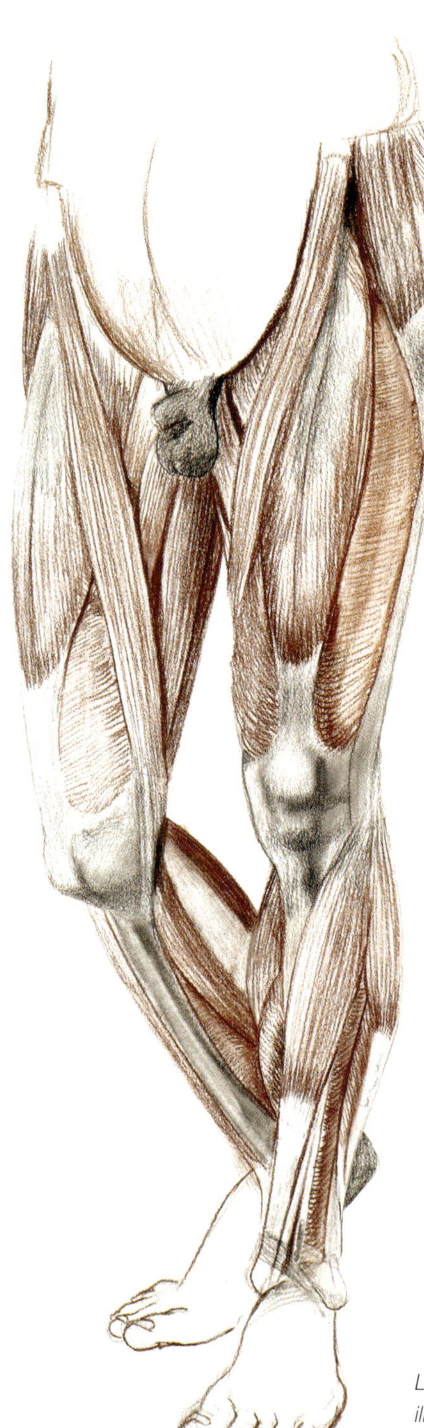

Laminated anatomical illustrations (similar to the illustrations shown in this book) provide a clear and detailed view of muscle distribution.

Wooden articulated hands are excellent models to practice drawing this complex part of the anatomy.

THREE-DIMENSIONAL FIGURES

The great advantage of three-dimensional figures (artists' mannequins, articulated or not) is the very many perspectives offered for drawing and the fact that they can be used with different types of lighting. The great artists of classical periods (Tintoretto and Poussin, among many others) used wax mannequins that they had made themselves to study the composition of their great works of art. There are articulated mannequins in different sizes that are especially designed for artwork, as well as heads and articulated hands for the same purpose. Some articulated toys are also very useful, as we will see throughout these pages.

DRAWING FROM A LIFE MODEL

This is the ideal option, but they are accessible only at art schools and centers. Drawing from a life model has no comparison and cannot be substituted by any other method: It constitutes the best study of anatomy for the artist, and it is the culmination of his or her learning process.

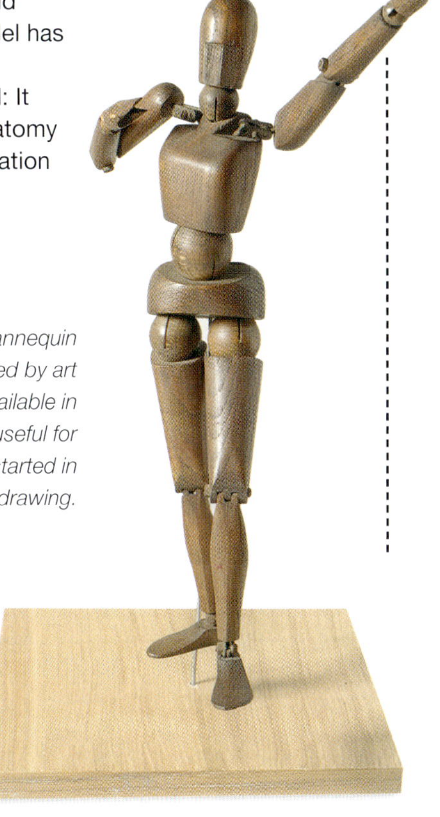

The wooden articulated mannequin is a device commonly used by art students. They are available in small sizes, which can be useful for those who are getting started in figure drawing.

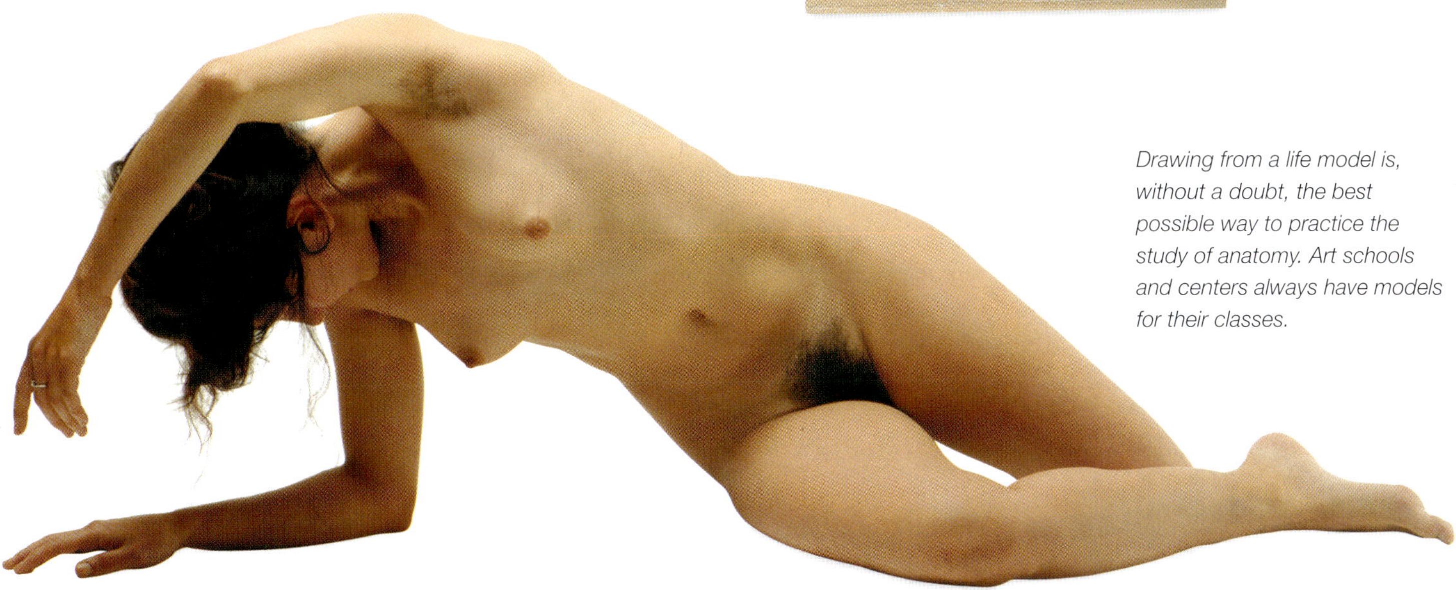

Drawing from a life model is, without a doubt, the best possible way to practice the study of anatomy. Art schools and centers always have models for their classes.

Proportions of the Human Body

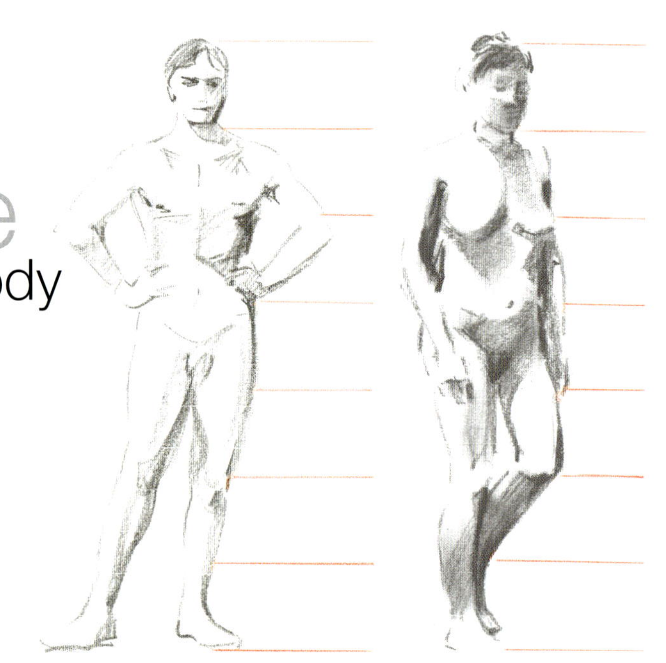

During many art periods it was believed that the responsibility of the artist was to represent figures according to a fixed idea about beauty, and that that idea could be formulated through objective guidelines. This belief gave way to the canons of proportions that stipulated the height and proportions of beautifully built bodies. Nowadays, these principles are not followed blindly by artists, but they continue to be a useful reference for successfully approaching figure drawing.

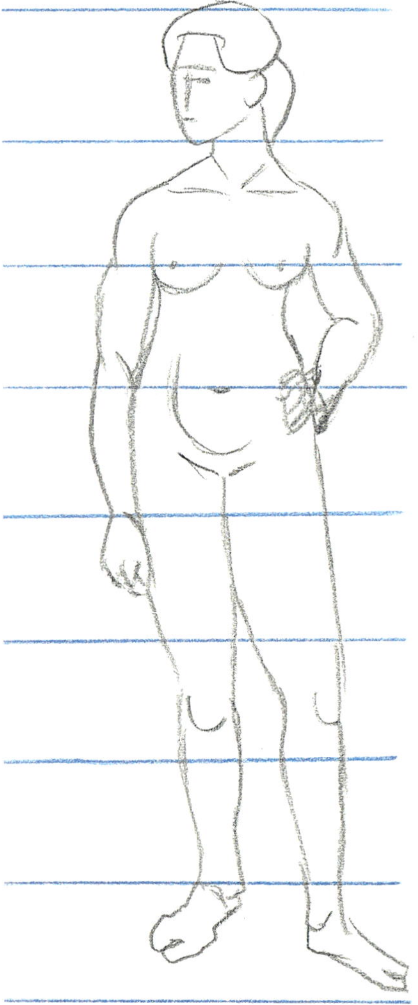

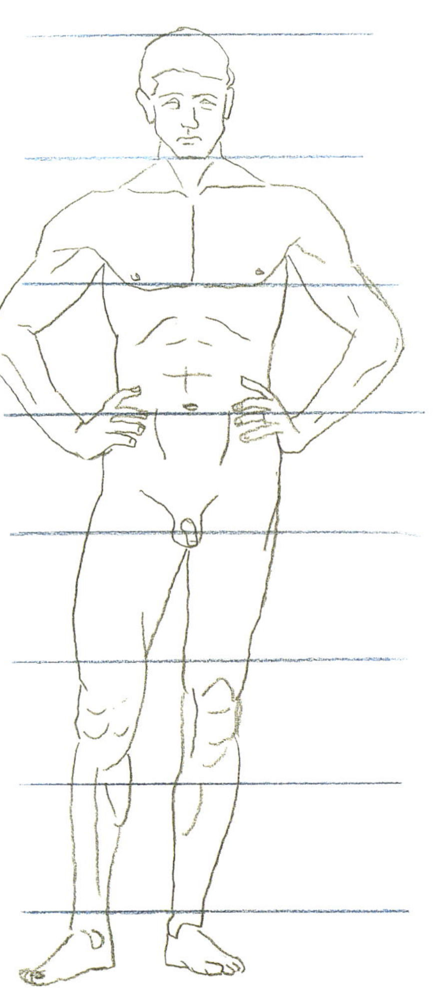

Most of the figures that we find in the real world do not extend beyond a height of seven heads. This makes them less thin but more convincing from a realistic point of view.

Tradition establishes the canonical height for figures at seven and a half heads, for either males or females. In certain idealized representations, height can reach eight heads.

THE CANON OF PROPORTIONS

The canon of proportions establishes the dimensions of each body part in a way that makes the figure harmonious and correctly composed. Our sense of proportion is based on the idea of harmonious relationships of all the parts of the body. The idealized classical canon dictates a height of eight heads, but in real life we can see that the proportion of seven and a half heads is more natural. From the many possible patterns, this is the most useful one for drawing figures that are well proportioned and not too stylized.

RELATIONSHIP BETWEEN BODY DIMENSIONS

The harmonious proportion of a seven-head figure affects the overall proportion of the entire body. Ideally, the total height of the figure fits exactly inside a circle with the center in the pubic area; and the two resulting halves fit into their own circles whose centers are located in the sternum and at the top of the patella, respectively. The total height is the same as the total width of the figure with the arms extended; the center of this width is located between the two clavicles, and each one of these two new circles has its center on the elbow.

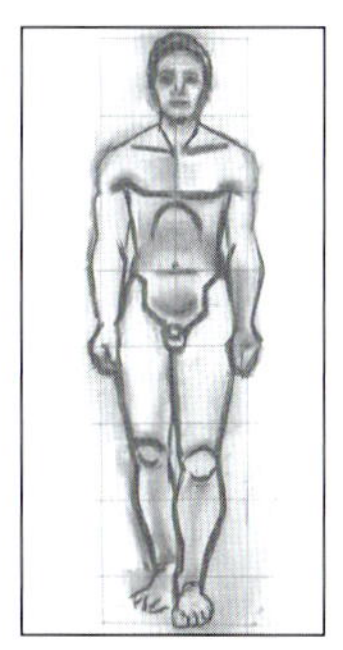

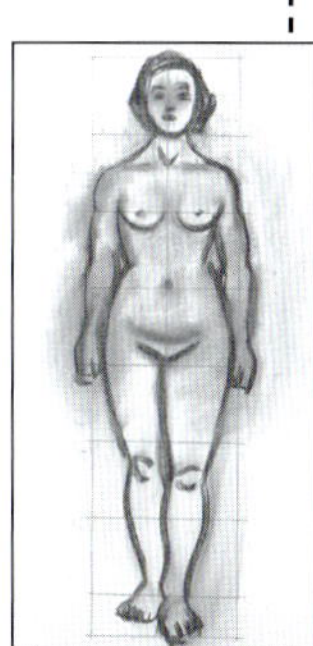

Drawing by memory is a good way to practice. We can use charcoal or any other medium and use seven and a half modules high by two wide as a pattern.

The geometric center of a well-proportioned body is located in the pubic area. Each one of the halves of the body's length is half the distance from one end of the arm to the other when they are both extended..

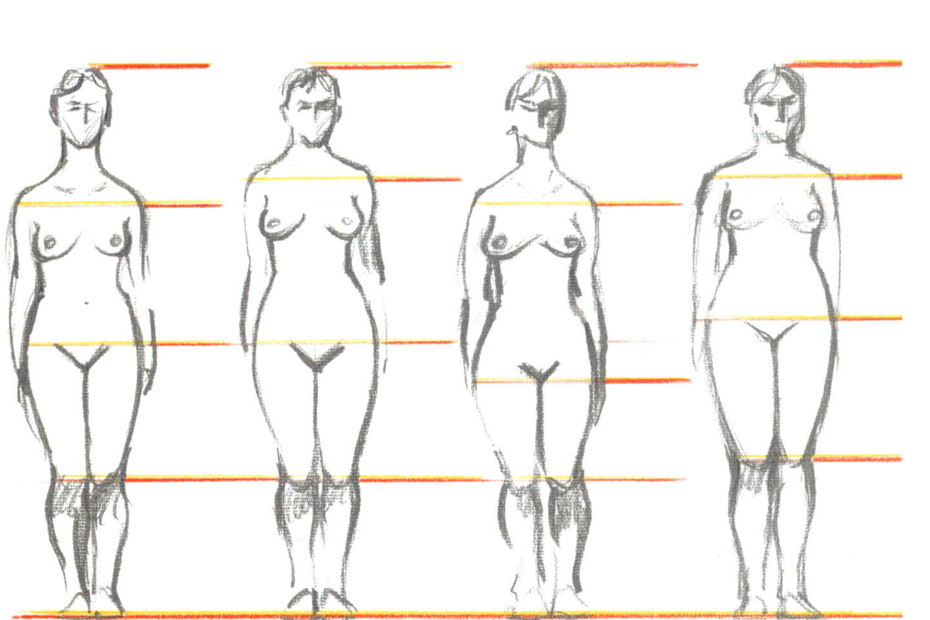

By dividing the body into four modules with breaks at the shoulders, hips, and knees, we can see how the figures, having the same height, have different proportions between modules without causing any problems anatomically.

Formulas for Constructing the Figure

To plan an anatomical drawing correctly, the artist must approach the human body as if it were a piece of architecture made of harmonious parts. This not only facilitates the drawing of the figure but also guarantees the correct proportion of the final drawing. It would be a mistake to draw a figure by copying all its details systematically, one after the other. The correct approach is to incorporate such details into generic forms or into reference lines that provide an overall view of the entire figure from the beginning. This way, it is much easier to keep refining the shapes and the forms and to introduce all the necessary corrections as the work progresses.

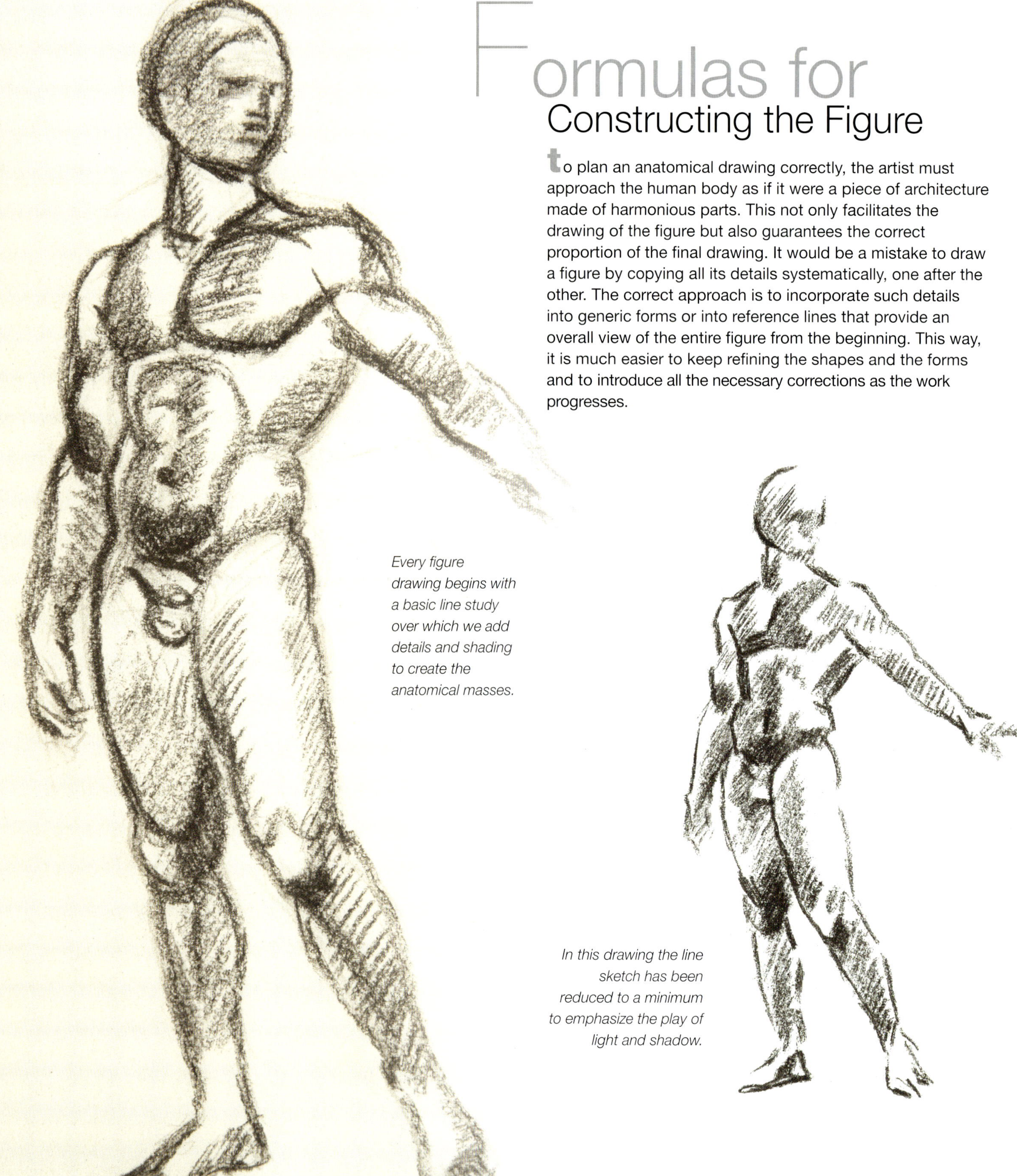

Every figure drawing begins with a basic line study over which we add details and shading to create the anatomical masses.

In this drawing the line sketch has been reduced to a minimum to emphasize the play of light and shadow.

USEFUL GUIDELINES

There is no single formula for constructing a figure. Each artist uses his or her own guidelines, the ones that best fit his or her own way of working. Generally, artists who give great relevance to the line use references based on the axes of movement, while those who tend to emphasize light and shadow contrasts normally use modules or blocks, simple volumetric pieces that suggest the overall volume of the anatomy from the onset of the work.

TESTING DIFFERENT METHODS

It is a good idea to test the usefulness of various methods for drawing the same figure. This is the only way the artist will know which one of them best conforms to his or her style or way of working. The idea is always to choose the least problematic solution, one that facilitates the work rather than makes it more difficult.

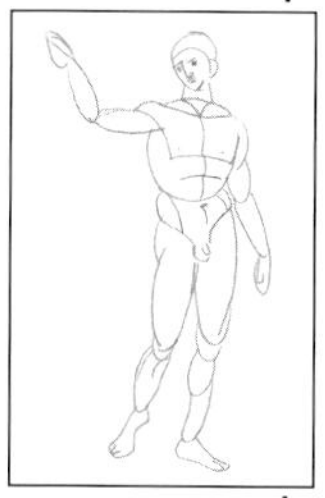

It does not matter which method is used to construct the figure if the result is pleasing and proportionate overall.

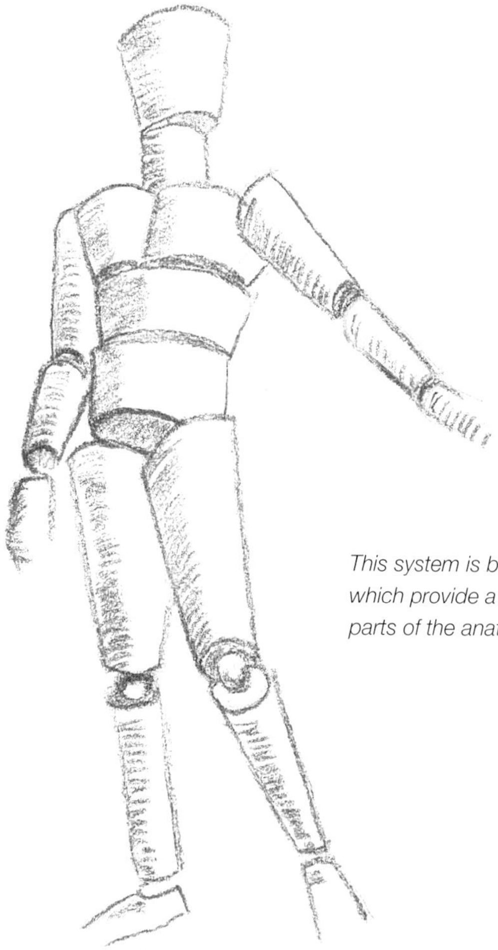

This system is based on the use of cylinders, which provide a systematic view of the basic parts of the anatomy.

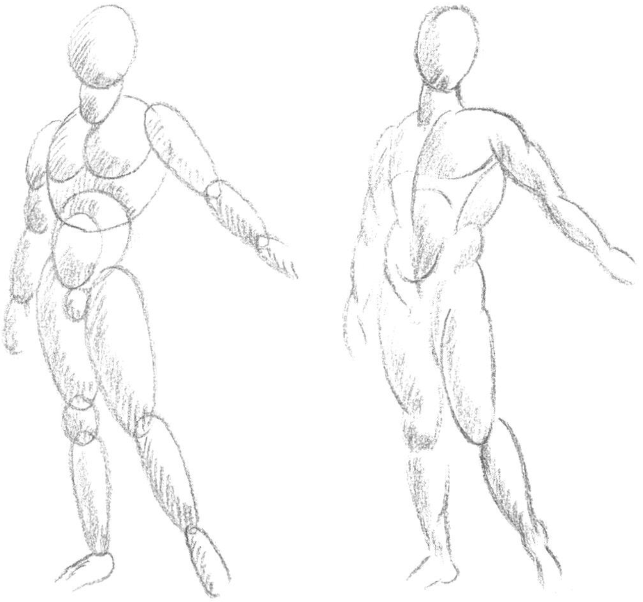

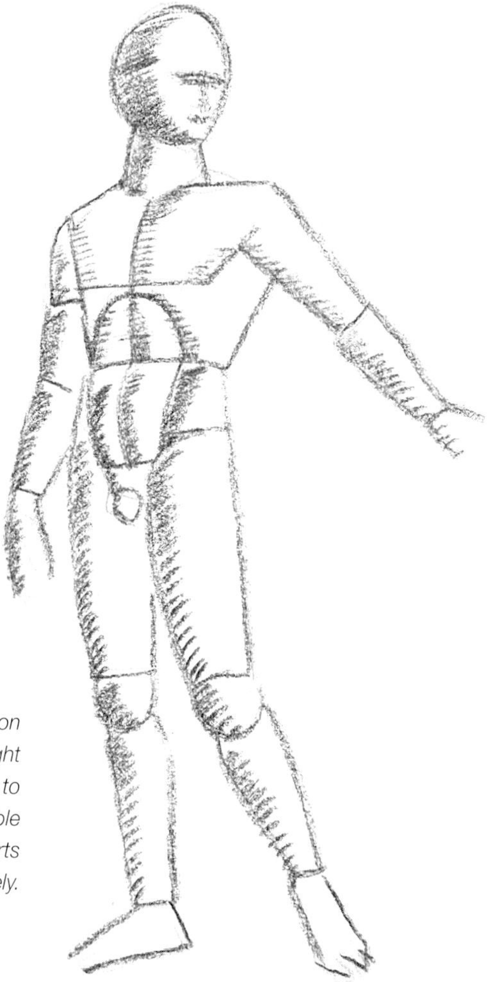

The methods based on flat shapes with straight sides are very simple to use and make it possible to adjust all the parts proportionately.

Using ovals is very helpful for understanding the basic volume groups of anatomy.

Constructing with Axes

This schematic approach to drawing consists of establishing the axes of the figure's movement as a preliminary step to drawing. The axes are the axis of the torso, the axes of the arms, and the axes of the legs. The axes of the torso extend from the head to the pubic area, and their possible flexion points are located in the neck, the chest, and the waist. These axes are all vertical, running through the body lengthwise. To establish the width, the artist can use transversal axes that connect the previous ones. There are two vital transversal axes: the shoulders and the hips. Both can swing up or down depending on the pose and can vary in size depending on the areas seen in perspective.

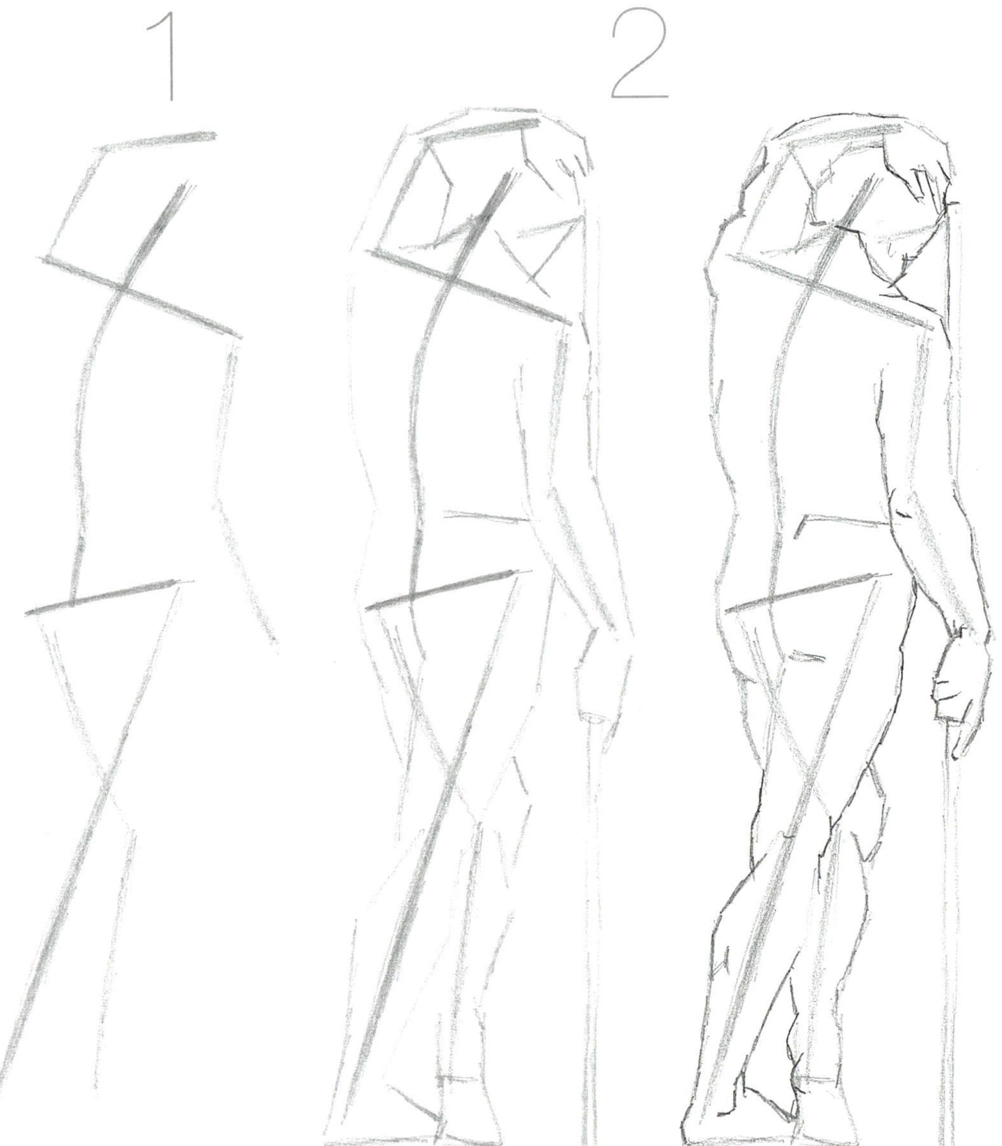

1. These are the basic axes for any pose: the axis for the neck and head, the axis for the torso (spinal column), and the axes for the arms and legs. These lines must be articulated starting at the axes of the shoulders and the hips.

2. The contours of the figures should be sketched very lightly, following the direction and angle of the basic axes.

3. Each new line must define a fold, a mass, or a turn of the different parts of the figure.

BALANCING THE AXES

In general, in most standing figures, the axis of the shoulders moves in an opposite direction to the hips: If the right shoulder is up, the right hip is down, and vice versa. These transversal axes also mark the position and the direction of the basic forms of the torso and the arms. Once this line structure is drawn, the basic characteristic lines of the different parts of the anatomy can be drawn around each axis. Then the muscles are added over these flat forms to continue drawing until the figure is finished.

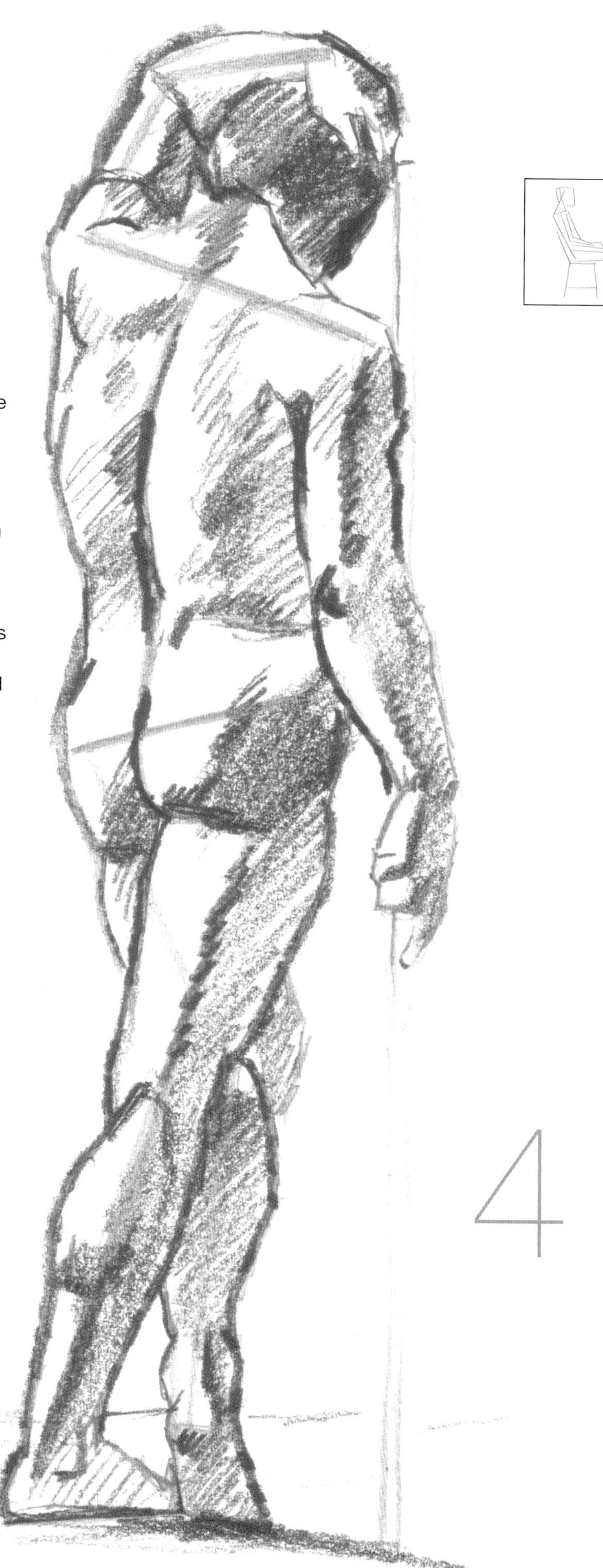

4. Representing the volumes with shading is the last phase of the work, and it is based completely on the previous line structure.

The drawing of the figure's axes makes it possible to capture the essence of its position in synthesis before studying the anatomical characteristics of the model. A few lines are usually sufficient.

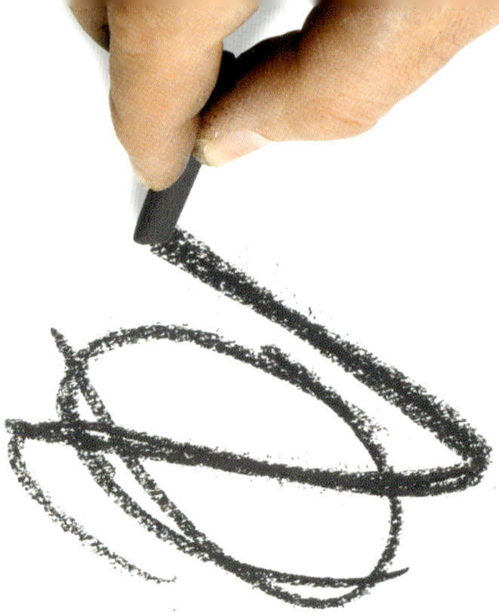

Constructing with Modules

Modules are shapes, normally rectangles, that define different parts of the anatomy: The longest ones can suggest the arms and the legs, while the square ones can be used for drawing the torso. These modules separate the joints from each other: the shoulders, the neck, the elbows, the waist, the inner thighs, and the knees. A very complete structure can be drawn with just a dozen or so of these modules. The challenge lies in establishing the correct proportion of each module and in the articulation of each with all the others. If these factors are worked out from the beginning, drawing the figure will be extremely easy.

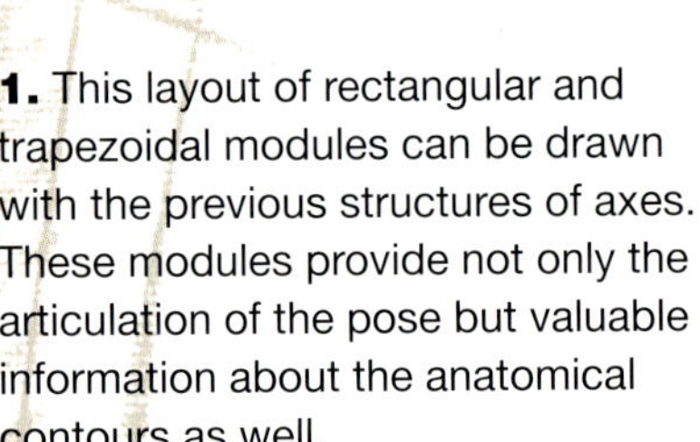

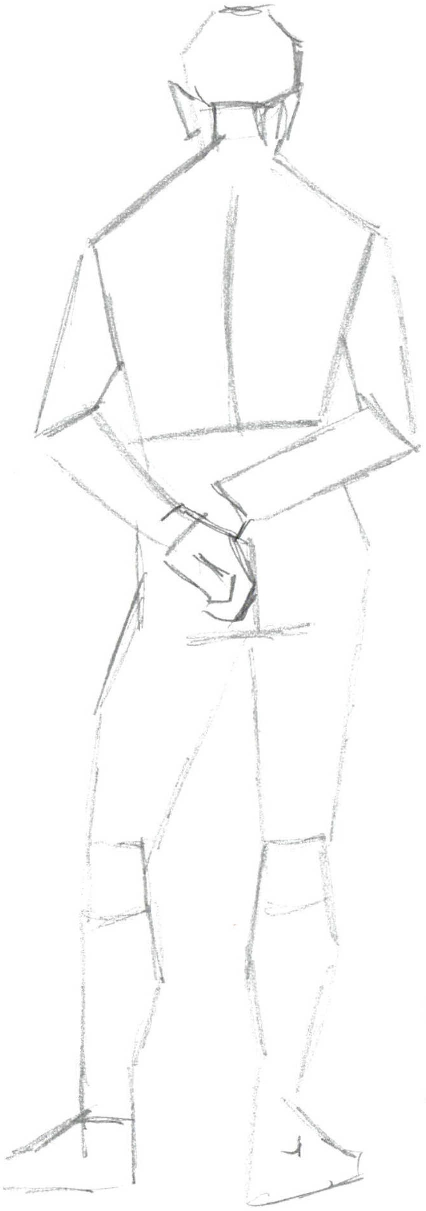

1. This layout of rectangular and trapezoidal modules can be drawn with the previous structures of axes. These modules provide not only the articulation of the pose but valuable information about the anatomical contours as well.

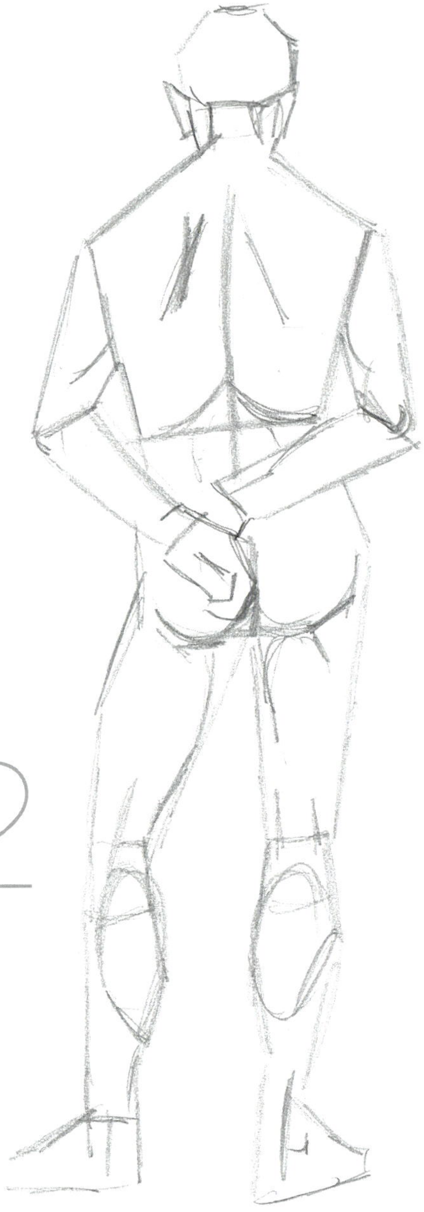

2. The modular structure is enriched with anatomical notations that are increasingly precise and that reveal the characteristic anatomy of the figure.

3

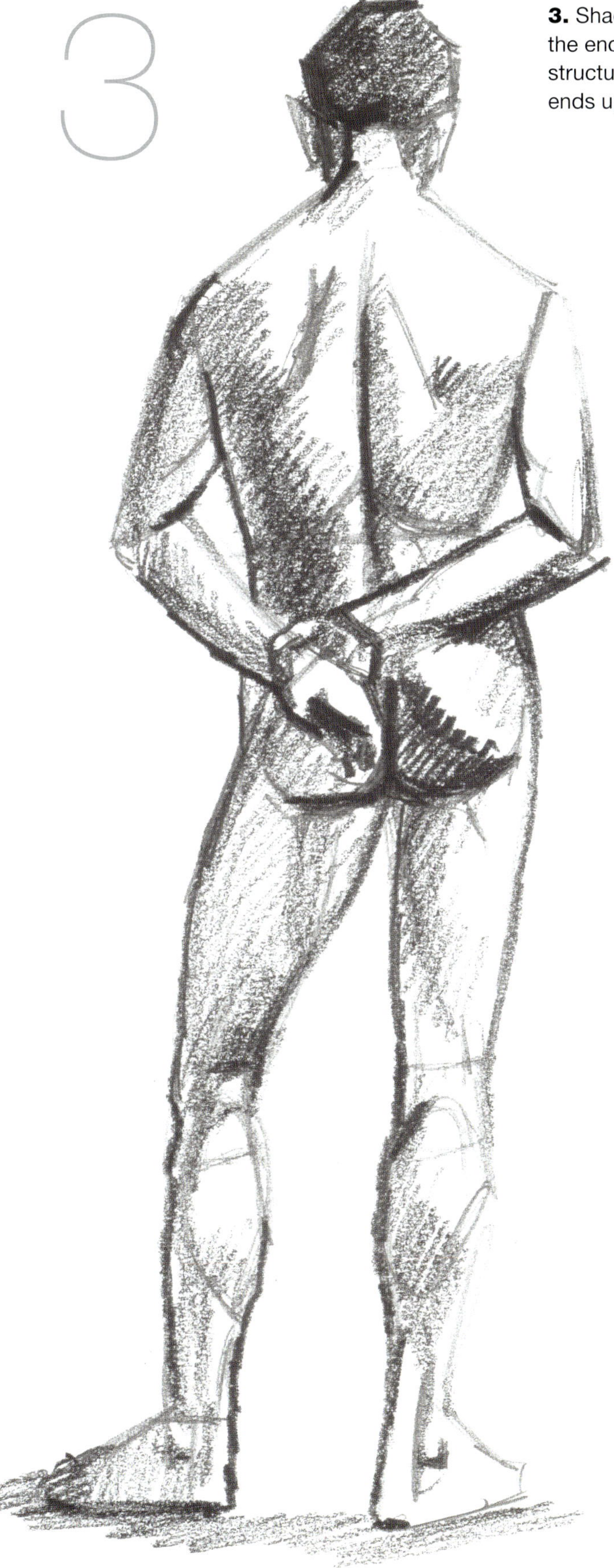

3. Shading should always be left for the end because shading over structures that lack precision inevitably ends up ruining the drawing.

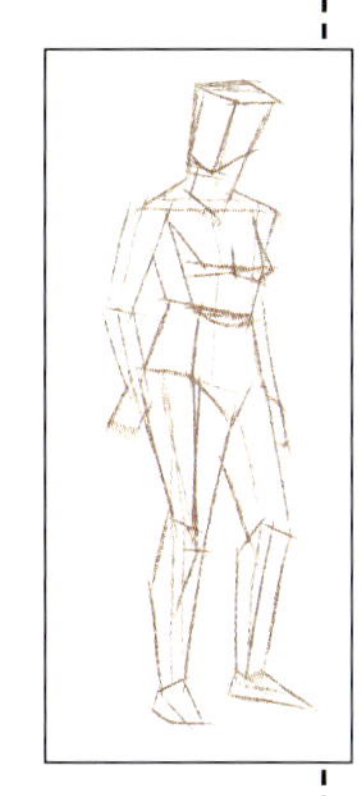

The modular structure does not necessarily have to be flat: the modules can be articulated prisms that approximate the pose. This is a preliminary three-dimensional modular diagram for the female figure represented in these pages.

OTHER TYPES OF MODULES

The advantage of rectangular modules is that they indicate the direction of the figure's movement clearly; besides, they are easy to draw. However, these are not the only modules available; oval modules, which suggest the volume of the anatomy much better and connect with each other much better as well, can also be used. Both types of modules can even be combined in more complex structures to depict difficult poses. In either case, the structure must resolve all the problems related to the figure's proportions and movement before one proceeds with anatomical representation itself.

If we use three-dimensional modules, shading can be integrated from the beginning of the drawing process.

1

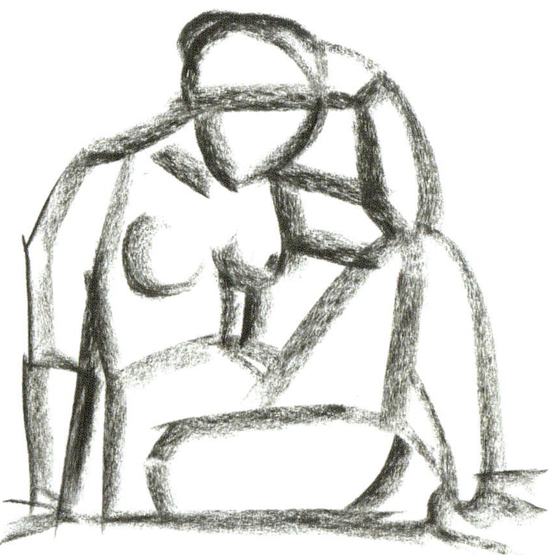

Synthesis
with Line

Anatomical modules, or blocks, are one of the many possibilities for constructing a figure. In fact, the same initial diagram can be a structure for constructing the figure, or it can be the final drawing. Ultimately, adapting the diagrammatic shapes to the particulars of the figure can end up producing a true work of art. In such a case, we can call it a synthesis of the anatomical form rather than a representational diagram. Thanks to synthesis, we can obtain a satisfactory result that resolves all the technical questions in a simple and elegant manner.

1. Using the tip of a stick of charcoal, we make a quick sketch that lacks anatomical details but that is well proportioned.

2. We erase the first diagram with a clean cotton rag. A trace of the drawing will always remain on the paper that is sufficiently light to allow us to draw a figure with more precision than by working with the darker lines.

2

THREE-DIMENSIONAL FORMS

The method proposed for sketching the figure is based on lines and the two-dimensional shapes that result in figures indicated by contours and outlines. To achieve a closer representation of the volumes of the human figure, it is possible to introduce diagrams that suggest three-dimensionality. These should be based on curved lines rather than straight lines because the former suggest the roundness of the figure more accurately. The brief sketch shown on these pages suggests the use of a basic foundation using simple curves (ovals, parabolas, and so forth). The idea is to suggest the thickness of each anatomical area by using one or several of those curved forms following the initial calculation of proportions and dimensions and without attempting any modeling or shading technique for the volumes. Once this simple method has been understood and practiced, it will be possible for the artist to interpret any pose by using a wide range of lines and forms, from which he or she will be able to choose the most appropriate for each particular case.

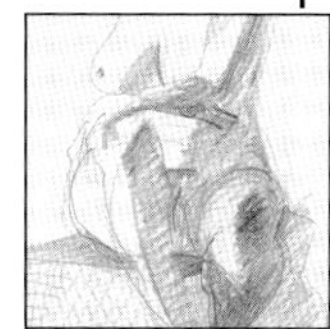

3

Drawing sketches is a required skill for the figure-drawing artist. It requires knowledge of human anatomy, and it allows drawing figures spontaneously, with emphasis on an overall pleasing structure rather than on conventional anatomy.

3. This line sketch can be perfectly valid as a drawing since all the important anatomical features of the figure are implicit and resolved.

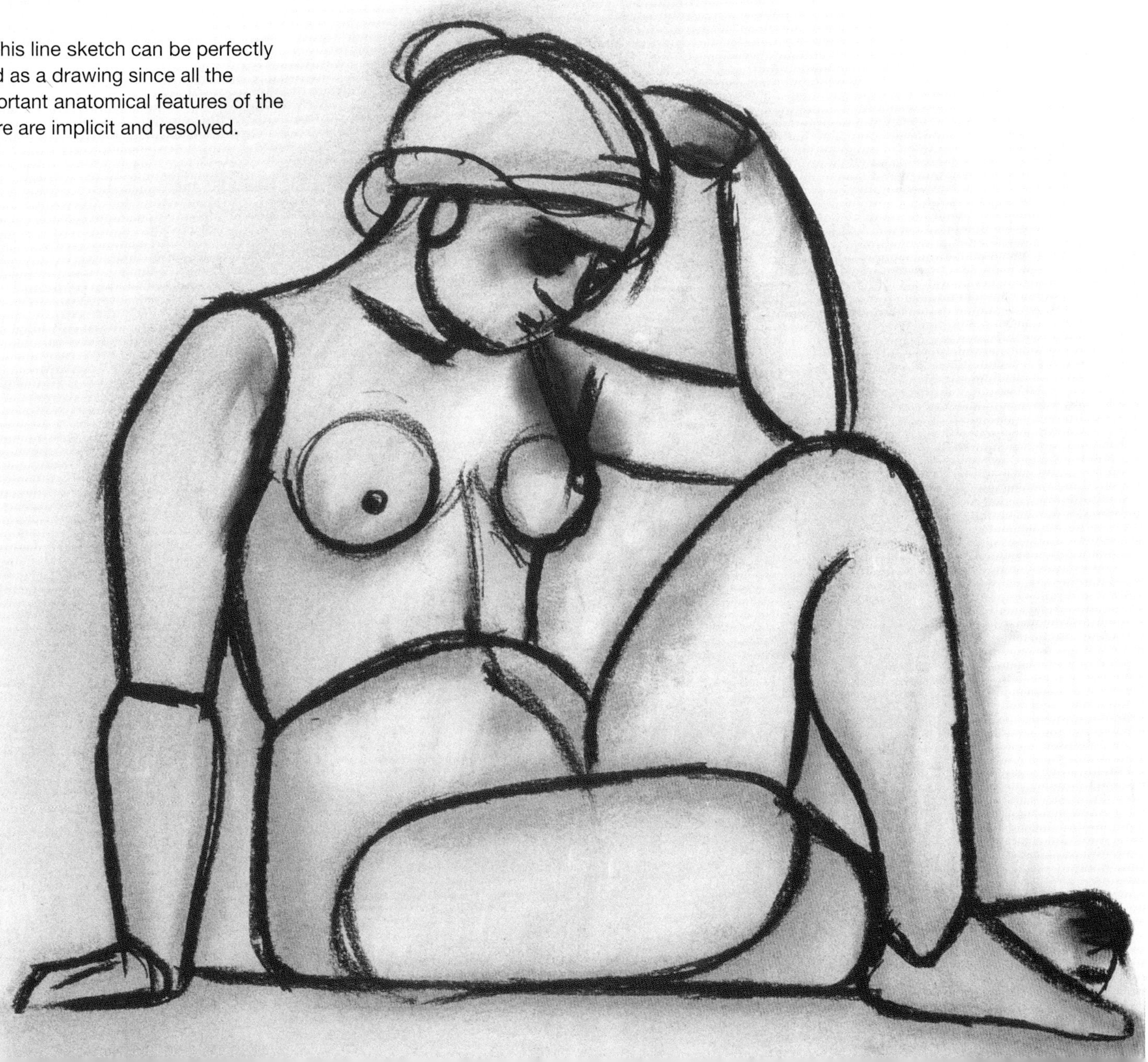

The Skeleton and the

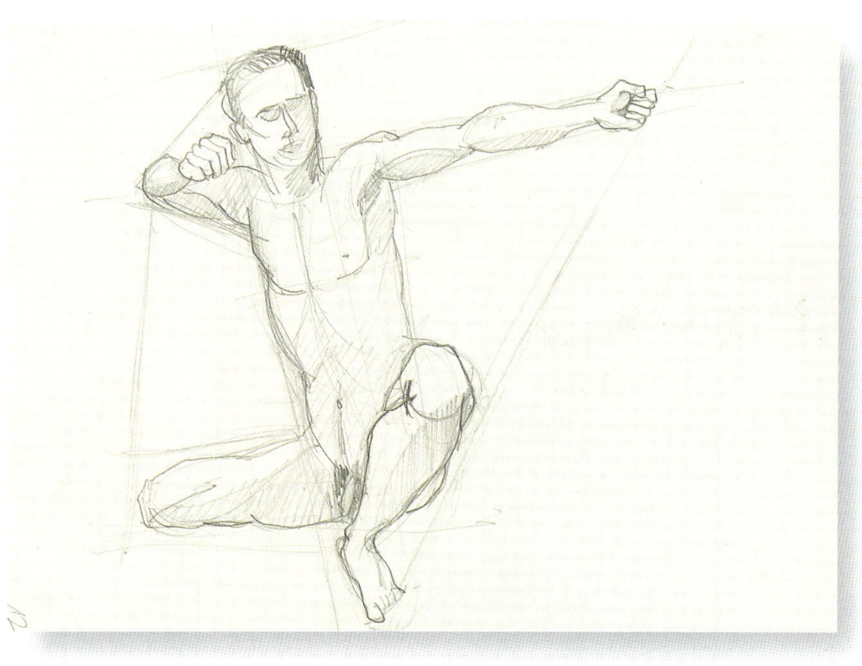

MUNTSA CALBÓ, *FIGURE, 1990.*
PENCIL ON PAPER

Muscles.

For the artist,

it is more important

to have an overall vision, even if it is a basic one, of the bone and muscle structure than to have a very detailed but incomplete knowledge of certain aspects of the skeleton and the muscles. A correct overview facilitates the synthesis of a drawing and makes it possible to draw the anatomy more in depth over a sound base. The idea of this chapter is to give the reader that conceptual base.

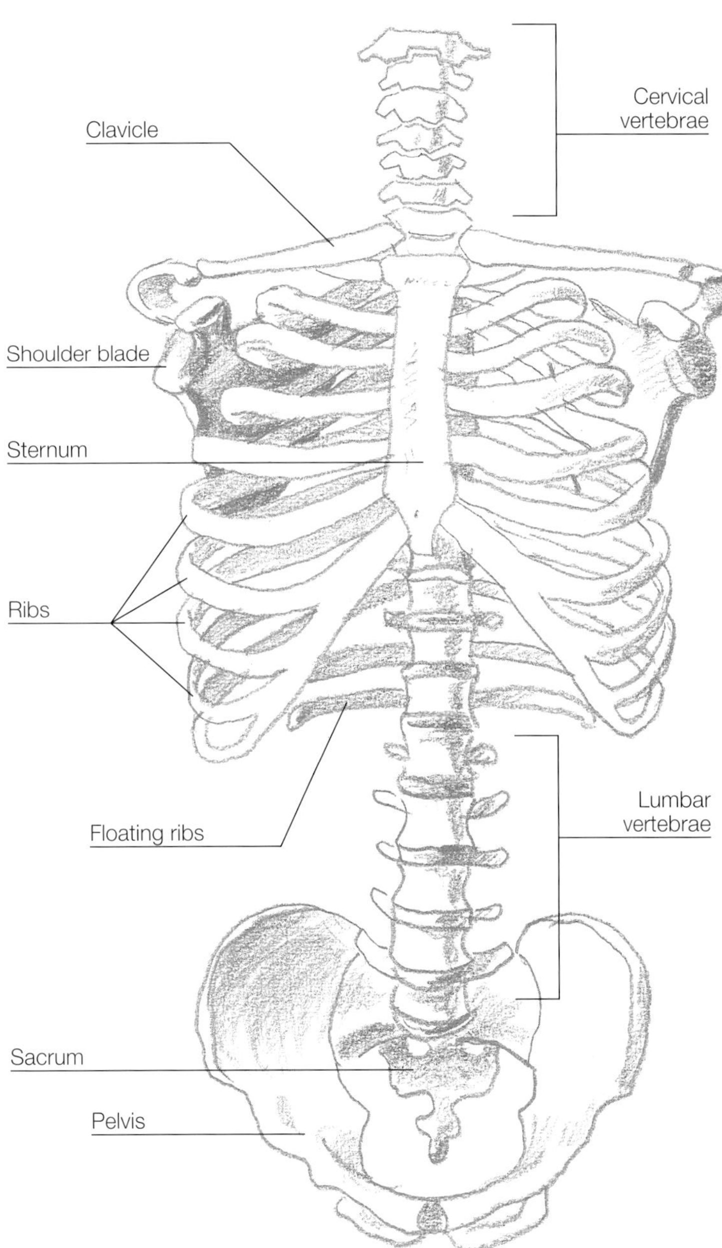

Anterior view of the torso.

The skeleton is a jointed bone structure that suspends the human body and supports and protects the internal organs. Almost all 233 bones that form the skeleton are jointed and serve as the base for muscle traction. Most of the bones are found in pairs (to the left and to the right of the body's centerline); the bones that are the exception to this rule, such as the cranium, the pelvis, and the vertebrae, are formed by two symmetrical halves

Parts of the Skeleton

BONES OF THE TORSO

The torso is the central part of the body. The bones of the torso are those that form the thoracic cavity, the clavicles, the shoulder blades or scapulas, the spinal column, and the pelvis.

THE THORACIC CAGE

This is formed by pairs of ribs lined up at both sides of the sternum. The ten pairs of upper ribs and the large pectoral muscles are attached to the sternum. The two lower pairs of ribs are not attached and are called floating, or false, ribs.

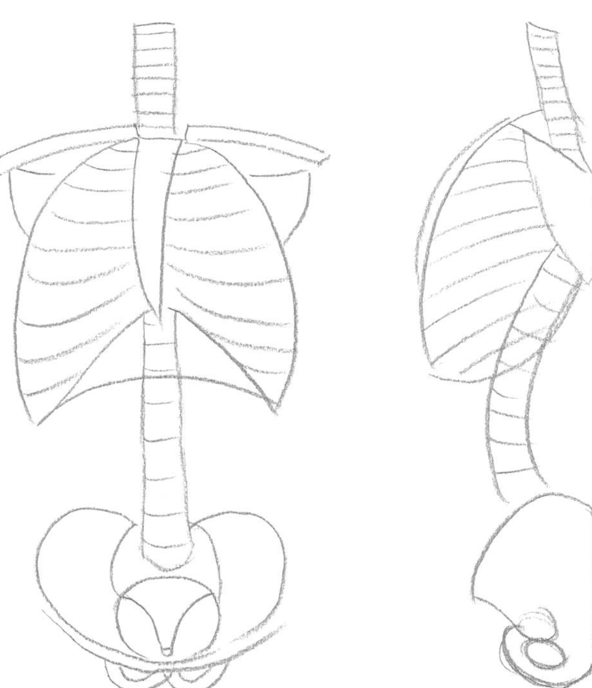

Useful diagrams for drawing the skeletal torso.

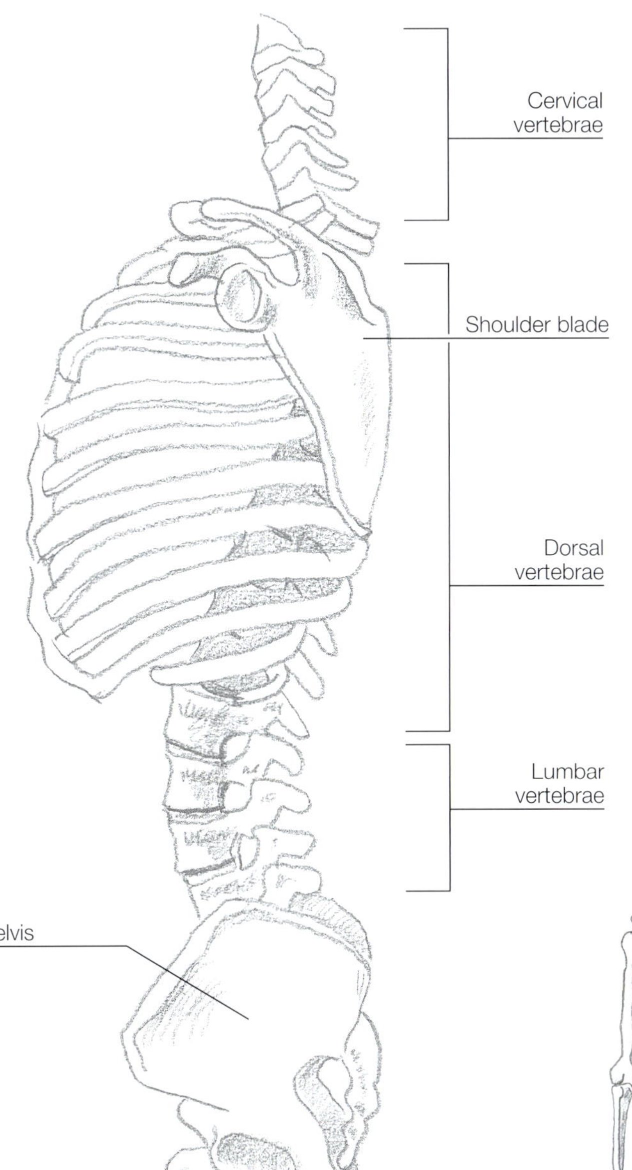

Side view of the torso.

THE CLAVICLES

These are S-shaped, short, round bones that connect the sternum with the shoulder blades. The shape of the clavicle is almost entirely visible under the skin, and this makes it easier for the artist to draw it.

THE SHOULDER BLADES

The shoulder blades, or scapulas, are flat, triangular bones that are slightly curved in the upper part to fit into the rib cage. They are jointed with the clavicle and with the humerus.

VERTEBRAL COLUMN

The vertebral column is a movable bone column formed by 24 independent vertebrae divided into five regions: 7 cervical vertebrae, 12 dorsal vertebrae, 5 lumbar, the sacrum, and the coccyx.

PELVIS

The pelvis is a bony ring formed mainly by three parts: the sacrum and the illium bones. The pelvis in general has the shape of a two-body basin and supports the weight of the upper part of the skeleton.

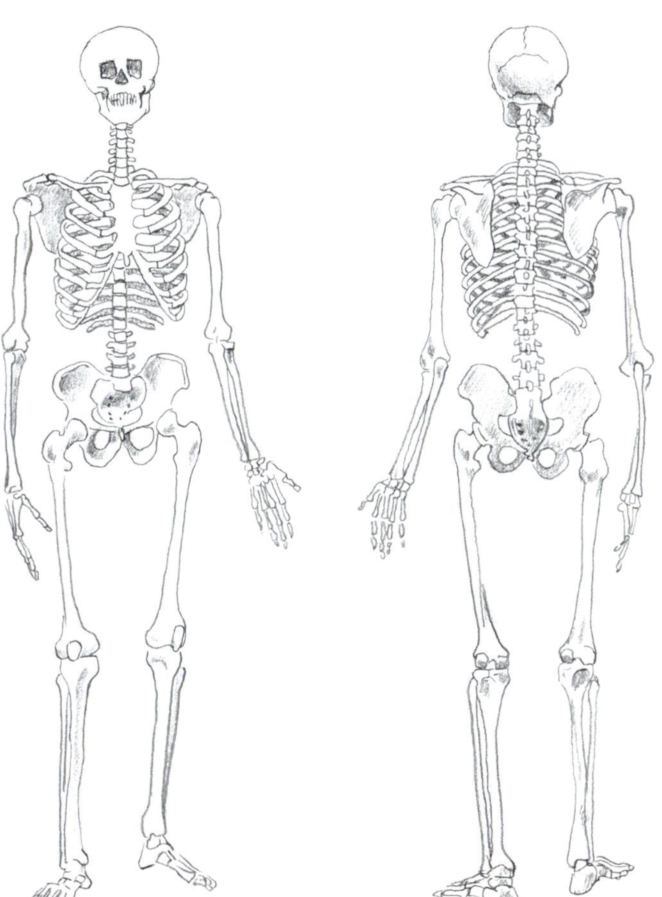

Anterior and posterior views of the human skeleton formed by 233 bones.

Arm Bones
and Joints

The upper extremities consist of the upper arm and the forearm. The humerus is the bone in the upper arm, and the ulna and the radius are located in the forearm. The humerus is the longest bone and is jointed at the upper end with the shoulder and at the lower end (the elbow) with the two remaining bones. The ulna and the radius are jointed in the lower end with the wrist bones. The length of these two bones is approximately three-quarters that of the humerus.

THE HUMERUS

This is the longest and most robust bone in the arm. On its upper extremity, the humerus is joined to the cavity of the scapula by a head-like round knob. The lower extremity of the humerus has two articulated surfaces in the shape of a pulley: one for the ulna on the inside and the other for the radius on the outside. The most significant protuberance of this extremity is located to the inside of the arm and is known as the *epicondyle*.

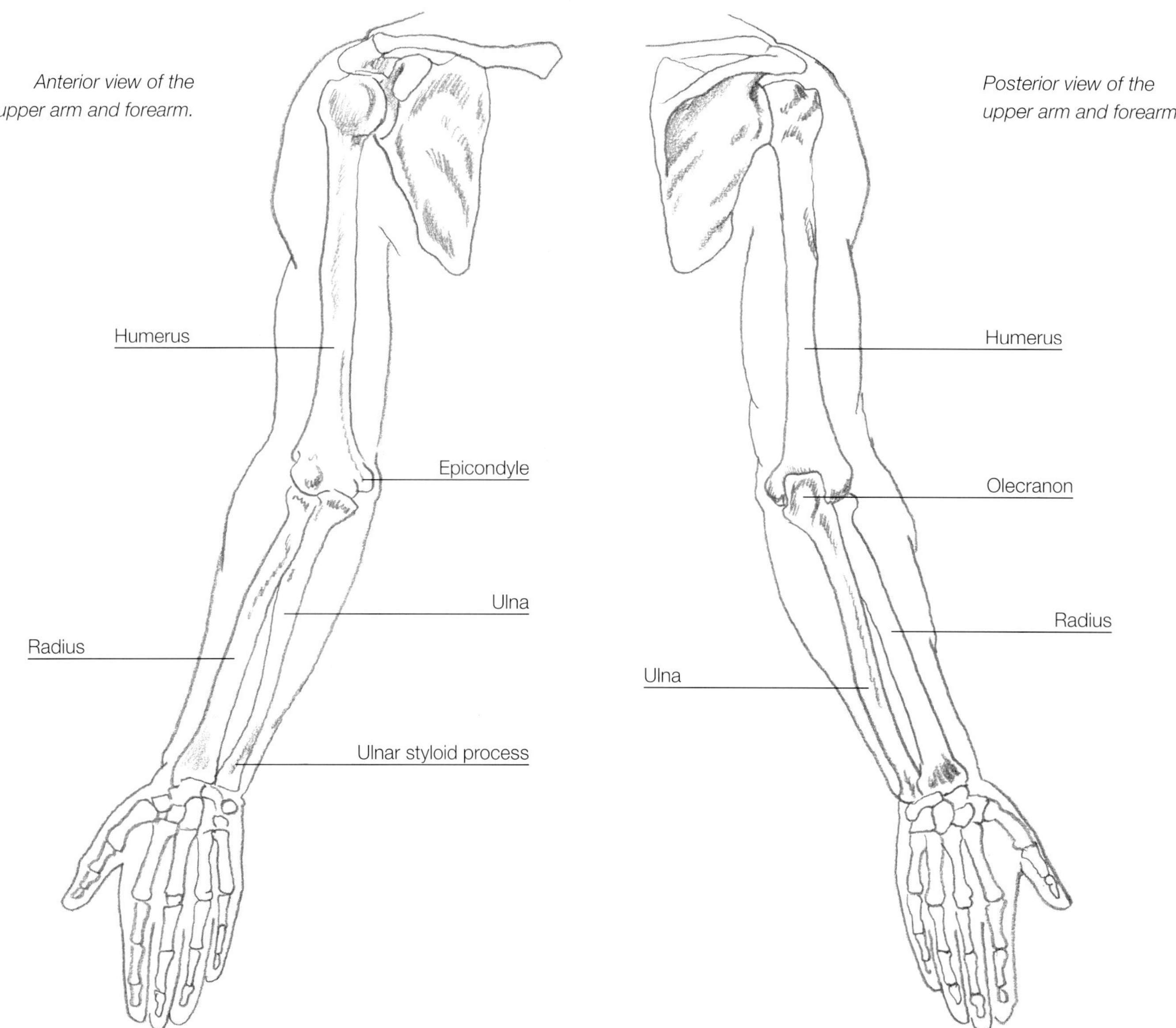

Anterior view of the upper arm and forearm.

Posterior view of the upper arm and forearm.

THE FOREARM

The forearm bones are the ulna and the radius. With the arm extended and the palm facing up, both bones appear side by side, with the ulna located toward the inner part of the forearm and the radius toward the outer part. The ulna's upper extremity, called the olecranon, is much larger than the lower end and is the part that gives the characteristic slightly pointed projection to the back of the elbow joint. The lower extremity also forms a significant protuberance on the outside of the forearm with the styloid process, which is normally visible in the area of the wrist and forms the angle of the hand. The bone of the radius is arched slightly outward and has a prism-like triangular shape. Like the ulna, the lower extremity of the radius has a process (radial styloid process), although it is not as prominent.

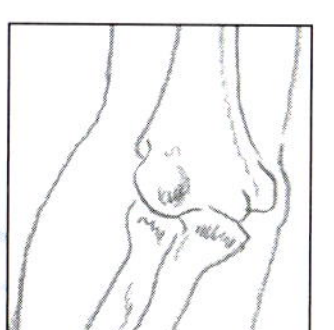

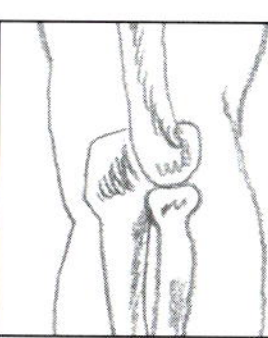

The elbow joints involve three different bones. Two of them are responsible for the significant protuberances that shape the exterior contour of that part of the anatomy: the humerus, which forms the projection of the epicondyle on the interior of the arm, and the ulna, which forms the olecranon to the posterior.

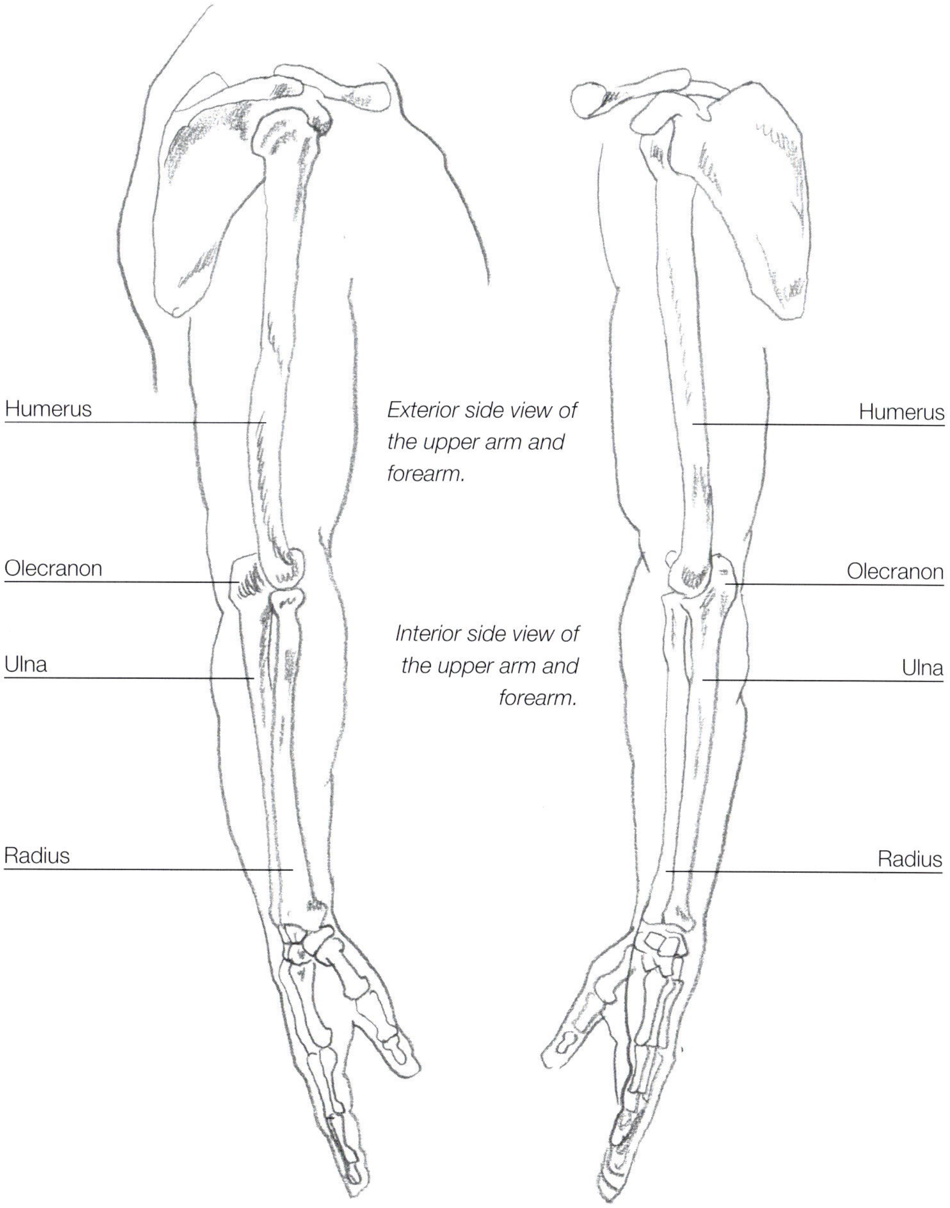

Humerus

Olecranon

Ulna

Radius

Exterior side view of the upper arm and forearm.

Humerus

Olecranon

Ulna

Radius

Interior side view of the upper arm and forearm.

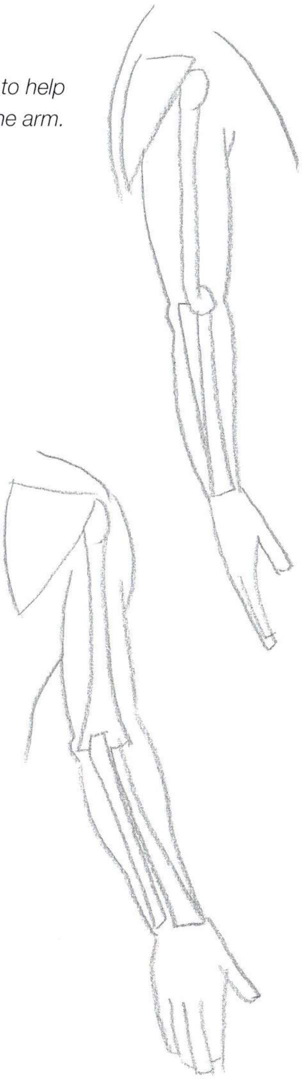

Diagrams to help draw the arm.

The Skeleton as a Guide for Drawing

The skeleton is the artist's best guide for constructing the figure. Reduced to its basic forms, it can be drawn quickly and can provide a perfectly articulated view of the figure's pose. In fact, this bone structure looks quite similar to the diagram of the axes seen on earlier pages and could be considered a more complete view of that diagram. The advantage of this basic skeleton is that it provides a better explanation of the complete anatomy of the figure than does a simple diagram of the movement axes of the spinal column, hips, shoulders, arms, and legs.

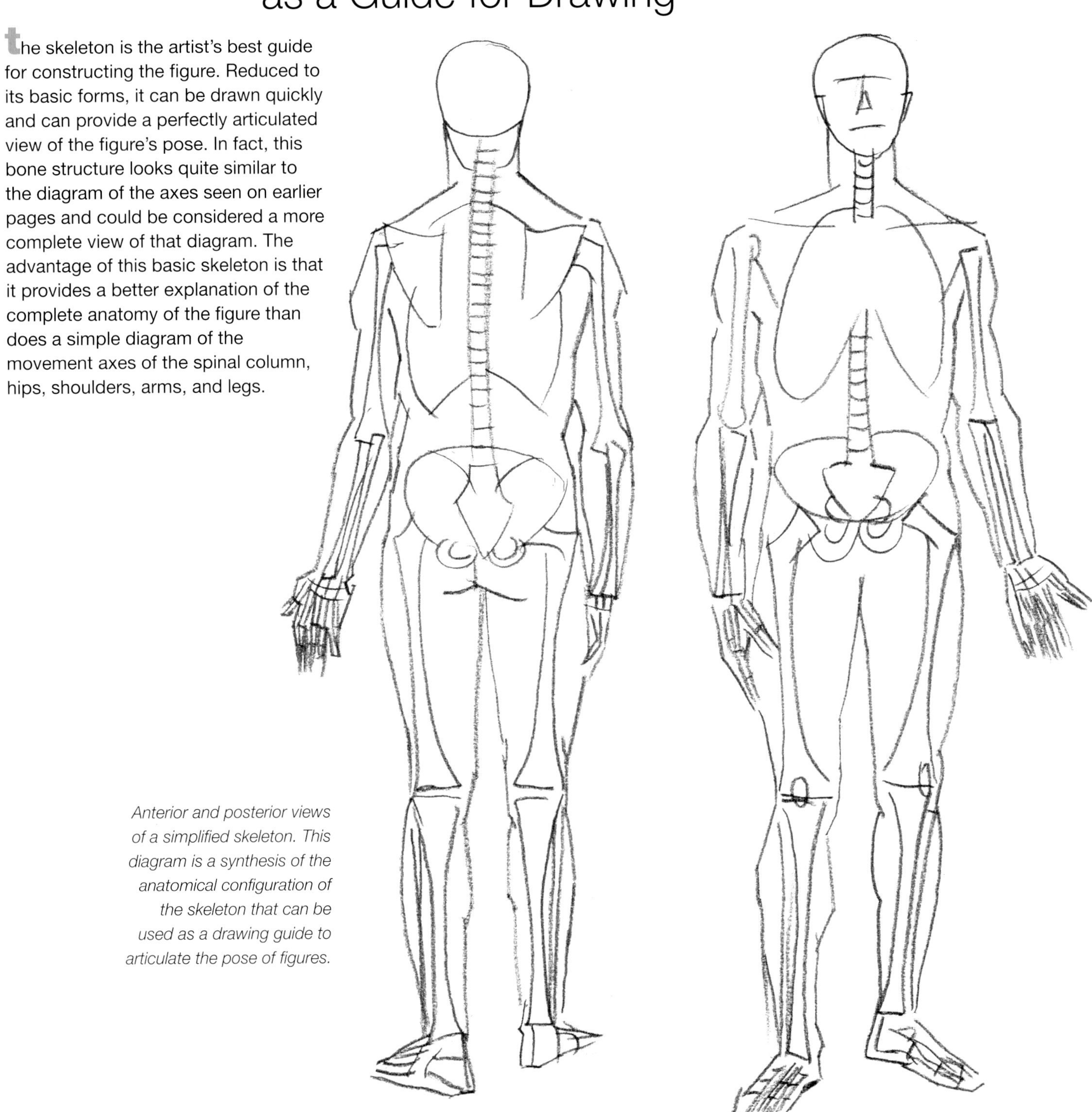

Anterior and posterior views of a simplified skeleton. This diagram is a synthesis of the anatomical configuration of the skeleton that can be used as a drawing guide to articulate the pose of figures.

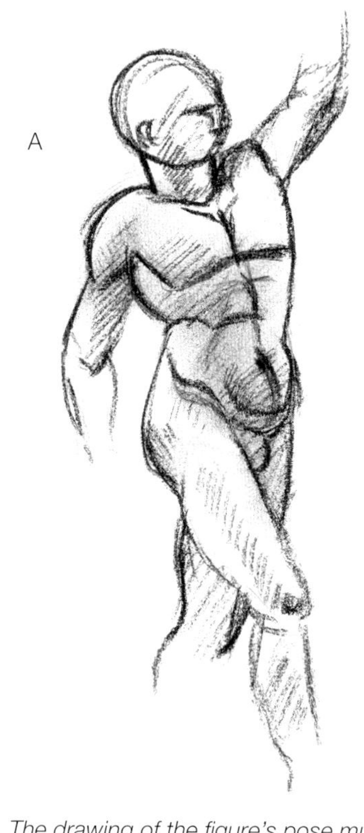

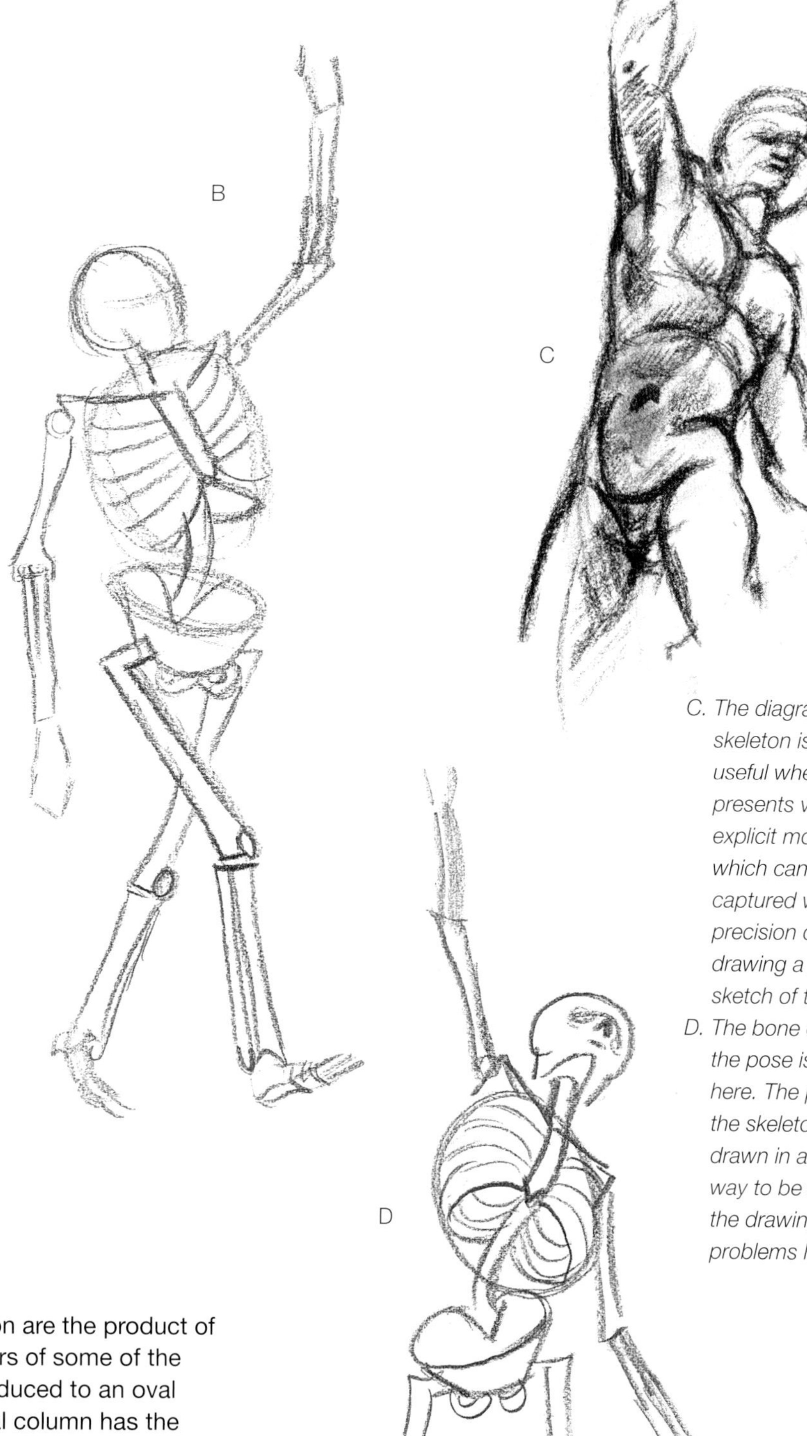

A. The drawing of the figure's pose must be dictated by a clear general understanding of the articulation of the limbs. This is the only way that movement can be represented clearly from the beginning of the drawing

B. This bone diagram corresponds to the drawing illustrated here and shows how all the factors of proportion and movement of the figure are present in its schematic version.

C. The diagram of the skeleton is particularly useful when the pose presents very explicit movements, which can be captured with precision only by drawing a general sketch of them first.

D. The bone diagram of the pose is shown here. The pieces of the skeleton must be drawn in a convincing way to be able to do the drawing without problems later.

SYNTHESIS OF THE BONES

The schematic forms of this basic skeleton are the product of the synthesis of the characteristic contours of some of the significant bones. The thoracic cage is reduced to an oval shape cut out on its lower part. The spinal column has the shape of a sinuous band or tube that marks the movement of the back, and it is finished with the oval indicating the head; the pelvis is a wide disc that determines the placement and movement of the hips. These large elements are the starting point for the two humeri (arms) and the two femurs (legs).

Constructing from the Skeleton

Using the bone diagram has an added advantage since it can be used as the basic foundation for articulating the figure: it makes it possible to establish stability and balance for all the parts. In other words, it makes it possible to draw the figure standing up straight without making it lean toward one side or the other. Balance is an essential factor when drawing the figure: it matters very little that the figure represented is completely correct anatomically if it does not look like it is standing upright.

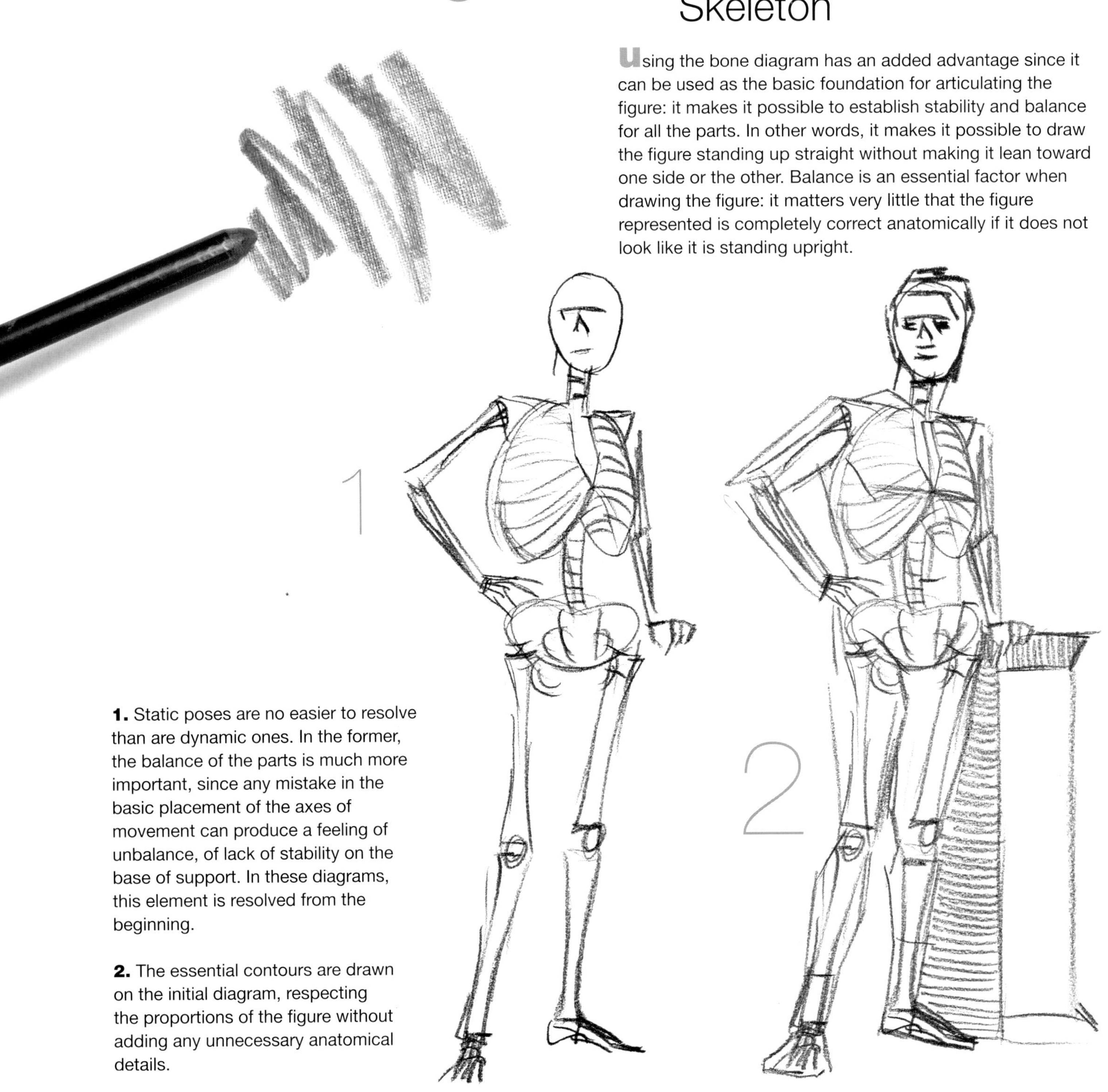

1. Static poses are no easier to resolve than are dynamic ones. In the former, the balance of the parts is much more important, since any mistake in the basic placement of the axes of movement can produce a feeling of unbalance, of lack of stability on the base of support. In these diagrams, this element is resolved from the beginning.

2. The essential contours are drawn on the initial diagram, respecting the proportions of the figure without adding any unnecessary anatomical details.

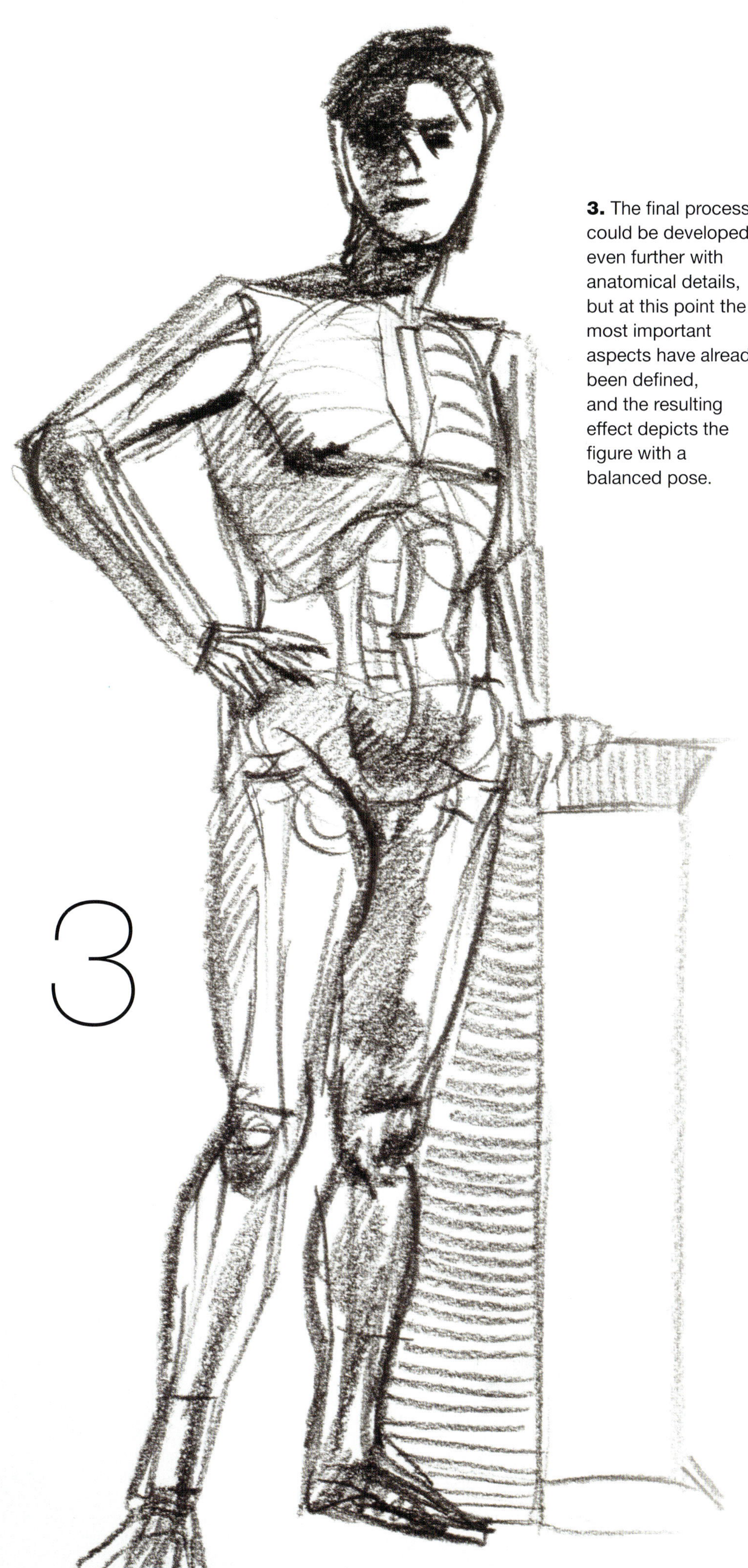

3. The final process could be developed even further with anatomical details, but at this point the most important aspects have already been defined, and the resulting effect depicts the figure with a balanced pose.

Using the bone structure to articulate the figure means that the characteristic axes of the movement of the shoulders, the spinal column, and the hips have already been established.

THE DRAWING PROCESS AND ITS DEVELOPMENT

The basic outline of a standing figure must be balanced from the beginning; if the first lines do not express this balance, it will be very difficult to achieve this through corrections in the subsequent phases of the work. The proposed diagram based on the skeleton can be applied to a standing pose by correctly expressing the placement of the feet and the movement of the shoulders and the waist. Using the knowledge learned from drawing nudes, the artist is able to detect any potential unbalance of the figure from the moment the first line is drawn and can correct it as he goes without having to check it. The slightly counterbalanced angle of the shoulders and the hips, putting the weight of the body on the figure's left leg, is the main element of balance in this pose. We must also point out that sometimes the figures appear out of balance even though everything is perfectly in place. In such cases, the visual effect is the most important aspect, so the drawing must be worked until complete balance is achieved.

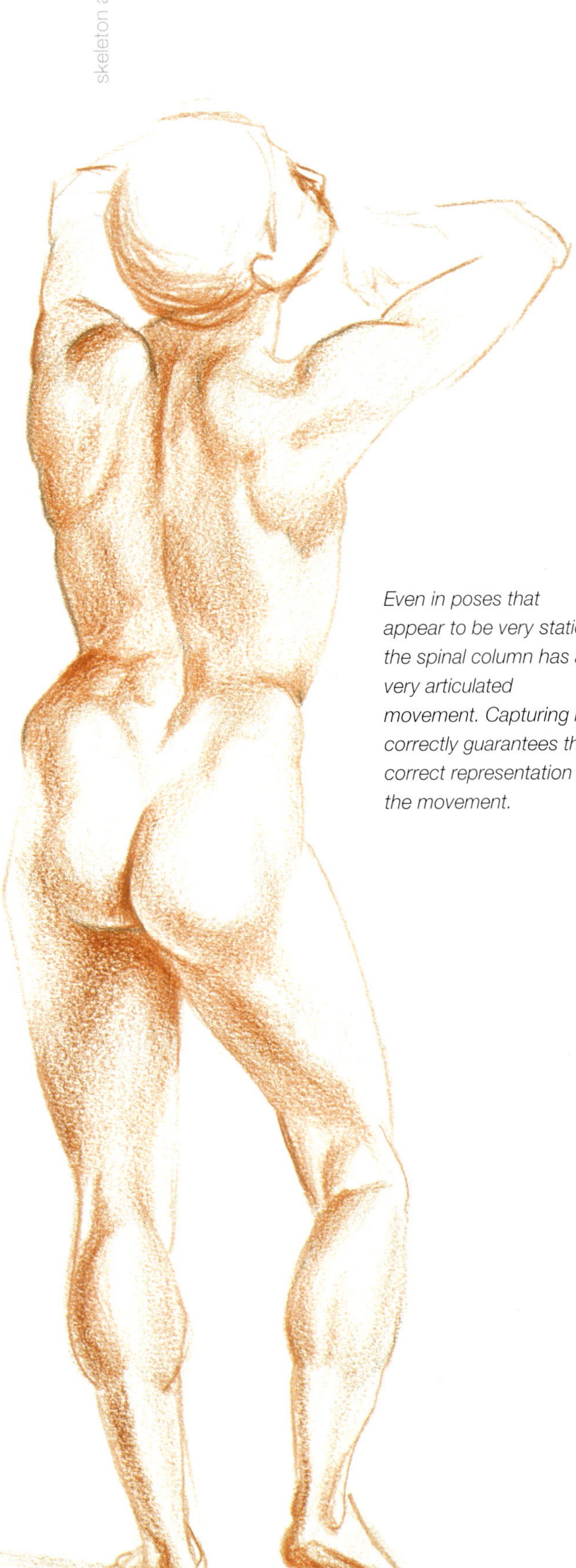

Even in poses that appear to be very static, the spinal column has a very articulated movement. Capturing it correctly guarantees the correct representation of the movement.

The spinal column is one of the basic references for drawing the figure. Its undulating outline determines the movement of the entire torso, and the movements of the limbs can be established from it.

The Line of the Spinal Column

It is very important to consider the curves that result from each pose, and it is advisable to avoid a completely straight line, even in the most static poses. Here we show various diagrams of the spinal column that reflect the poses of the figures.

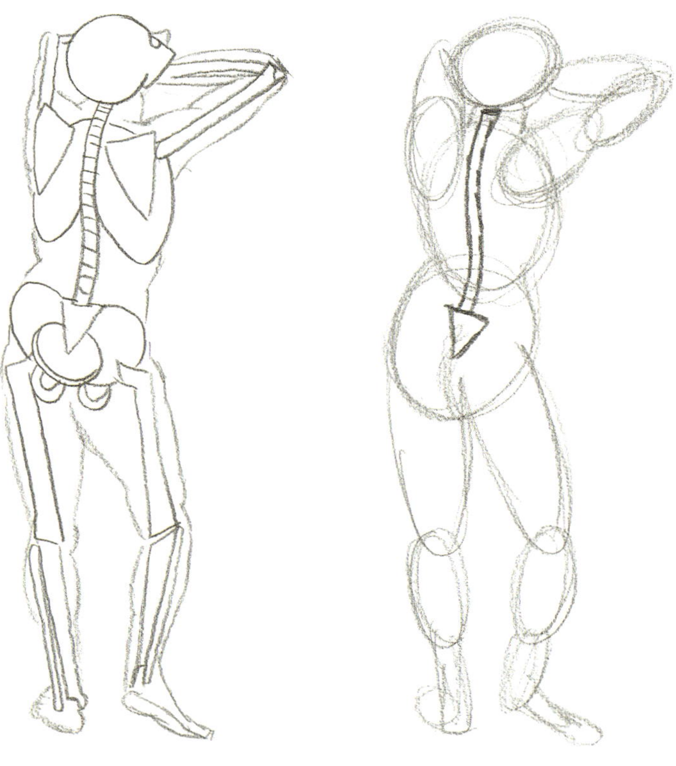

These two drawings show the bone distribution and the specific movement of the spinal column for the pose shown on this page.

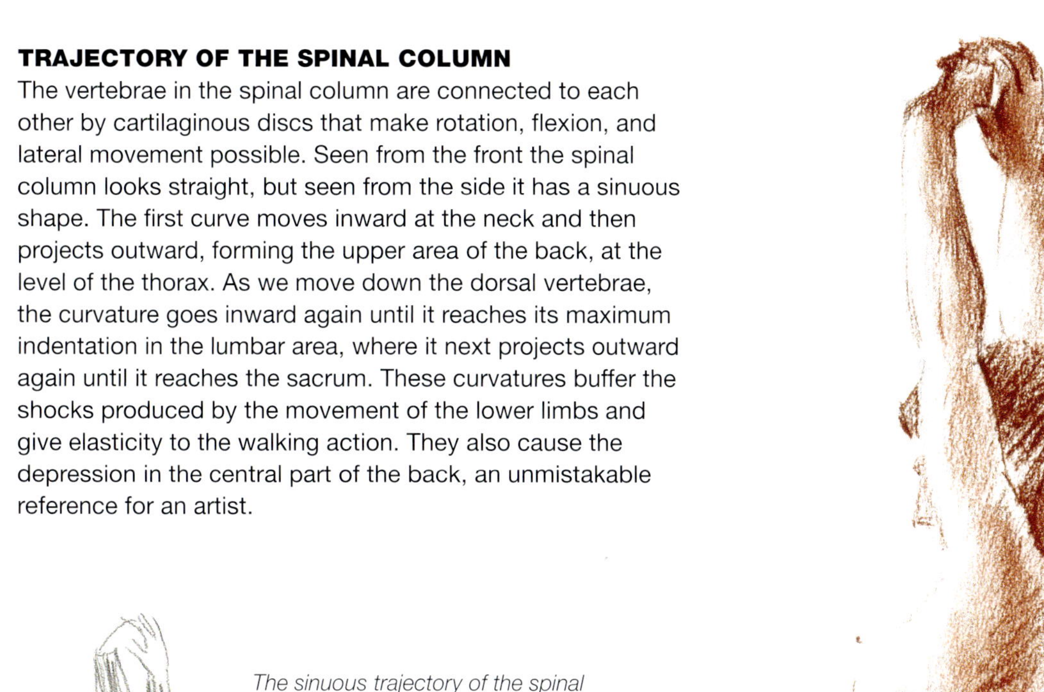

TRAJECTORY OF THE SPINAL COLUMN

The vertebrae in the spinal column are connected to each other by cartilaginous discs that make rotation, flexion, and lateral movement possible. Seen from the front the spinal column looks straight, but seen from the side it has a sinuous shape. The first curve moves inward at the neck and then projects outward, forming the upper area of the back, at the level of the thorax. As we move down the dorsal vertebrae, the curvature goes inward again until it reaches its maximum indentation in the lumbar area, where it next projects outward again until it reaches the sacrum. These curvatures buffer the shocks produced by the movement of the lower limbs and give elasticity to the walking action. They also cause the depression in the central part of the back, an unmistakable reference for an artist.

The depression of the spinal column is particularly pronounced in the lumbar area. This gives the artist an excellent anatomical reference when drawing a back view of the hips.

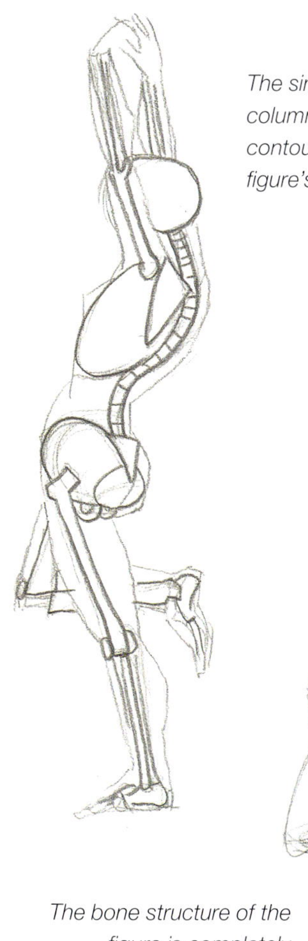

The sinuous trajectory of the spinal column radically determines the contours of the drawing of this figure's back.

The bone structure of the figure is completely dependent on the form adopted by the spinal column in this pose.

This pose presents a strong movement of the spinal column that responds to the spread of the weight and tension to which the figure's limbs are subjected.

The Anatomy of Muscles

The muscles are fleshy masses made of fibers that put the body in motion when they contract as a result of a nerve stimulus. The number of muscles varies from 460 to 501 depending on how anatomists count them (many muscles can be considered either as units or as aggregates); they overlap each other and are arranged in layers or in planes. The muscles of the viscera and the motor muscles located deep in the body are not visible as contours of the body, which is the anatomical aspect that artists are most interested in. With the exception of the cutaneous muscles and the sphincter muscles, a muscle is always attached to at least two different bones.

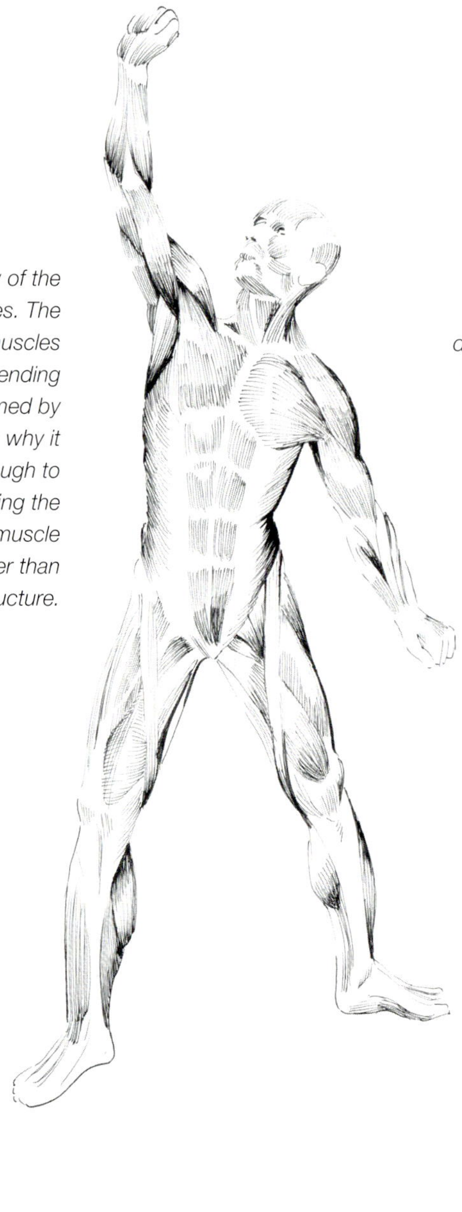

Anterior view of the muscles. The appearance of muscles varies greatly depending on the pose assumed by the figure. This is why it is more thorough to approach drawing the figure from the muscle perspective rather than from the bone structure.

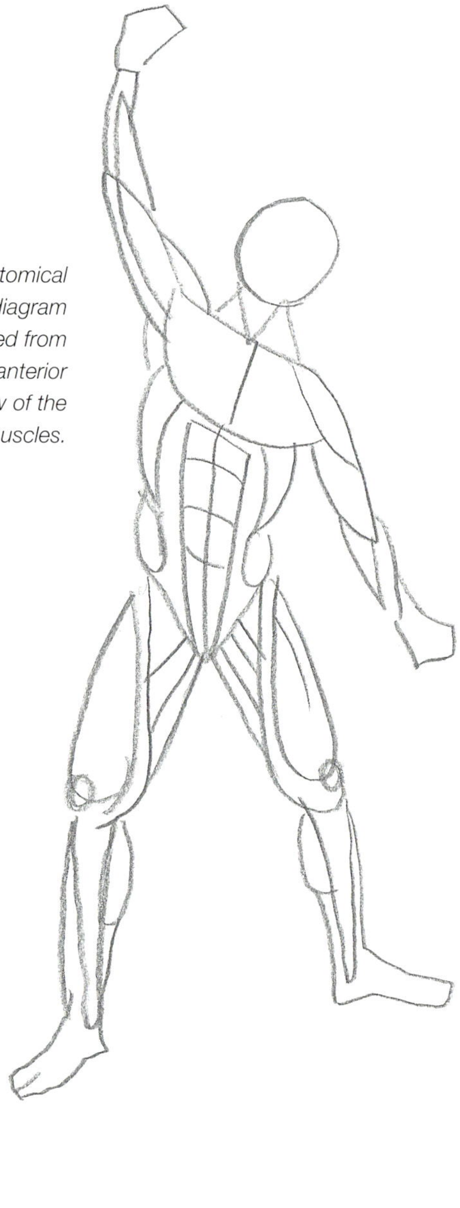

Anatomical diagram derived from the anterior view of the muscles.

SURFACE MUSCLES AND DEEP MUSCLES

Surface muscles are located, in general, under the skin, and therefore, their shape can be perceived on the body's outer contours. Deep muscles are not visible on the outer contour, but their contraction modifies the forms of the surface muscles, elevating them or displacing them. Deep muscles are usually attached to bones along their entire length, while surface muscles are attached at the ends.

THE MECHANICS OF MUSCLES

The muscles are attached with tendons and ligaments. They are divided into long muscles (those of the limbs), wide muscles (those that cause the trunk to move), short muscles (those that must deliver the most power), and the annular muscles (which surround the orifices of the body). When in movement, the muscles contract and shrink, becoming more prominent and moving nearer to the points where they are attached to the joints. Muscle mechanics follow the same laws as those that govern levers: the muscle exerts force to overcome a resistance (the weight that it must move) and the joint acts as the fulcrum of the system.

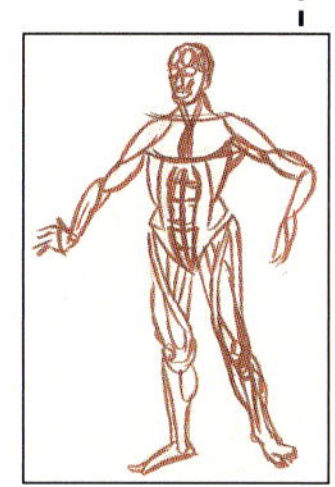

The diagram involving the distribution of the muscles is much more complex than the diagram of the skeleton. But it is worth drawing it before getting deep into the exploration of the anatomy, since this allows the artist to acquire a general view that can be refined later.

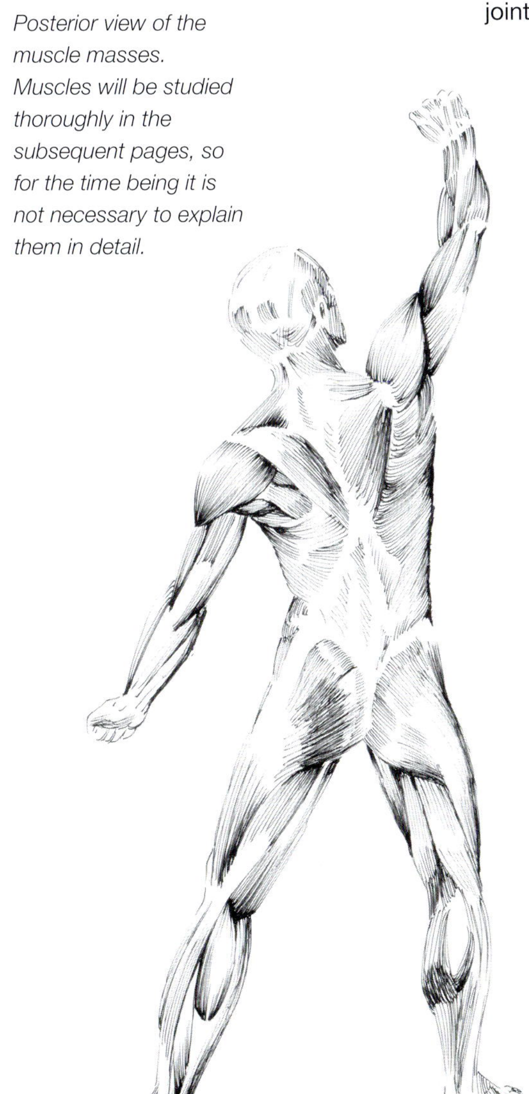

Posterior view of the muscle masses. Muscles will be studied thoroughly in the subsequent pages, so for the time being it is not necessary to explain them in detail.

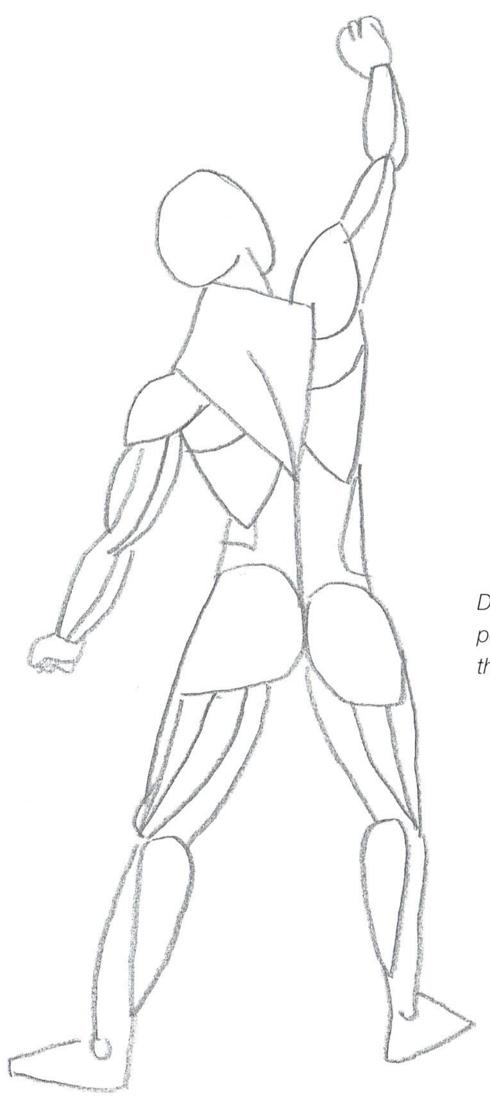

Diagram of the posterior view of the muscles.

Drawings and Diagrams of Muscles

In the following pages we will show a series of drawings accompanied by their corresponding muscle diagrams. We reiterate that drawing a diagram of the muscles is much more complicated than making a bone diagram, because the former is a covering for the latter: Drawing the axes or articulated bones is always done first. Figures drawn following only the muscle structure run the risk of looking too "robotic," because a diagram is nothing more than the exaggeration of specific aspects, and the exaggeration of muscles always results in a mechanical look. However, it is interesting to practice this exercise to familiarize yourself with the distribution of the muscle masses of the body before studying them in detail, which we will do in the subsequent sections of this book.

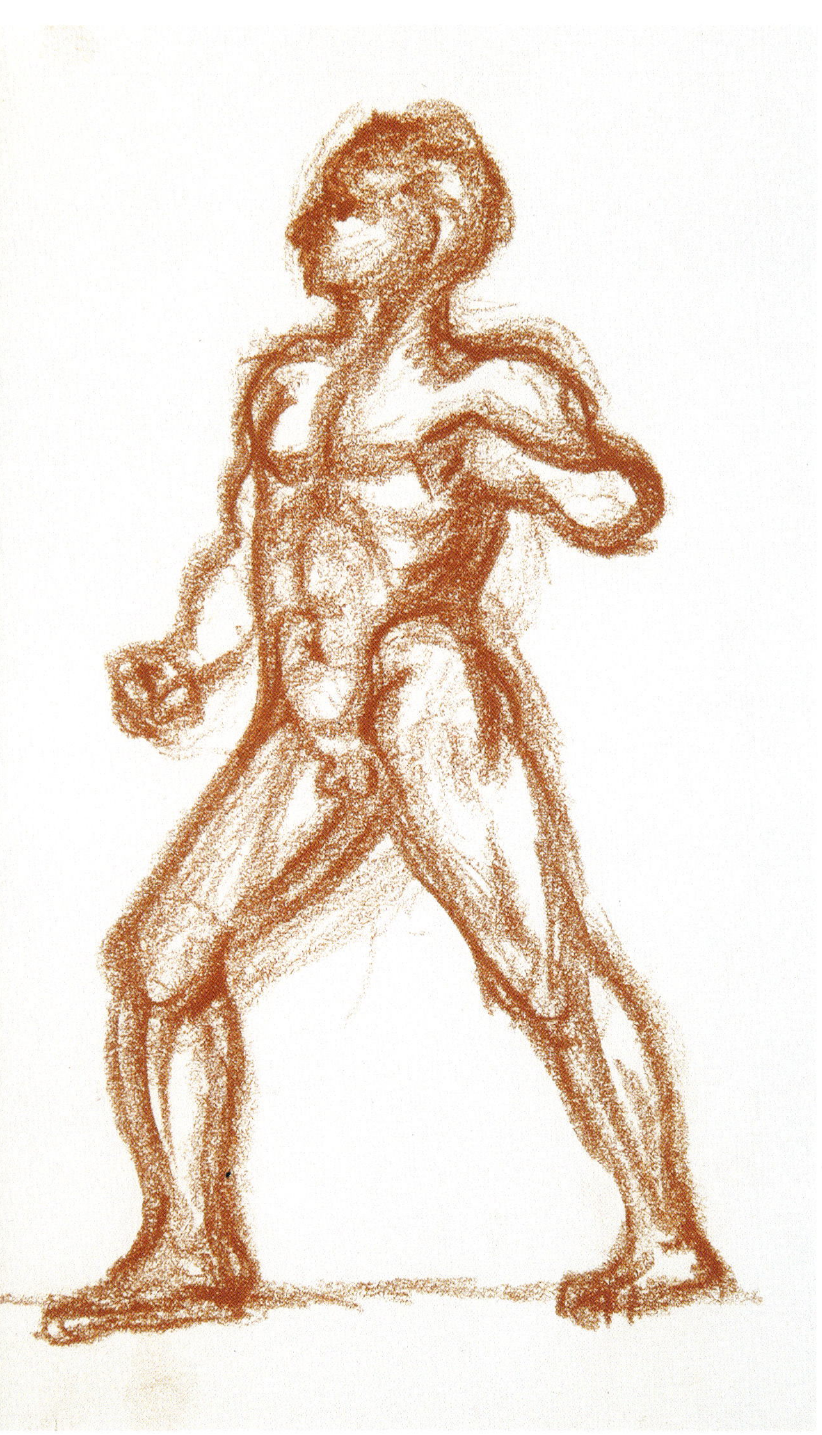

No matter how athletic a body may be, its exterior appearance never looks like the muscle diagram. It is very important for the diagram to give way to more convincing and less defined anatomical forms.

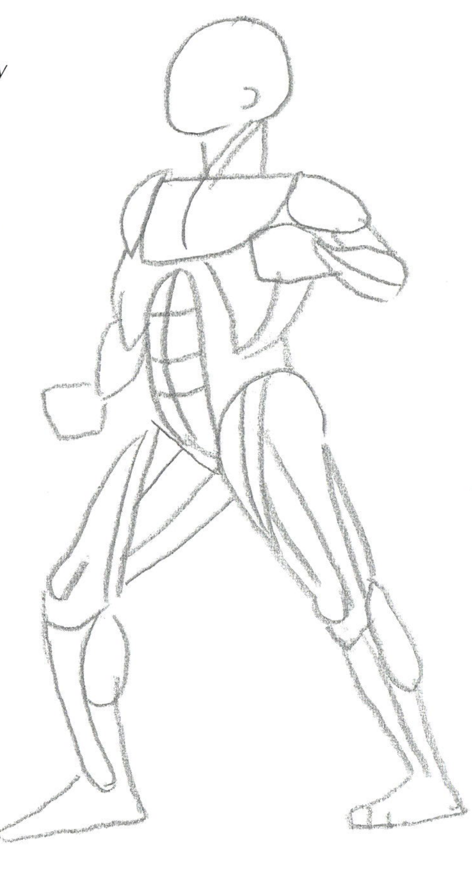

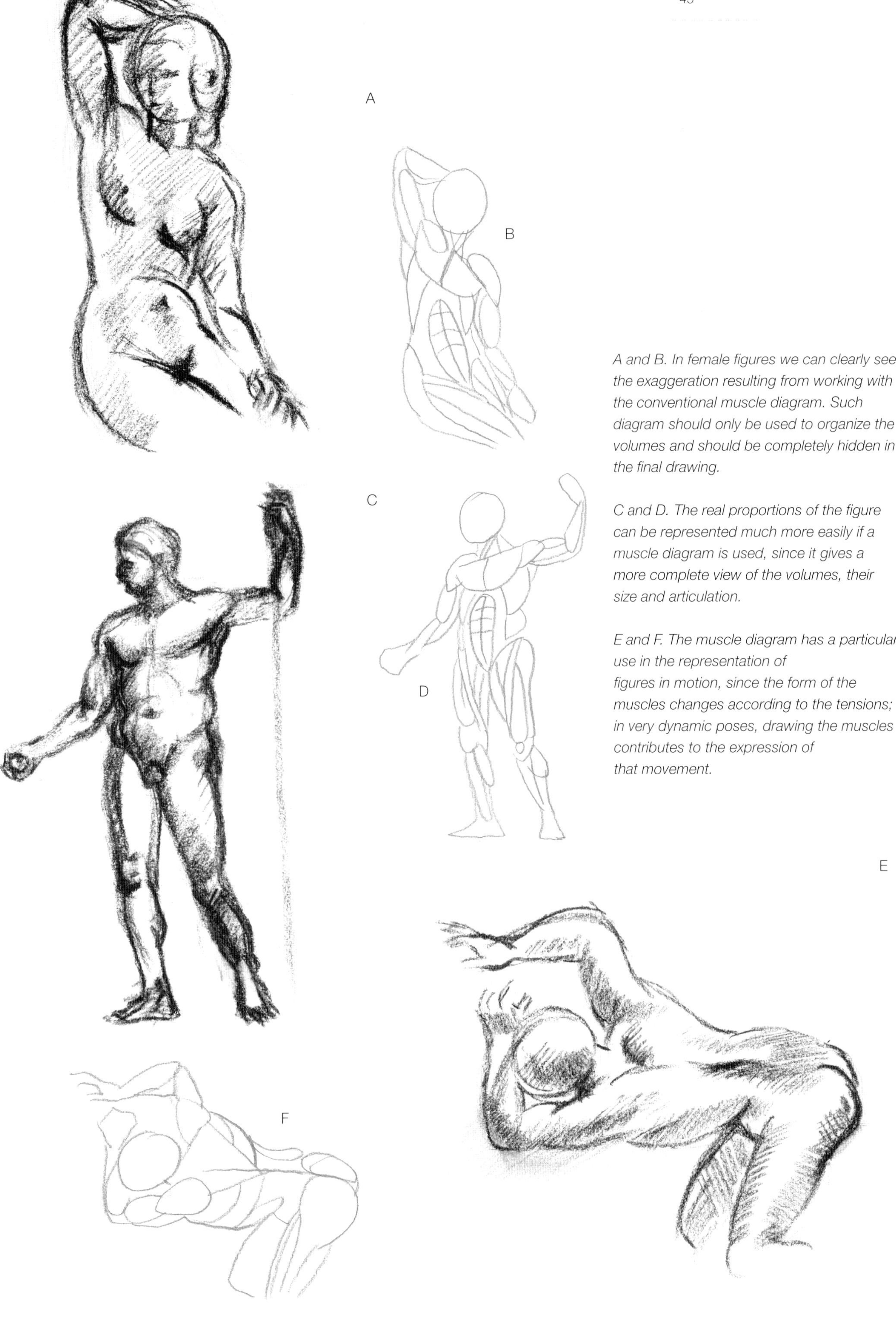

A and B. In female figures we can clearly see the exaggeration resulting from working with the conventional muscle diagram. Such diagram should only be used to organize the volumes and should be completely hidden in the final drawing.

C and D. The real proportions of the figure can be represented much more easily if a muscle diagram is used, since it gives a more complete view of the volumes, their size and articulation.

E and F. The muscle diagram has a particular use in the representation of figures in motion, since the form of the muscles changes according to the tensions; in very dynamic poses, drawing the muscles contributes to the expression of that movement.

Muscles of the Torso, Arms, and Legs

"THE FORM OF THE HUMAN ANATOMY DOES NOT BELONG TO A SPECIFIC MOMENT IN HISTORY, IT IS ETERNAL AND CAN BE ADMIRED BY PEOPLE FROM ANY ERA."
August Rodin (1840-1917)

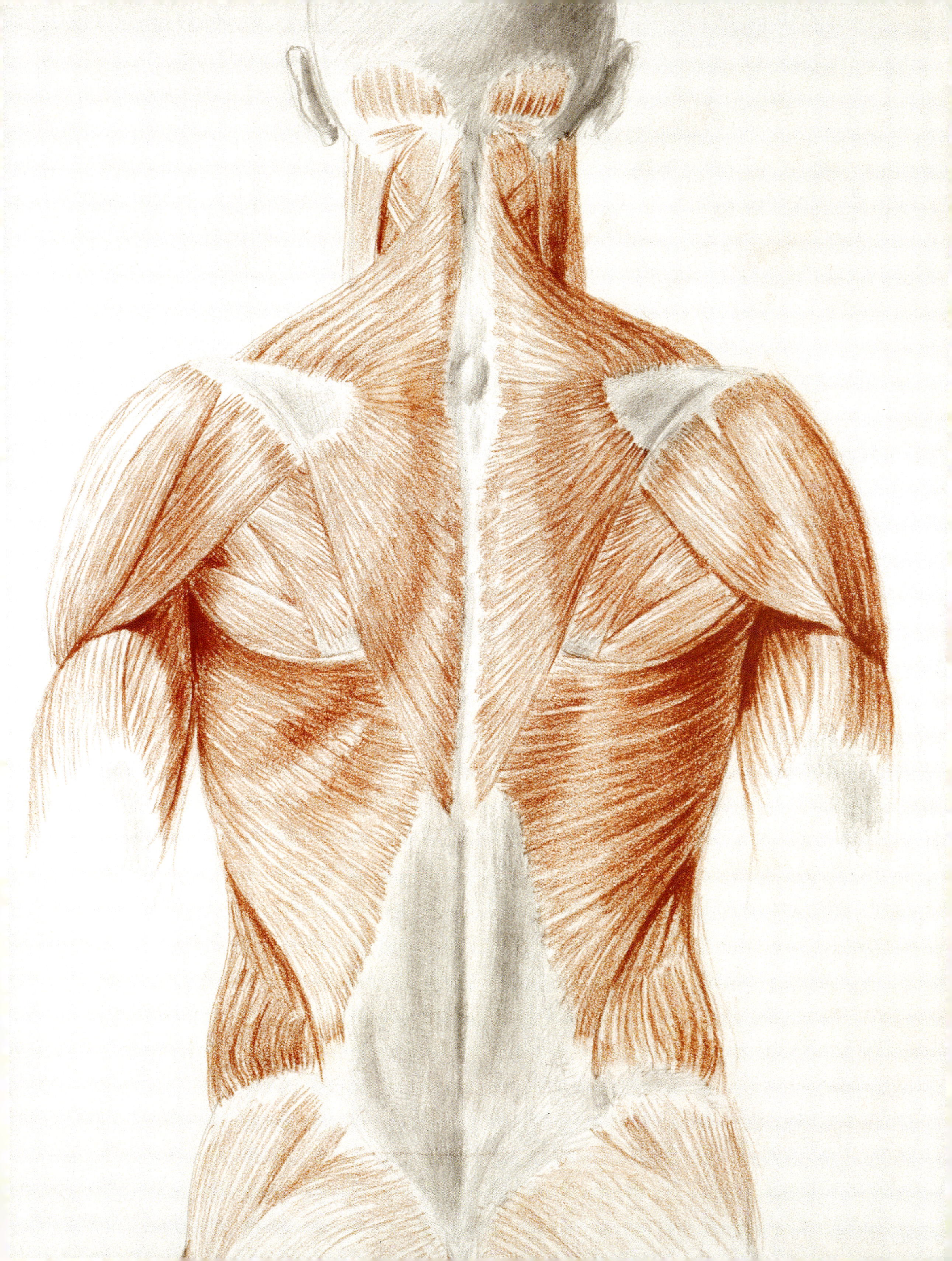

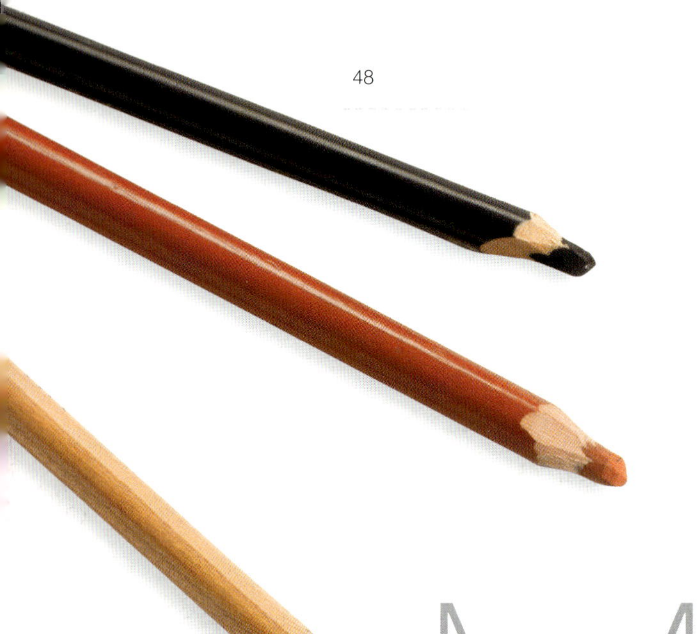

Muscles of the Torso

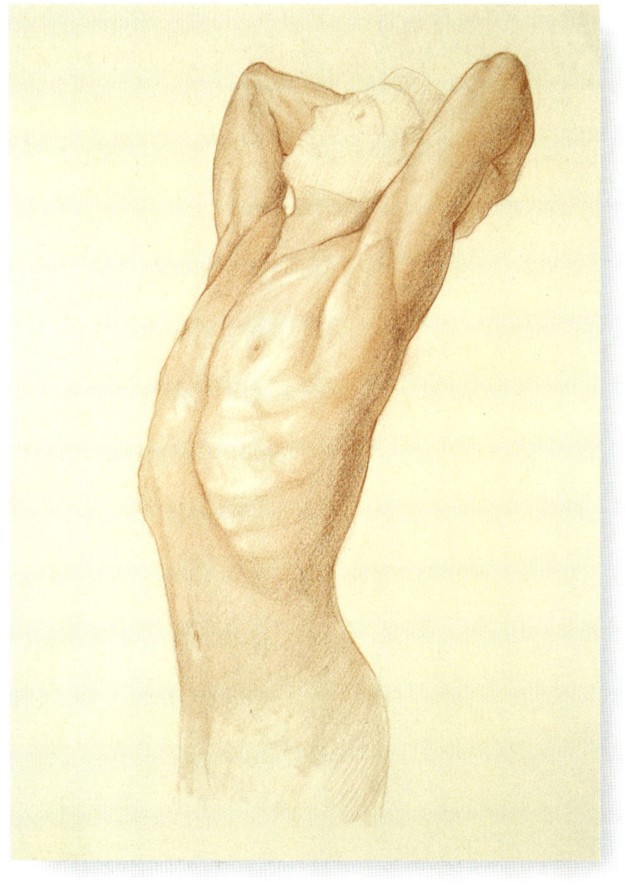

HÉCTOR FERNÁNDEZ. TORSO, 2002. SANGUINE

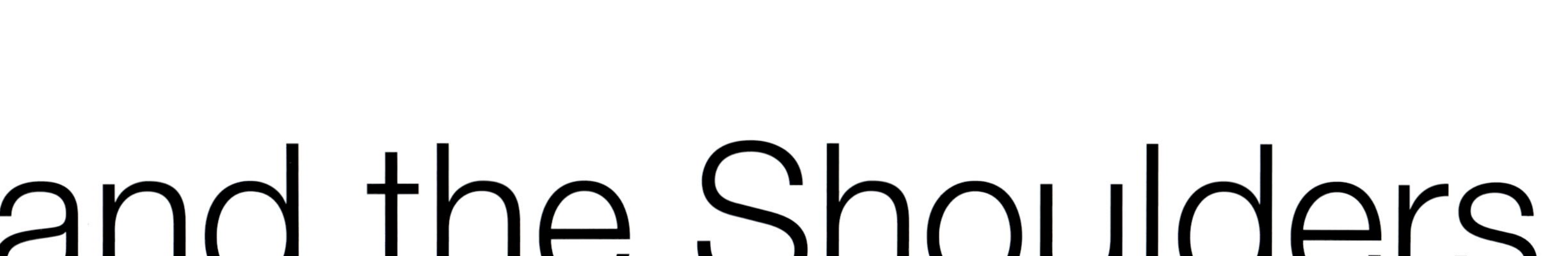

and the Shoulders.

In this section

on muscles, we study

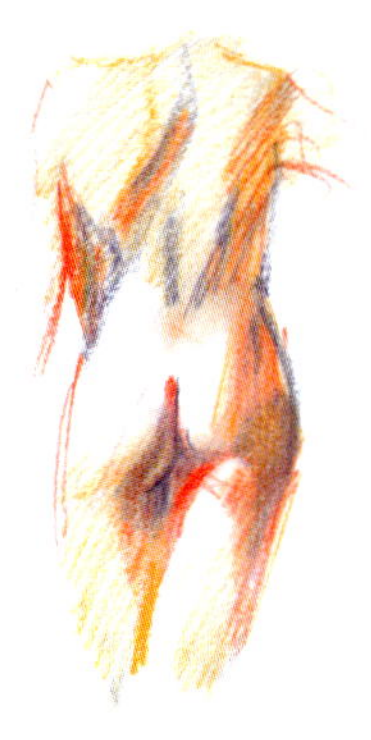

in detail the distribution of the muscles of the torso, shoulders, and arms of the figure. But only the ones that can be perceived from the outside: the surface muscles. These are generally located right under the skin, and therefore, their shapes can be made out through the skin. The deep muscles are not visible from the outside, but their contraction modifies the shapes of the surface muscles by raising them or displacing them. For reasons of interest and space, the deep muscles will not be included. The complexity of the subcutaneous muscles is sufficient for understanding anatomy from an artistic point of view.

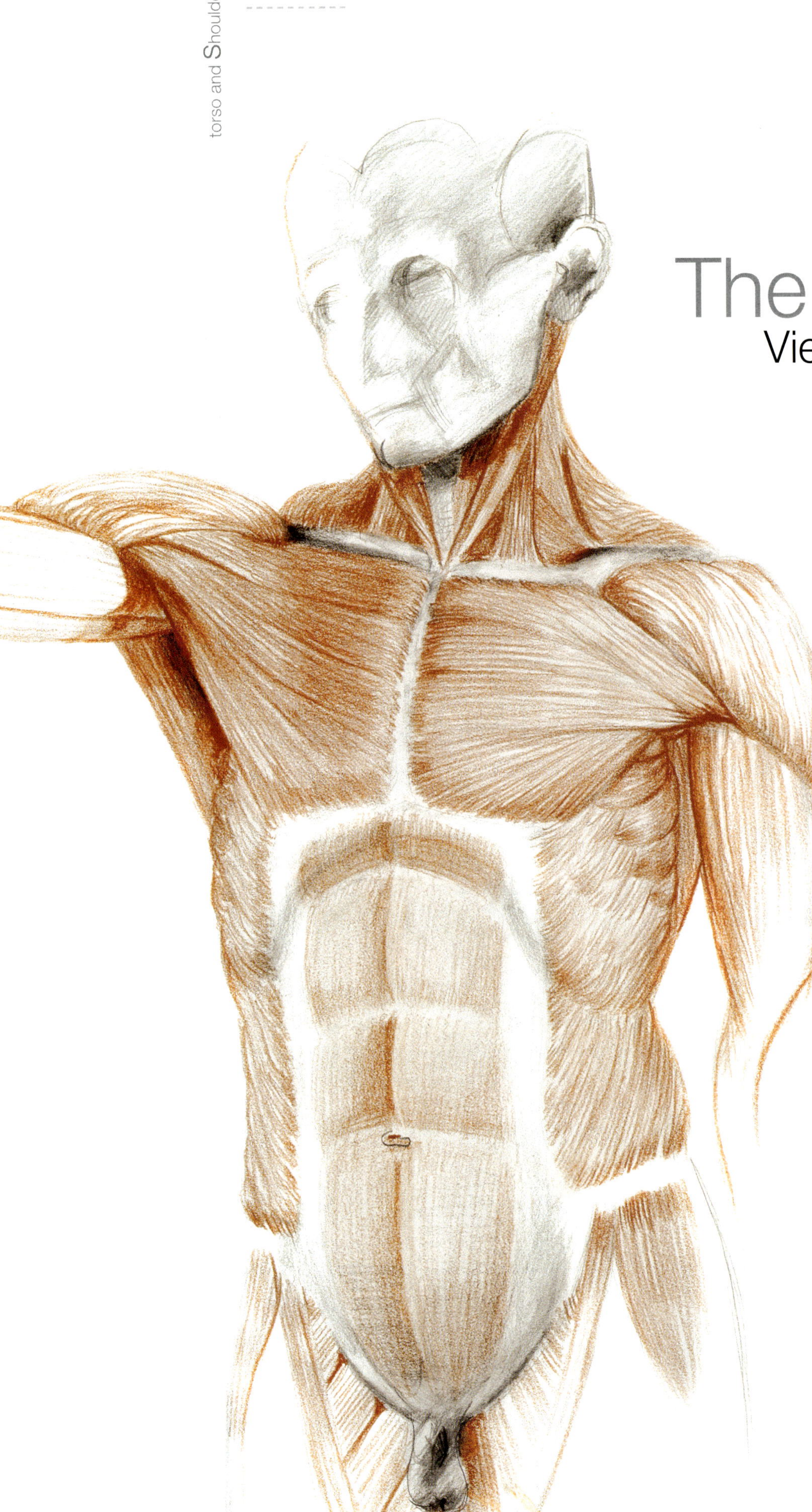

The Torso
Viewed from the Front

The torso, formed by the thorax and the abdomen, is the most significant part of the anatomy from the artistic point of view. The fact that most of the fragments of well-known classical statues are torsos has greatly influenced the symbolism associated with this part of the body: it embodies the attributes of strength, beauty, and aesthetic perfection of human anatomy. Proof of this is the expression "aesthetic armor" used to define the frontal representation of the torso in the French Academy of the seventeenth and eighteenth centuries. Its identification with armor comes from the military uniform used by the Roman legions, but also from the fact that the thorax and the abdomen together are the symbols of the most relevant classical aesthetic aspects in the representation of the anatomy.

The muscles of the thorax and the abdomen form an anatomical element that is almost the hallmark of the ideal human body. It constitutes the nucleus of anatomical drawing, to which it conveys expressivity and artistic power.

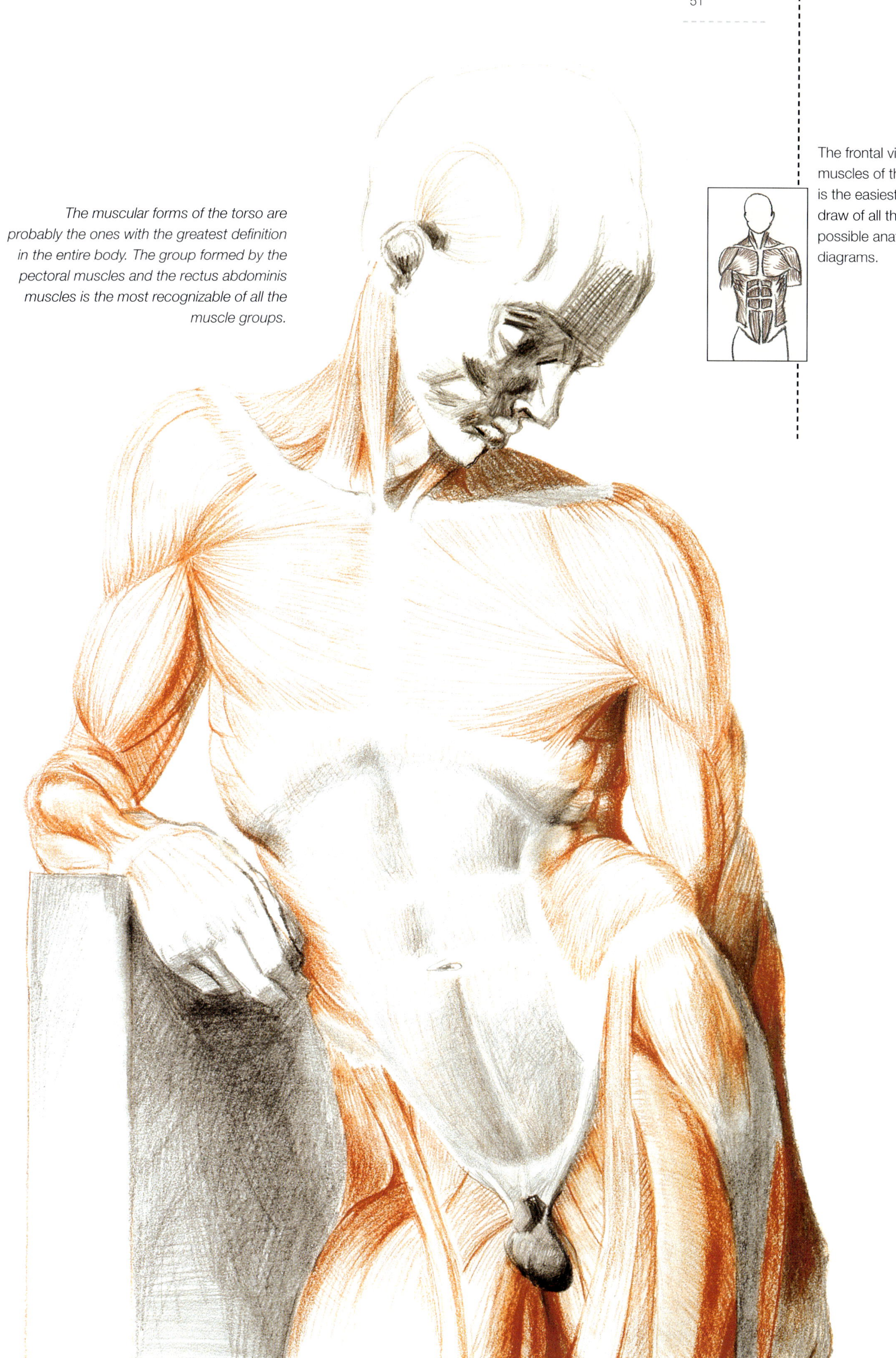

The muscular forms of the torso are probably the ones with the greatest definition in the entire body. The group formed by the pectoral muscles and the rectus abdominis muscles is the most recognizable of all the muscle groups.

The frontal view of the muscles of the torso is the easiest one to draw of all the possible anatomical diagrams.

Drawing the Muscles of the Torso and the Shoulder

The torso and the shoulder are covered by wide muscles that are especially powerful in the areas of the attachments with the limbs. The most relevant pectoral muscles are the pectoralis major, which contributes to the characteristic outline of the chest, and the serratus anterior, more noticable in side view on each side of the thoracic cage. The most significant shoulder muscle is the deltoid, which provides the characteristic contour of this part of the anatomy, in anterior view as well as posterior view. The shape of the torso seen from the front is characterized by the wide arch that indicates the cartilage of the ten ribs and the epigastric cavity, defined below the sternum.

Other important references are the contour of the clavicles and the lower neck sternal notch.

THE DELTOID

This muscle covers the articulation of the shoulder by wrapping around it. It is voluminous and strong, and its shape determines the athletic appearance of male drawings. It originates along the scapular spine, as well as in the acromion and around the anterior edge of the clavicle, and it is inserted in the external superior area of the humerus, below the tuberosities of the superior end of this bone. The deltoid consists of three bodies, or minor fascicles, that are tightly braided, which make it especially compact and powerful.

The deltoid raises and lowers the arm and protects the articulation of the shoulder and makes it stationary.

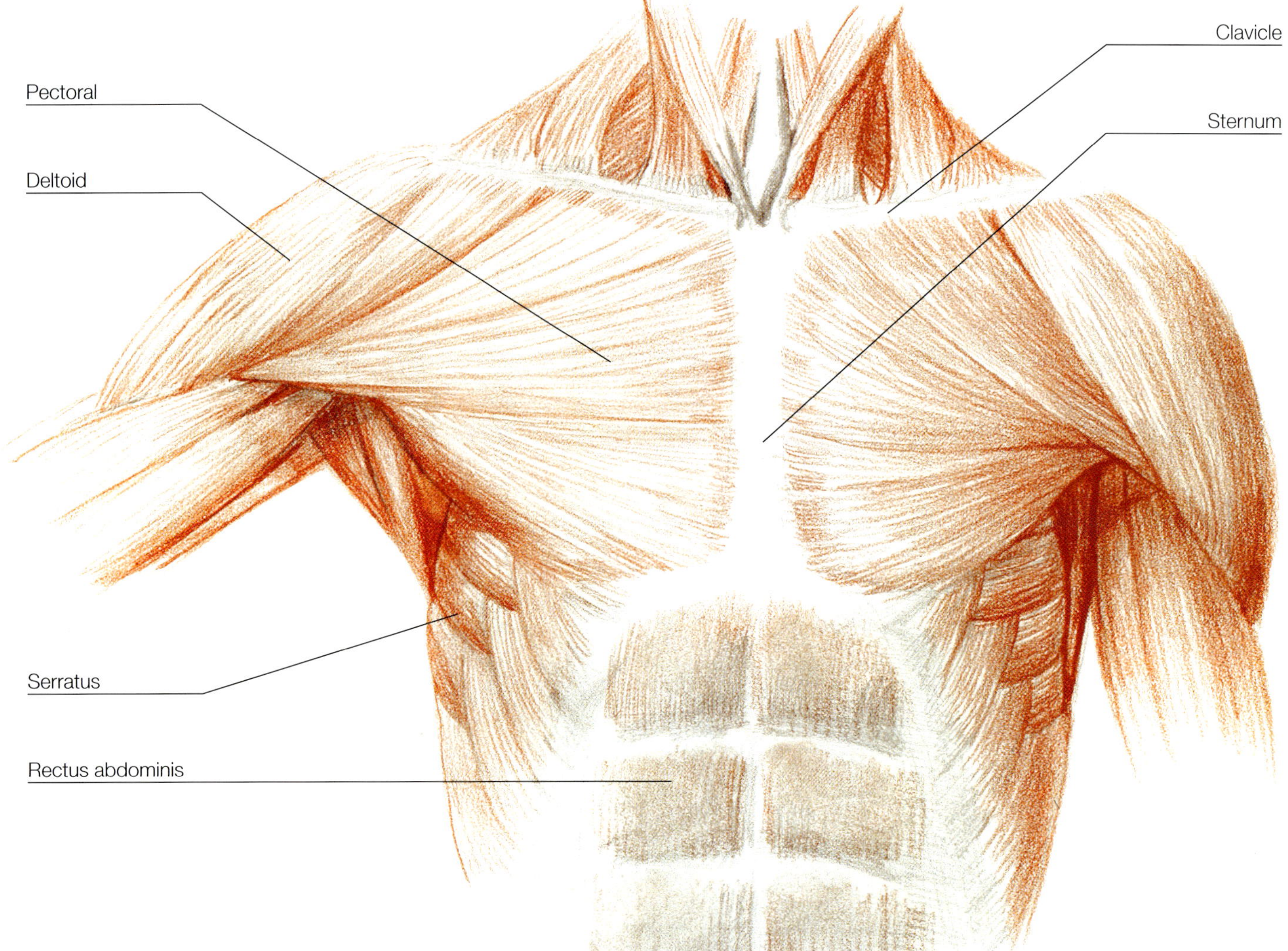

In the torso the outlines of the pectoral muscles stand out above all, which give the male thorax its wide and square shape.

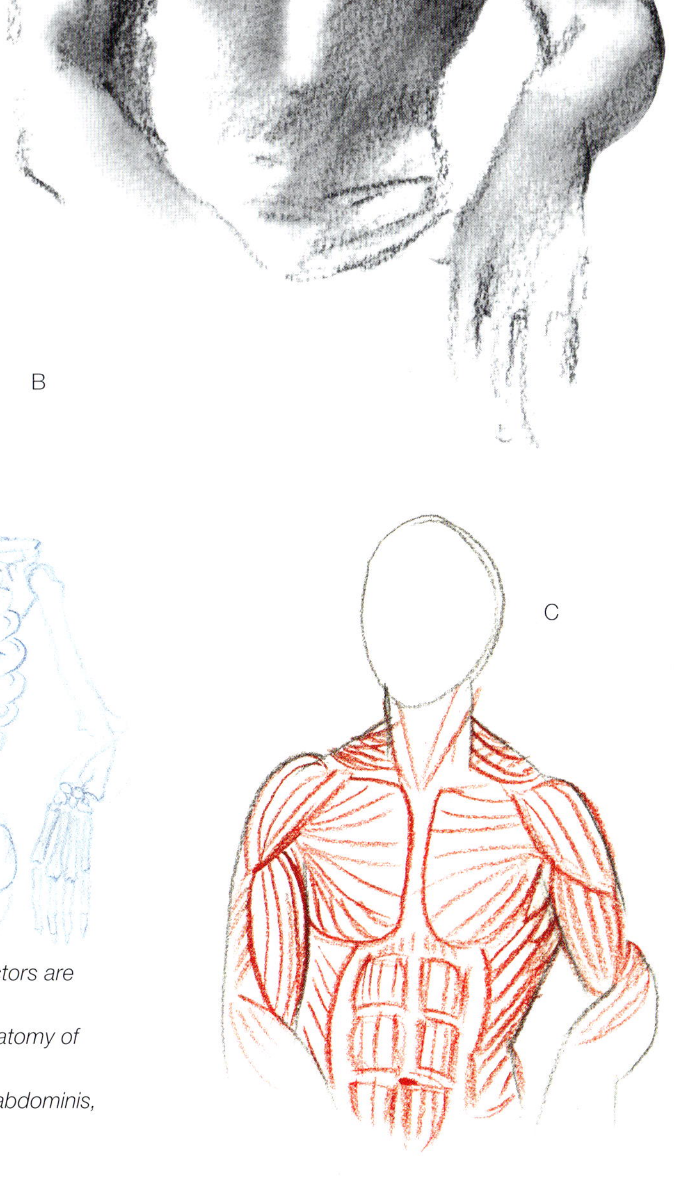

PECTORALIS MAJOR

The pectoralis major is a broad, fan-shaped muscle that originates in the clavicle and at the head of the humerus, and attaches along the sternum and in the cartilages of the first six ribs. It is attached to the humerus with the help of a wide, flattened tendon that wraps around it. This is a powerful muscle that causes the adduction of the arm (when the arm is raised, it tends to approximate it to the body's midline), as well as its internal rotation (toward the interior of the body). Upon elevating the arm, the pectoralis major forms the interior wall of the cavity of the axilla (armpit), an anatomical factor of special interest for the artist because it provides a characteristic outline to the body's silhouette. In female figures, the pectoral muscles are located under the breast and are therefore less relevant than in the male figure.

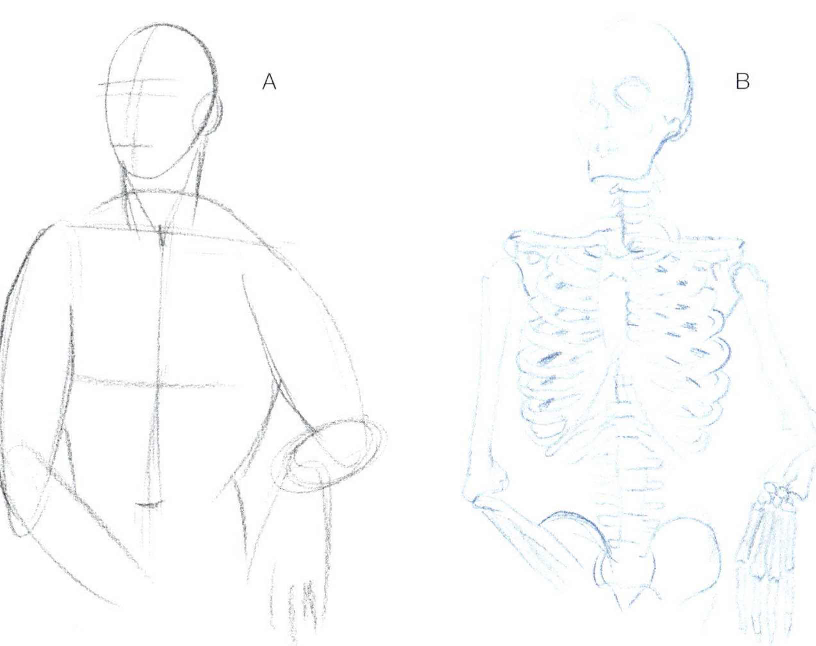

A. Basic diagram for drawing the figure illustrated here. The anatomical factors are defined with simple lines.

B. Bone diagram of the figure. The thoracic cage dominates the overall anatomy of the drawing.

C. Muscle diagram of the figure that includes the deltoid, pectoral, rectus abdominis, and oblique muscles.

The posterior side of the torso is formed basically by the bones of the spinal column, which articulate with most of the other bone areas. The back is formed by several very powerful muscular masses that are responsible for keeping the figure upright and for giving it adequate support. Most of these muscles are broad and flat, and they overlap with each other, forming the visible characteristic shape of the back.

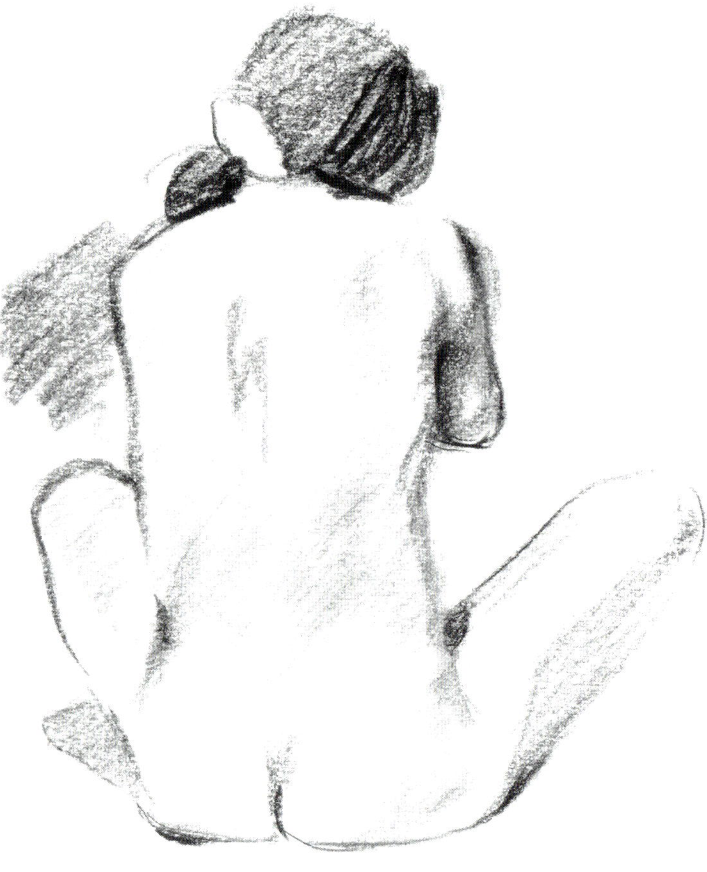

The Torso
Viewed from the Back

ANATOMICAL PROTRUSIONS OF THE BACK

The most notable of the anatomical aspects that determine the contour of the back are the exterior tip of the clavicle (visible at the edge of the shoulders), the protrusion of the seventh (and last) cervical vertebra located between the two shoulder blades, the depression of the spinal column, the protrusions of the scapular (rhomboid major and minor, and the infraspinatus muscle) muscles, and, in many cases, the protuberances of the lumbar vertebrae.

The back of the female figure has much softer contours than the male. Even so, the protuberances of the shoulder blades and the depression of the spinal column are visible, as well as the volume of the upper part of the thoracic cage.

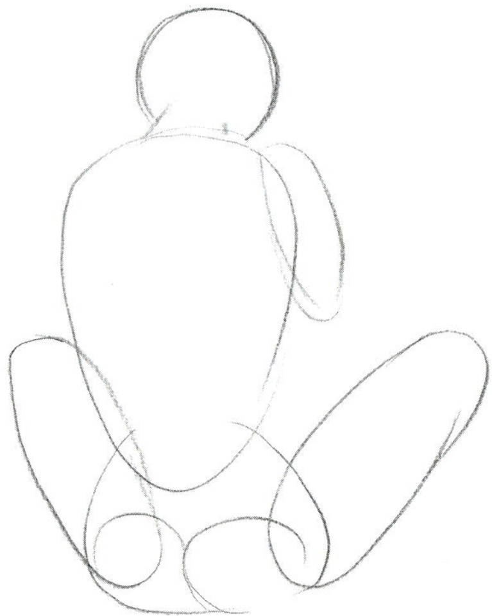

Line sketch of the drawing above with references to the main anatomical elements.

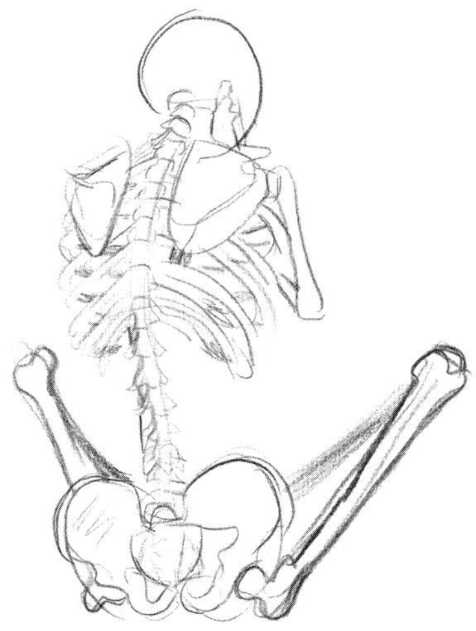

Bone diagram of the female back showing the direction of the spinal column and the position of the pelvis extracted from the adjacent drawing shown here.

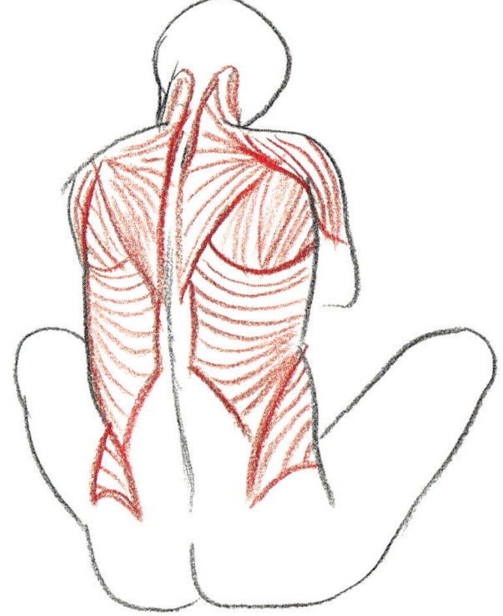

Muscle diagram of the adjacent drawing.

The muscular configuration of the back can be summarized with a simple diagram that shows clearly the outlines of each muscle group.

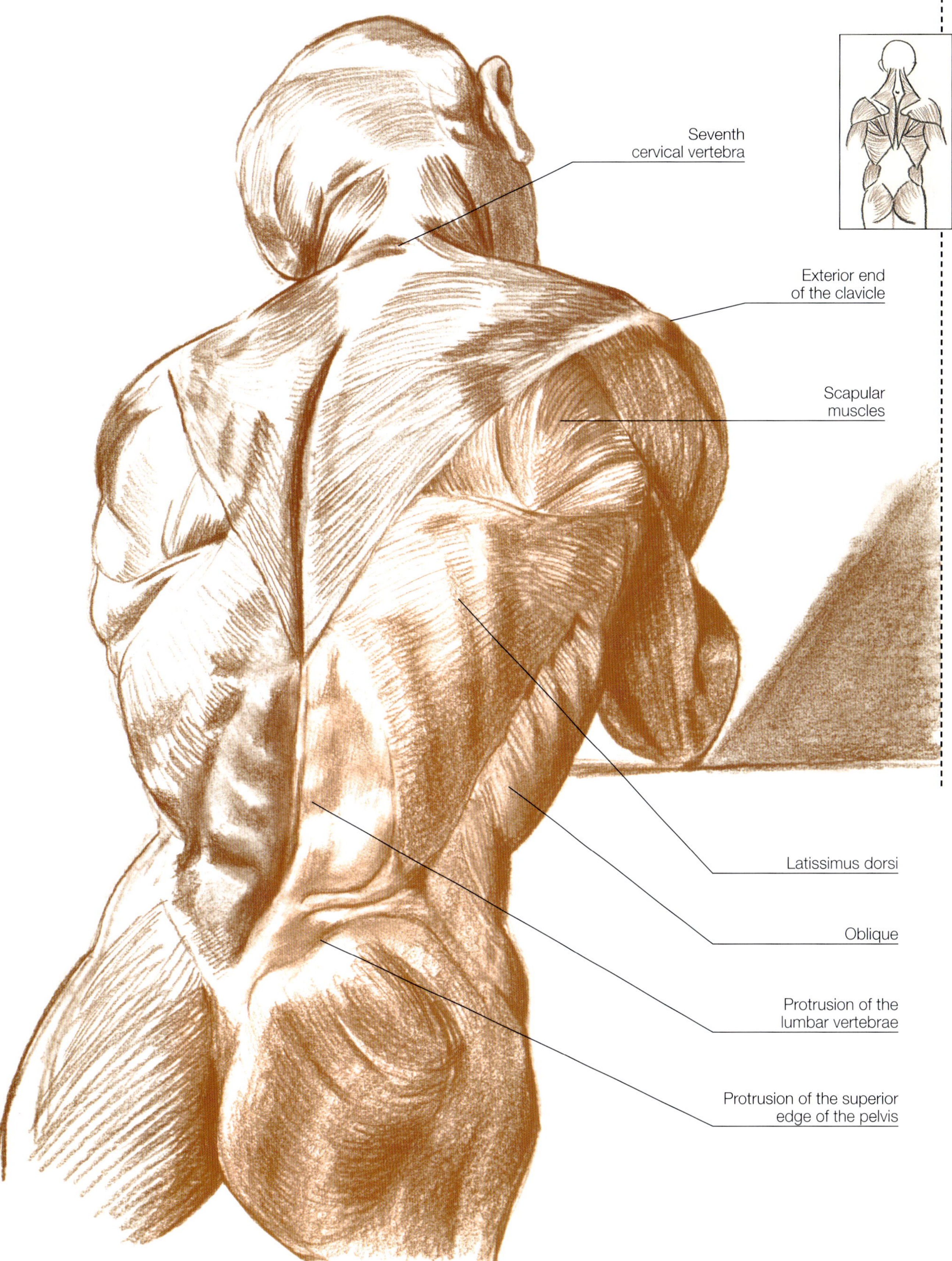

Drawing the Muscles of the Arm

The upper arm and forearm form a complex muscle system, especially in the case of the forearm, because that is where all the muscle groups responsible for the movement of the hand and the fingers are located. To this complexity, we must add the rotational movements of the forearm (pronation and supination), which alter the muscle disposition in a significant way, for example, by making certain muscles of the external or internal side of the arm become more pronounced under specific circumstances. The muscles in the upper arm are larger and easier to locate, and they maintain their respective positions during the course of movement.

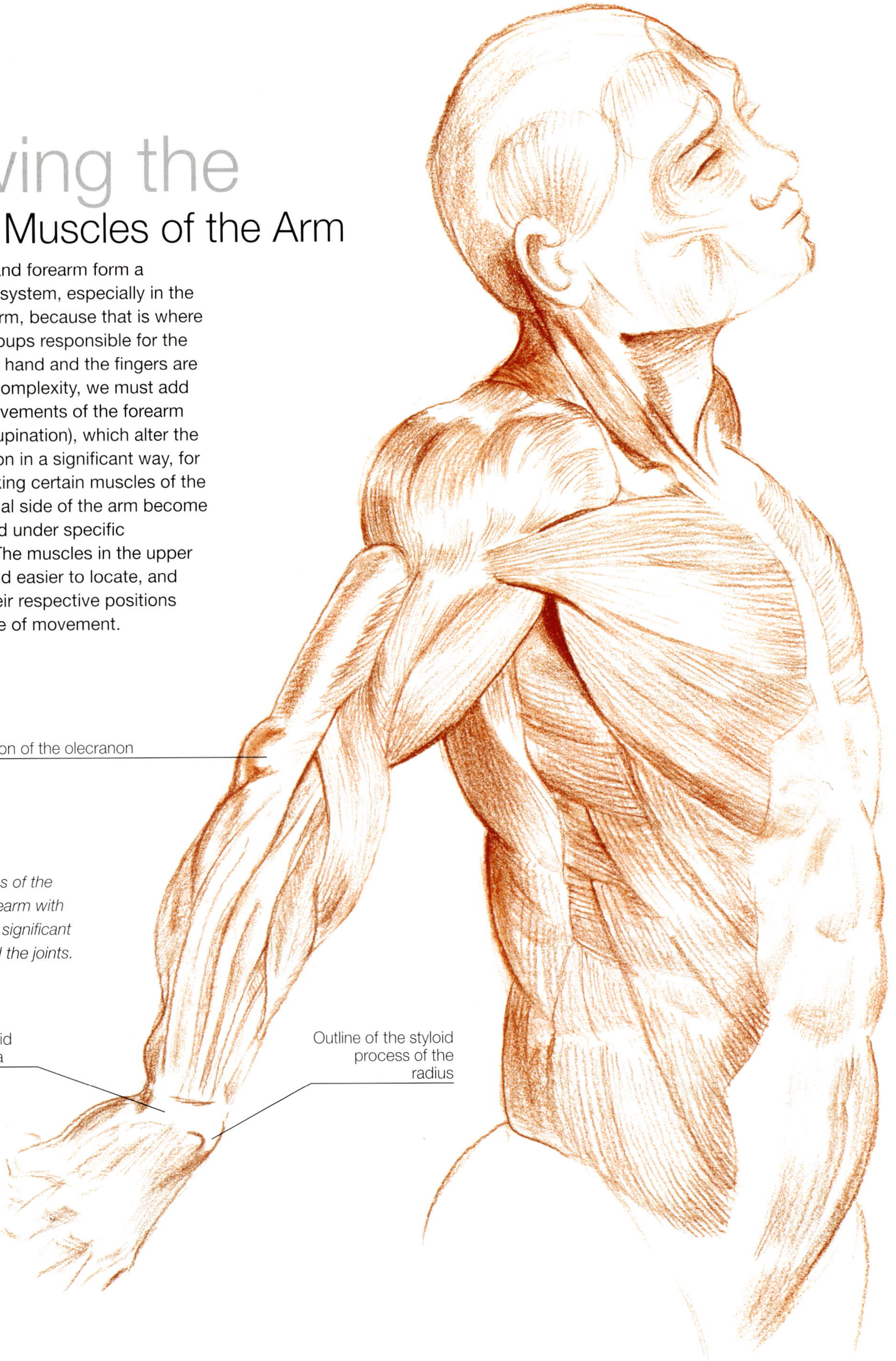

Protrusion of the olecranon

View of the muscles of the upper arm and forearm with labels on the most significant protrusions around the joints.

Outline of the styloid process of the ulna

Outline of the styloid process of the radius

FEATURES OF THE ARMS

The outline of the arm reflects its bone and muscle anatomy in certain areas. The protrusions of the bones are most noticeable in the elbow and the wrist, while the outline of the muscles is particularly visible (when the arm is not in tension) in the shoulder and the upper arm. As is logical, the muscles become much more evident under tension, especially in the upper arm (deltoid and biceps), but the tendons that run along the exterior side of the wrist can also be distended.

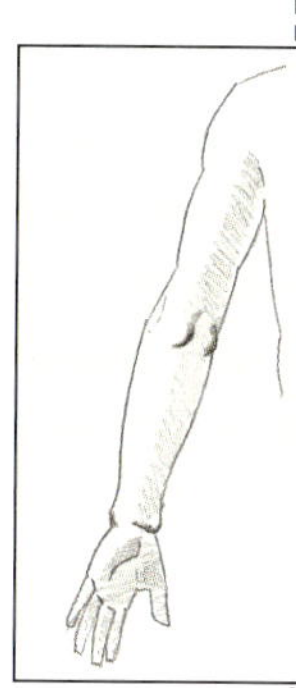

The most interesting protrusions of the arms for the artist are located in the articulations of the elbow (olecranon and epicondyle) and of the wrist (styloid processes of the ulna and of the radius).

Protrusion of the clavicle

Protrusion of the olecranon

Protrusion of the epicondyle

Protrusion of the styloid process of the radius

Protrusion of the styloid process of the ulna

This is a rendering of the muscles of the arms, which have been exaggerated in certain areas to make their identification easier.

The arm is made up of four muscles, three in the anterior area and one in the posterior. The muscles of the anterior area are the biceps brachii, the brachialis, and the coracobrachialis (having no significance for the artist). The muscles of the posterior region are the triceps. They are all visible in the position illustrated here.

Muscles and Shapes of the Front of the Upper Arm and Forearm

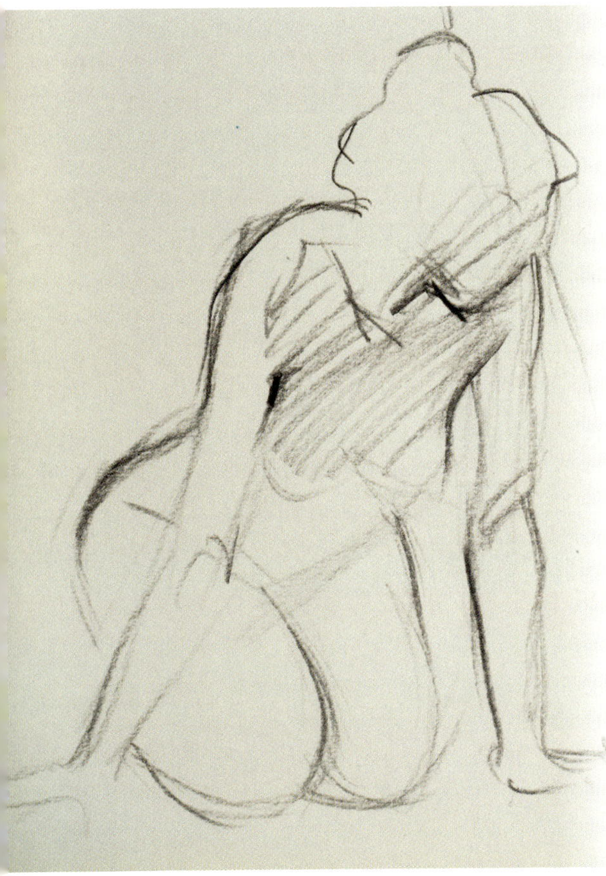

General contour of the upper arm and the forearm seen on their internal side. The following diagrams show the anatomical reasons for their volumes.

There are three areas or regions in which the muscles of the forearm are located: the anterior, the posterior, and the external. The anterior region is also called the palmar region because it occupies the same plane as the palm of the hand. It is made up of eight muscles, of which only four are located on the surface plane and visible in the exterior outline: the pronator teres, the flexor carpi radialis, the palmaris longus, and the flexor carpi ulnaris.

THE BICEPS

The biceps, or biceps brachii, is the most superficial of the muscles on the anterior side of the arm. It originates in two areas of the shoulder, which results in two muscle parts or heads (long and short heads). Both heads (also called long biceps and short biceps) join together in their lower part to form a single tendon, which passes in front of the articulation of the elbow and inserts in the upper end of the radius. The biceps promotes the flexion of the forearm and also its supination.

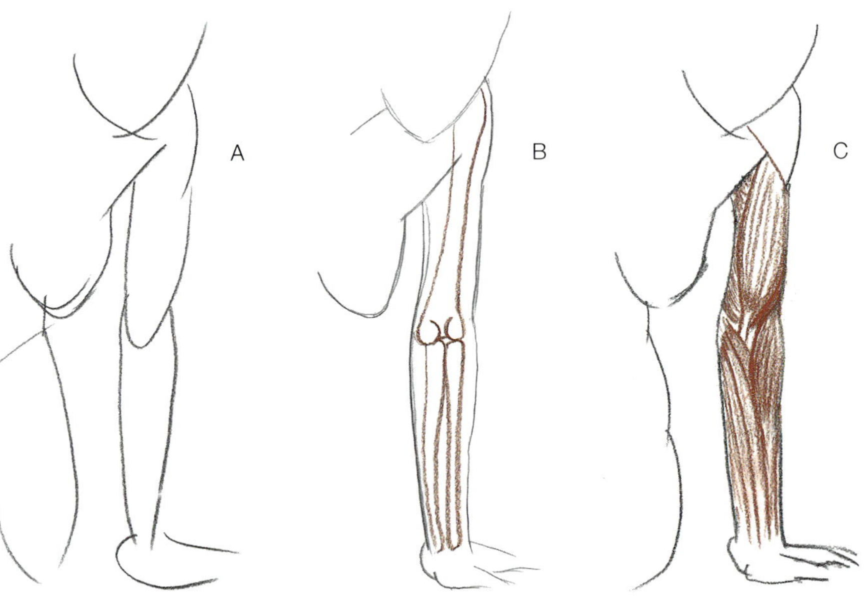

A. General diagram of the arm in the pose shown in the drawing above.
B. Respective positions of the humerus in the upper arm and the ulna (the innermost bone) and the radius in the forearm.
C. General diagram of the internal muscles of the upper arm and forearm and the mass of the supinator longus, which gives the arm its characteristic profile at the level of the elbow.

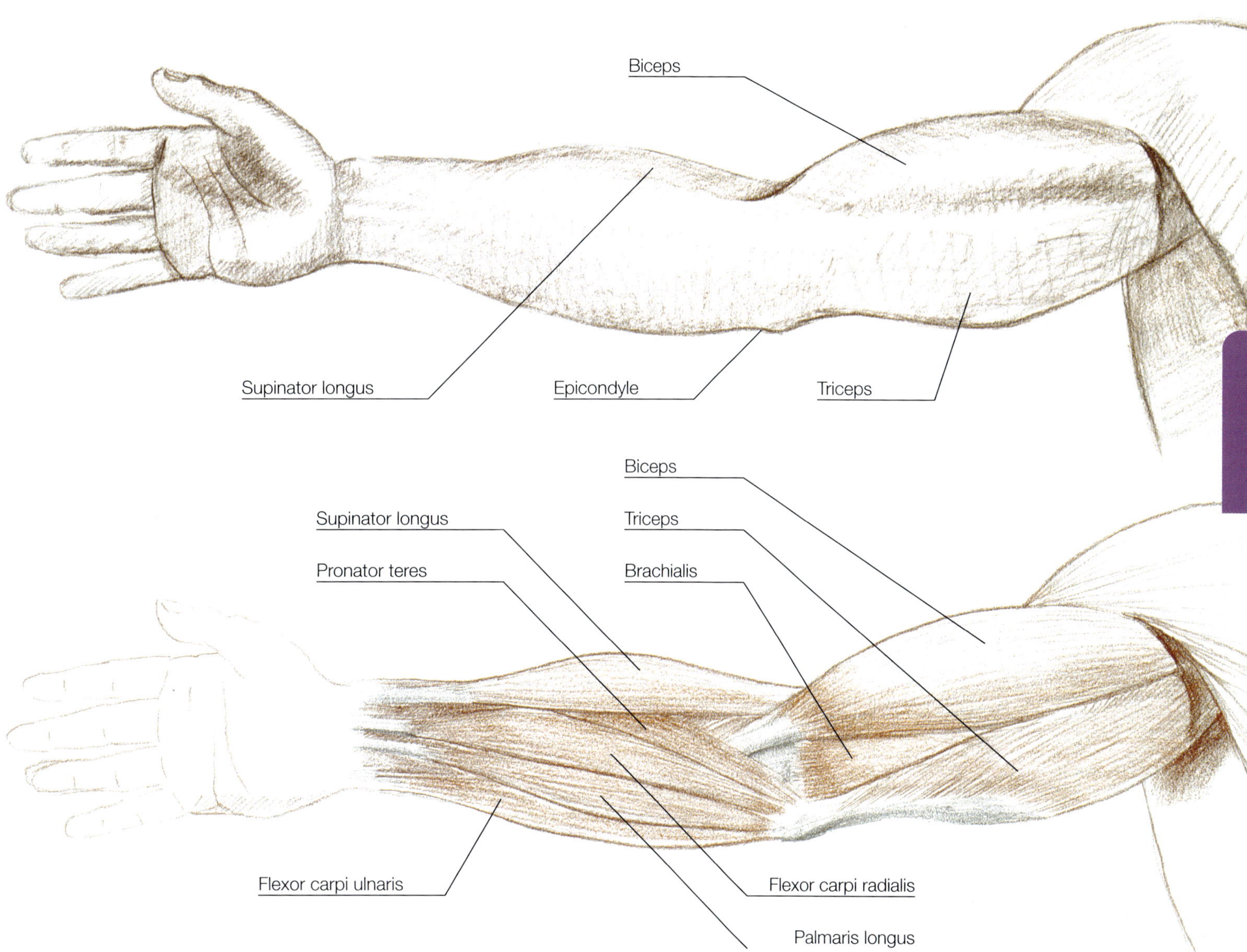

THE BRACHIALIS

The brachialis, or brachialis anticus, is a deep muscle with respect to the biceps, but is broader and extends beyond it on both sides. Its function is to flex the forearm.

THE TRICEPS

Also called triceps brachii, this muscle consists of three heads. These three heads join together in a powerful flat tendon (the tendon of the triceps). The triceps extends the forearm and contributes to keeping the head of the humerus stable in its joint.

THE PRONATOR TERES

This originates in the epicondyle and runs down diagonally toward its insertion in the middle area of the radius. It is partially hidden under the supinator longus in its lower area. Its function is to promote the pronation of the forearm by pulling the radius toward itself when it contracts.

FLEXOR CARPI RADIALIS

This is the muscle located next to the pronator teres. Both originate in the epicondyle. The flexor carpi radialis allows the wrist to bend forward, bringing the palm of the hand closer to the forearm.

THE PALMARIS LONGUS

It is located next to the flexor carpi radialis and closer to the internal side of the forearm. It originates in the epicondyle and ends in a broad tendon that inserts into the palm of the hand. Like the flexor carpi radialis, it promotes hand flexion.

THE FLEXOR CARPI ULNARIS

This muscle also originates in the epicondyle and is the innermost of the muscles in the anterior side. Its tendon descends along the ulna and inserts into a carpal bone. Its function is to take part in the bending and rotating of the wrist.

Muscles and Shapes of the Outside of the Arm and Forearm

The external area is the part that appears in the same plane as the back of the hand when we shake hands. On the external view of the upper arm, the triceps, which is the muscle that determines the external outline of this area, especially stands out, but the brachialis and the biceps are also partially visible. The posterior area of the forearm is the one that occupies the same plane as the back of the hand when the arm is relaxed while the figure is in the standing position. This region is shared by eight muscles, of which four are most noticeable: the anconeus, the extensor carpi ulnaris, the extensor digitorum communis, and the extensor carpi radialis longus. These muscles are especially visible on the exterior surface of the upper area of the forearm, that is, the one closest to the elbow.

This pose makes it possible to draw the exterior anatomy of the arm in an extended position.

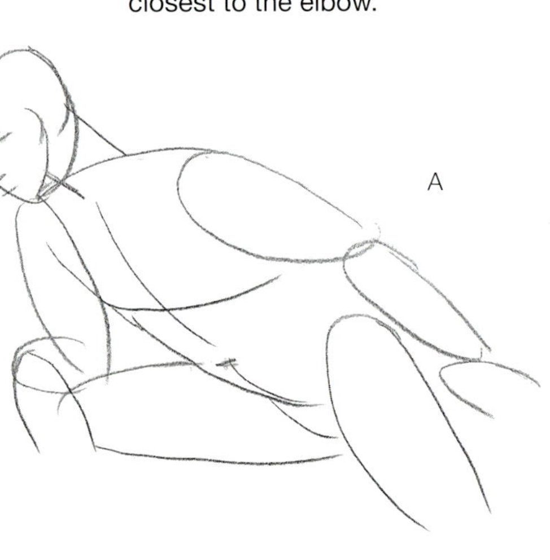

A. Generic diagram for drawing the figure above.

B. Bone diagram of the pose. The arm is shown in pronation position: the ulna and the radius cross each other.

C. In this muscle diagram, the biceps, the brachialis, and the triceps can be easily identified in the upper arm, as well as the flexor carpi radialis and the supinator longus in the forearm.

THE ANCONEUS

This is a small muscle that originates in the posterior side of the humerus and ends in the posterior side of the ulna. Its function is to extend the elbow.

THE EXTENSOR CARPI ULNARIS

This is located next to the flexor carpi ulnaris, a little bit more to the outside with respect to that muscle. It is an extensor and adductor for the hand, meaning it bends the wrist and pulls the back of the hand closer to the forearm and rotates it inward.

THE EXTENSOR CARPI RADIALIS LONGUS

This is a thin muscle whose function is, like the extensor carpi ulnaris, to extend and adduct the hand.

THE EXTENSOR DIGITORUM COMMUNIS

The common extensor of the fingers is the most robust of the muscles on the surface layer of the posterior region. It originates at the epicondyle of the humerus and and descends along the radius to divide into four tendons in the wrist. These tendons attach to the three phalanges of each finger, but not the thumb. This muscle takes part in the extension of the wrist and promotes the extension of the phalanges, bringing them closer to the bones of the metacarpus.

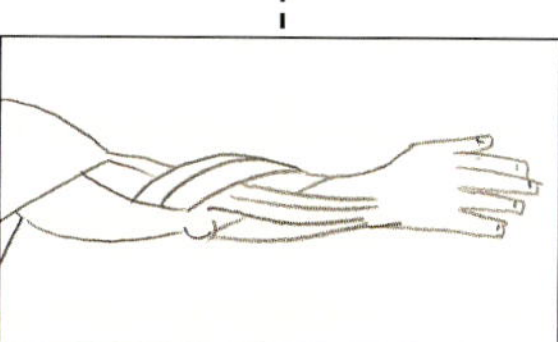

Generic diagram of the surface muscles of the external sides of the upper arm and forearm studied in these pages.

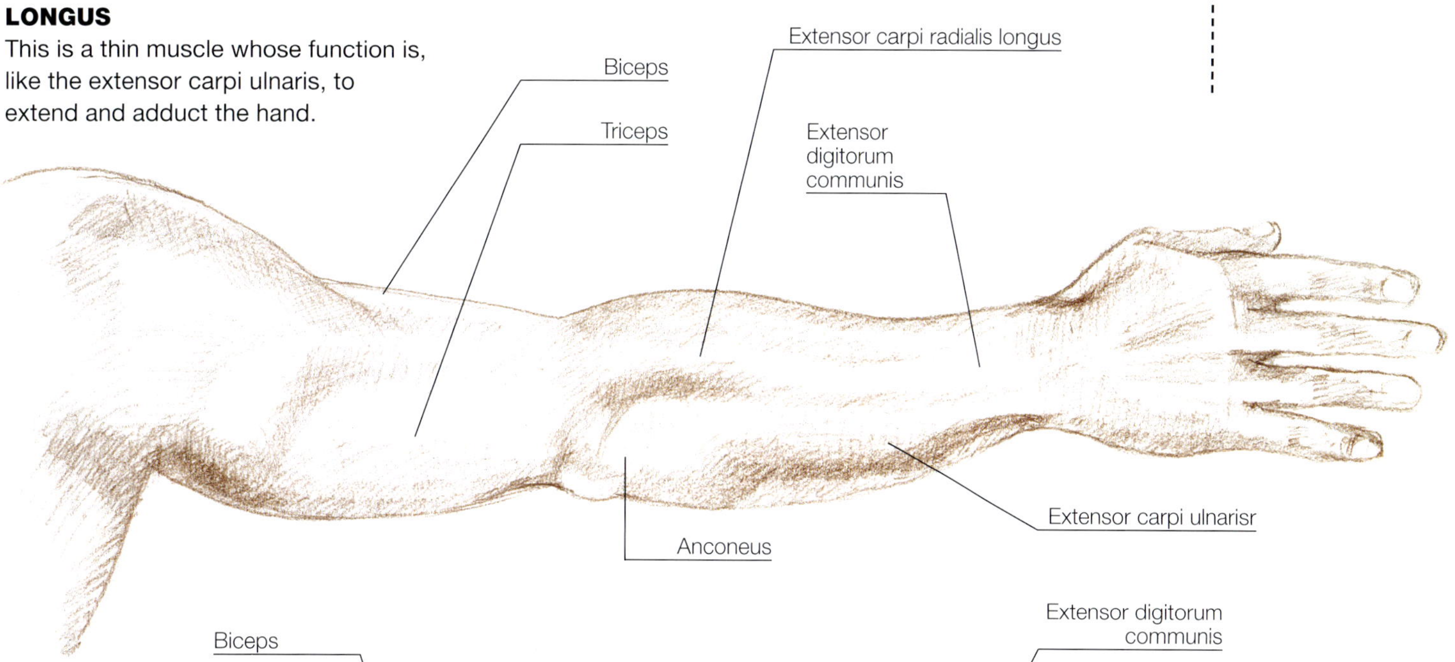

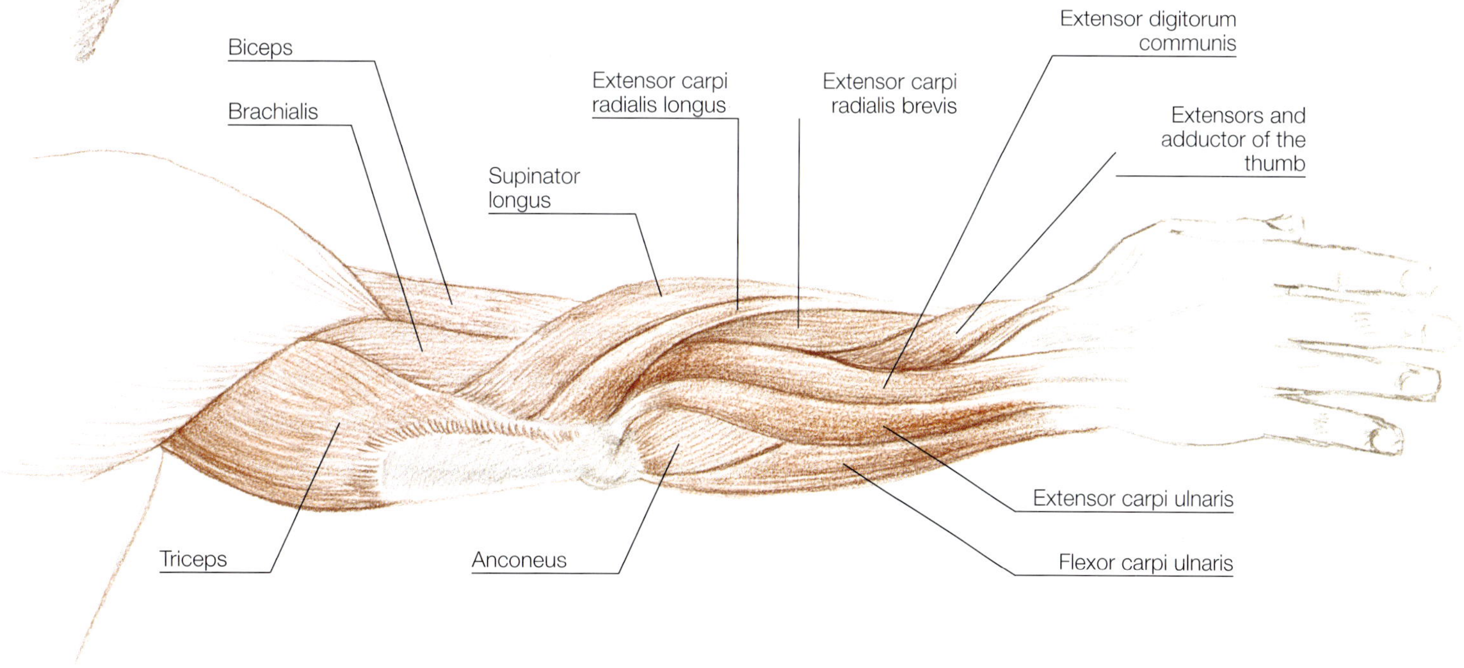

Other Views of the Arms

The distribution of the muscles in the arms (except in the cases of the biceps and triceps) is not easy to memorize. Each position presents a problem, which in most cases must be resolved by guessing the locations of the muscles from the interior and exterior views previously studied. Here, we show two views of the upper arm and forearm in a relaxed position while the figure is standing up: a view that reveals the front, the side, and the back.

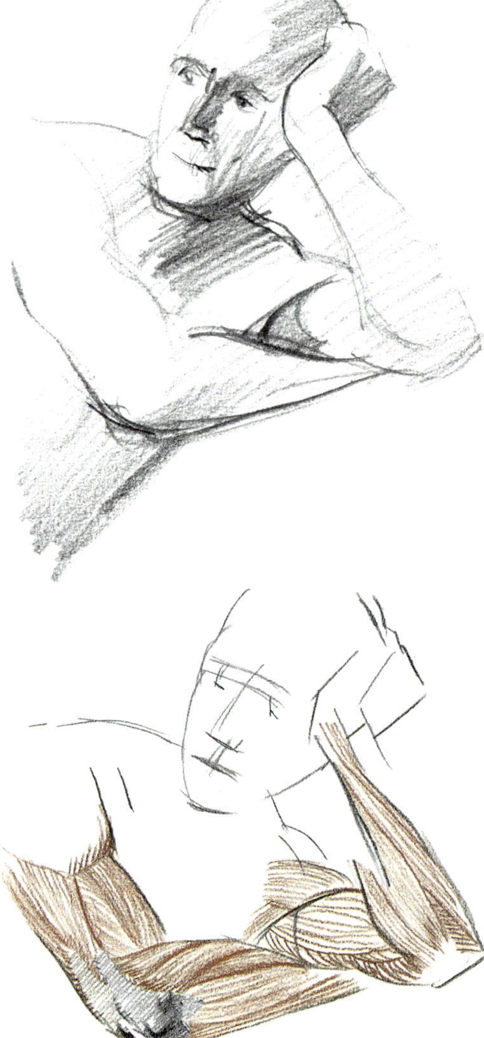

This pose of the figure shows the anatomy of the upper arm and the forearm in a way that is somewhat complex, but that can be worked out through the illustrations of the anatomy shown here.

In the muscle diagram of the drawing shown here, some of the muscles depicted in the illustrations are indicated.

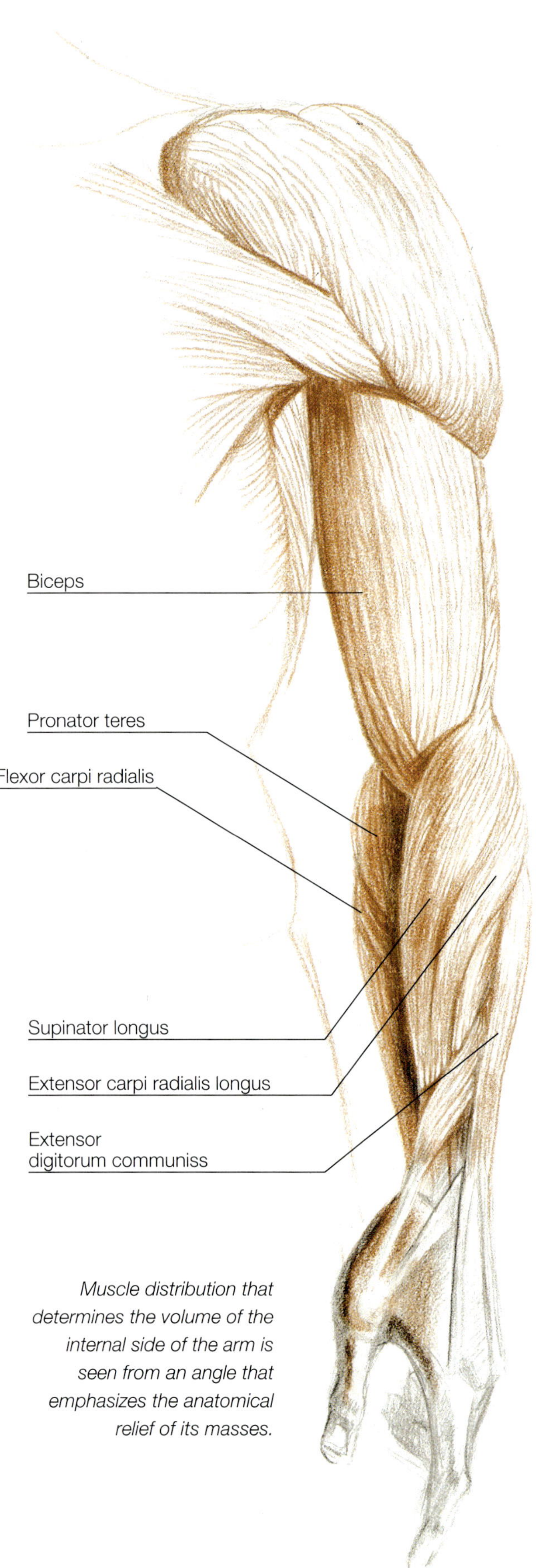

Muscle distribution that determines the volume of the internal side of the arm is seen from an angle that emphasizes the anatomical relief of its masses.

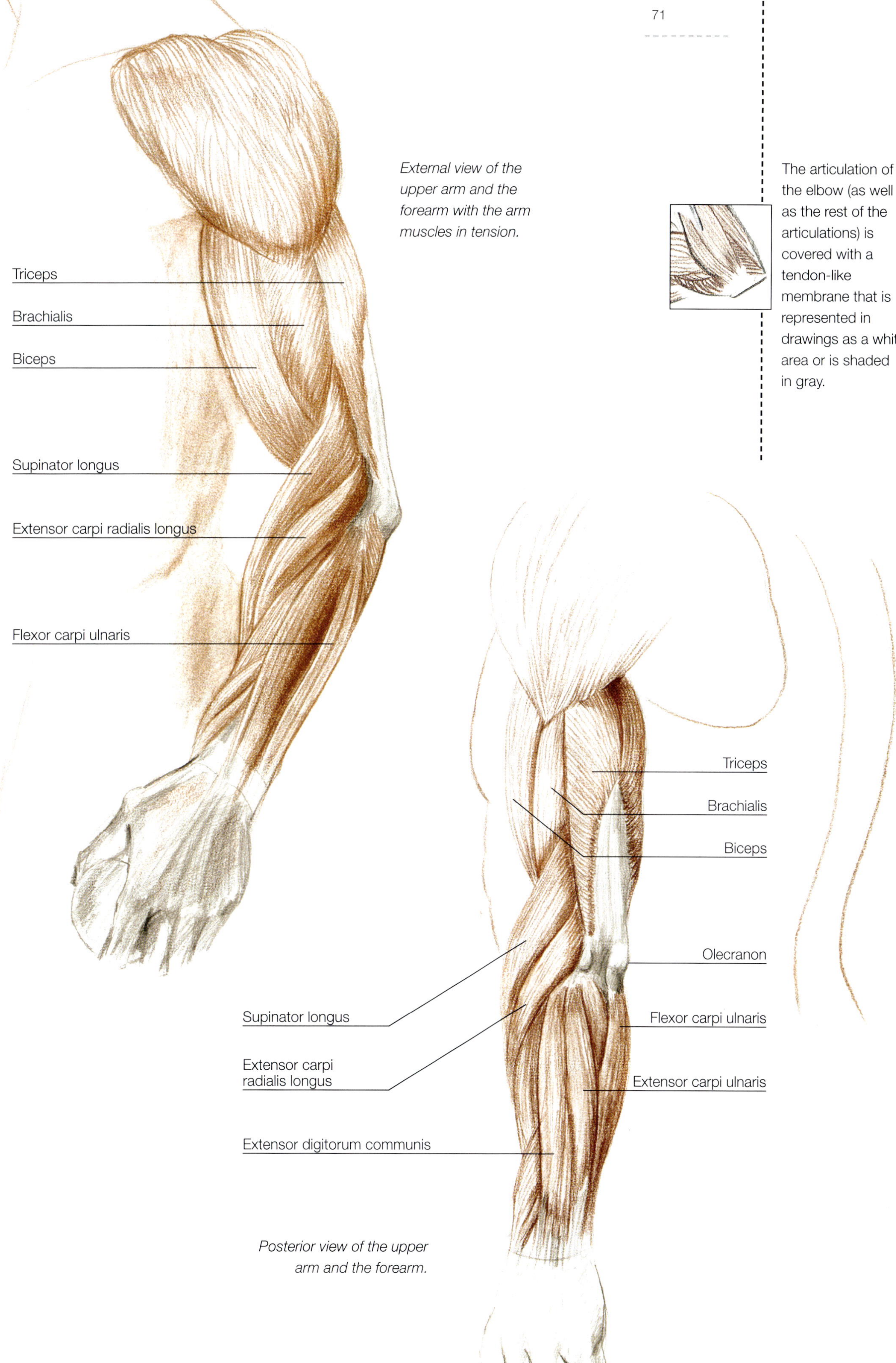

External view of the upper arm and the forearm with the arm muscles in tension.

The articulation of the elbow (as well as the rest of the articulations) is covered with a tendon-like membrane that is represented in drawings as a white area or is shaded in gray.

Posterior view of the upper arm and the forearm.

Study of the Drawing of the Arms

A

B

The practical application of the study of the arms' anatomy requires basic knowledge of the muscles, as well as careful observation of their behavior. These are generally important recommendations for drawing any figure, but especially for the arms, since many muscles are involved and a wide range of possibilities can arise during their movement. These pages show some of the drawings made from the model where different views of the arms have been drawn with precision and simplicity.

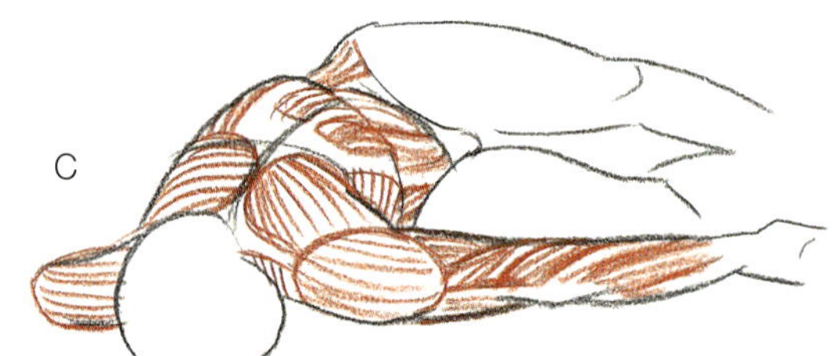

A. General diagram for drawing the figure illustrated here.

B. Bone diagram of the figure.

C. In this muscle reconstruction of the pose, we can see the muscles of the external side of the upper arm and forearm studied in previous pages

The extension of the upper arm and forearm illustrates all of the muscles' external shapes.

Arms crossed in front of the body are somewhat difficult to draw, but this can be resolved with adequate knowledge of the anatomy of the different sides of the upper arm and the forearm.

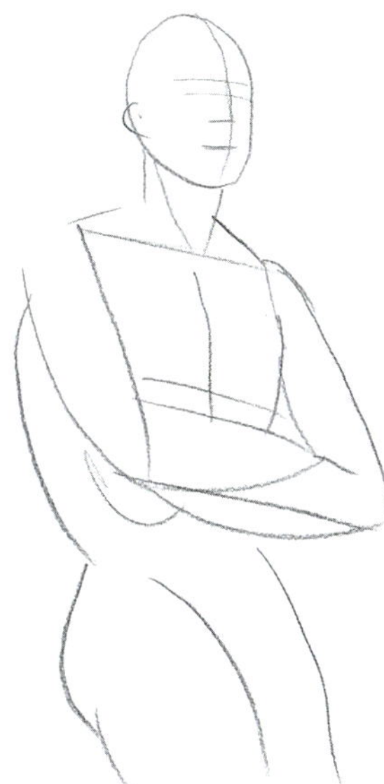

This diagram of the figure provides a good overall approach for drawing the arms.

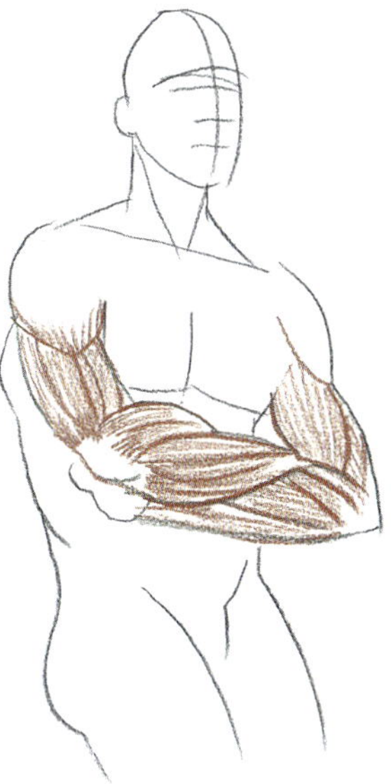

Diagram of the figure's muscles showing the torsion of the arm muscles in this position.

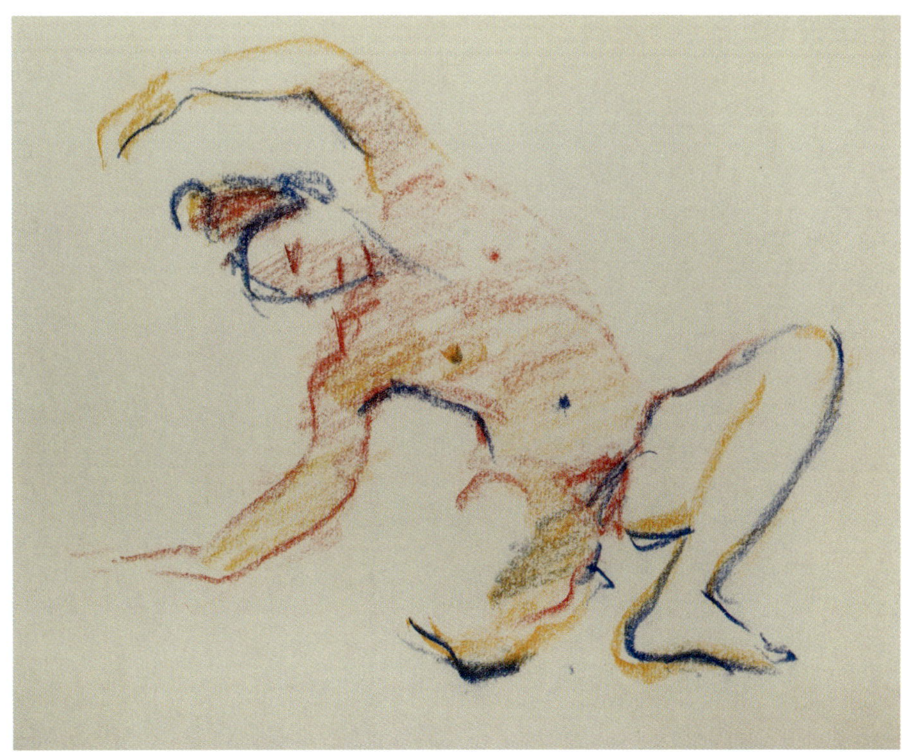

Knowledge of the position of the muscles of the upper arm and forearm helps resolve the drawing of any pose in terms of the figure itself and of the logic of the muscles involved in the movement.

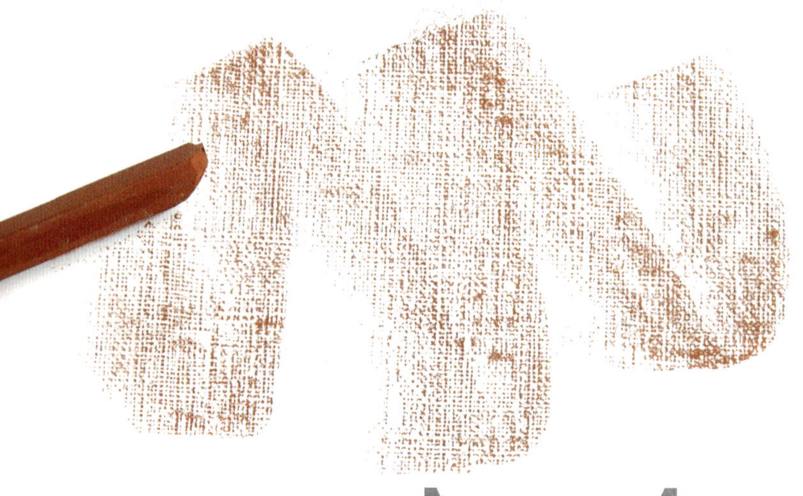

Muscles of the

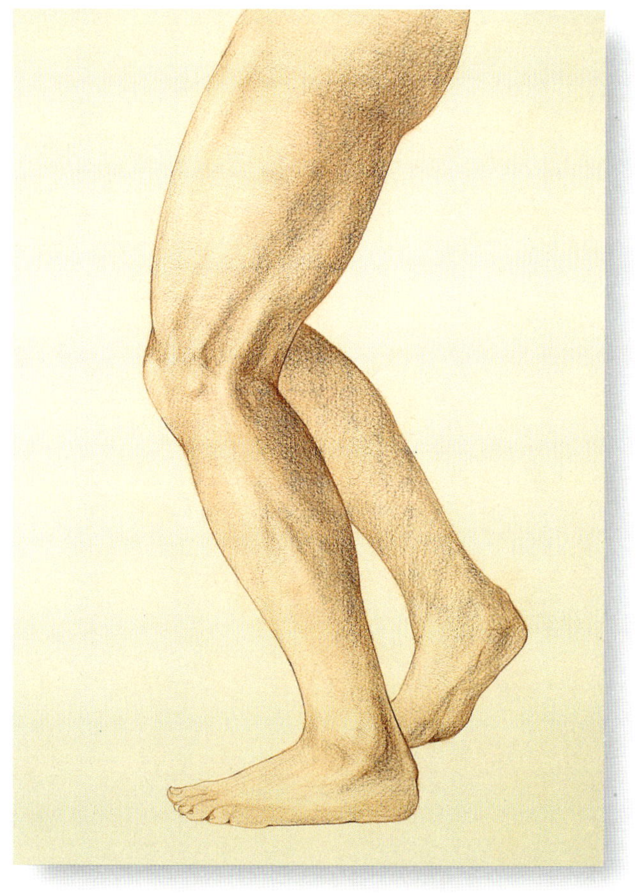

HÉCTOR FERNÁNDEZ. LEG, 2002. *SANGUINE*

Leg.

Anatomically speaking,

the legs are considered

the lower limbs, also called the *pelvic* limbs. Each leg can be divided into four parts: the pelvis, the thigh, the calf, and the foot. Regarding the pelvic area, these pages will address the posterior muscles, the gluteus, because its anterior part comprises almost entirely the muscles of the lower abdomen, studied in the pages related to the torso. The leg muscles are the most powerful muscles in the entire body because their function supports the whole body and allows it to walk.

Features
of the Legs

The bone and muscle projections of the legs are somewhat more pronounced than those of the arms if we compare them both at rest. Due to their supportive function, the muscles of the lower limbs are much more voluminous and visible under the skin than those of any other part of the body. Seen from the front, the mass of the quadriceps in the thigh stands out, as well as the protrusion of the knee and the tibialis muscle in the calf. Seen from the side, the mass of the gastrocnemius is especially visible in the calf; and seen from behind, the popliteal groove (in the articulation of the knee), the gastrocnemius, and the biceps femoris stand out, among others.

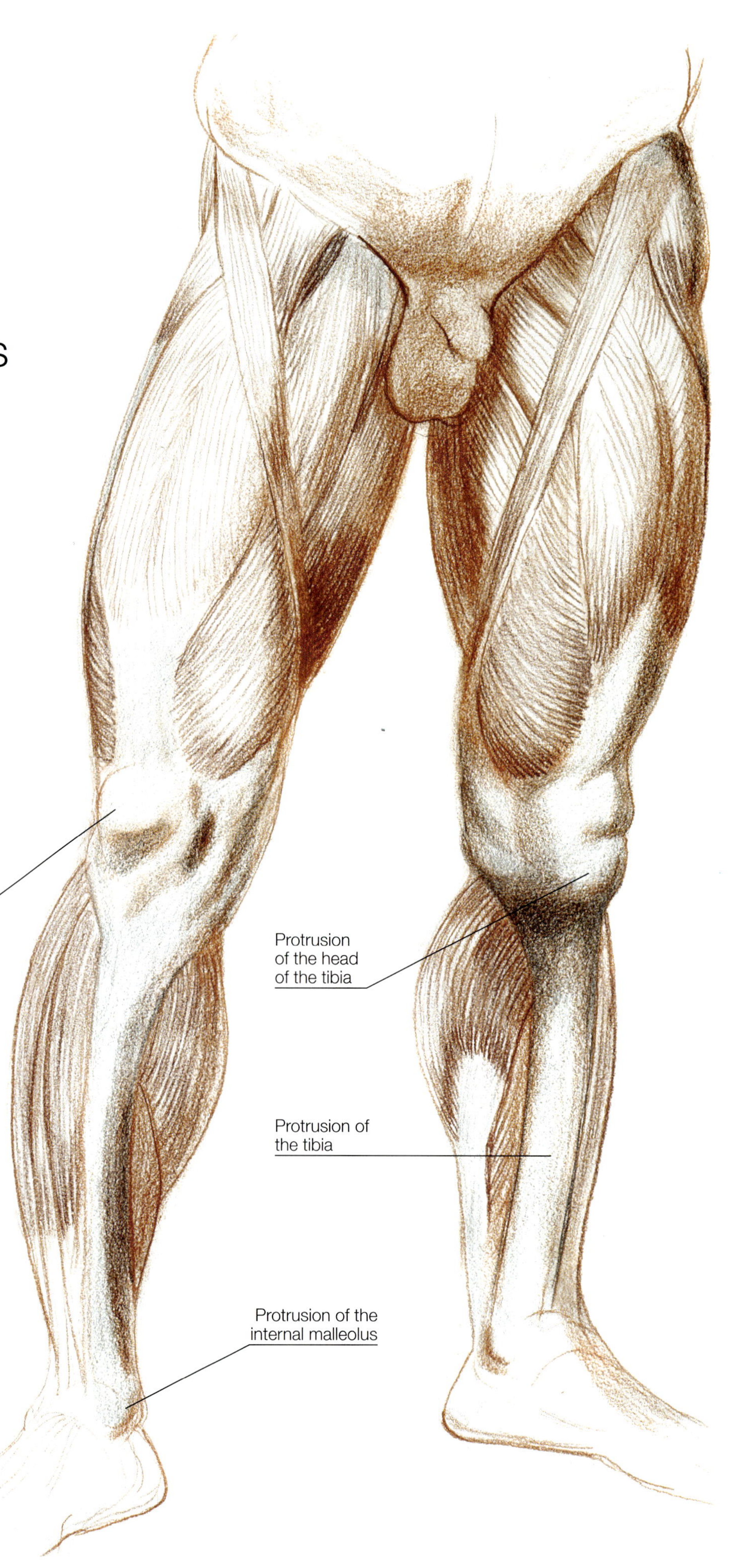

View of the external protrusions of the legs in the anterior region and, partially, in the internal region.

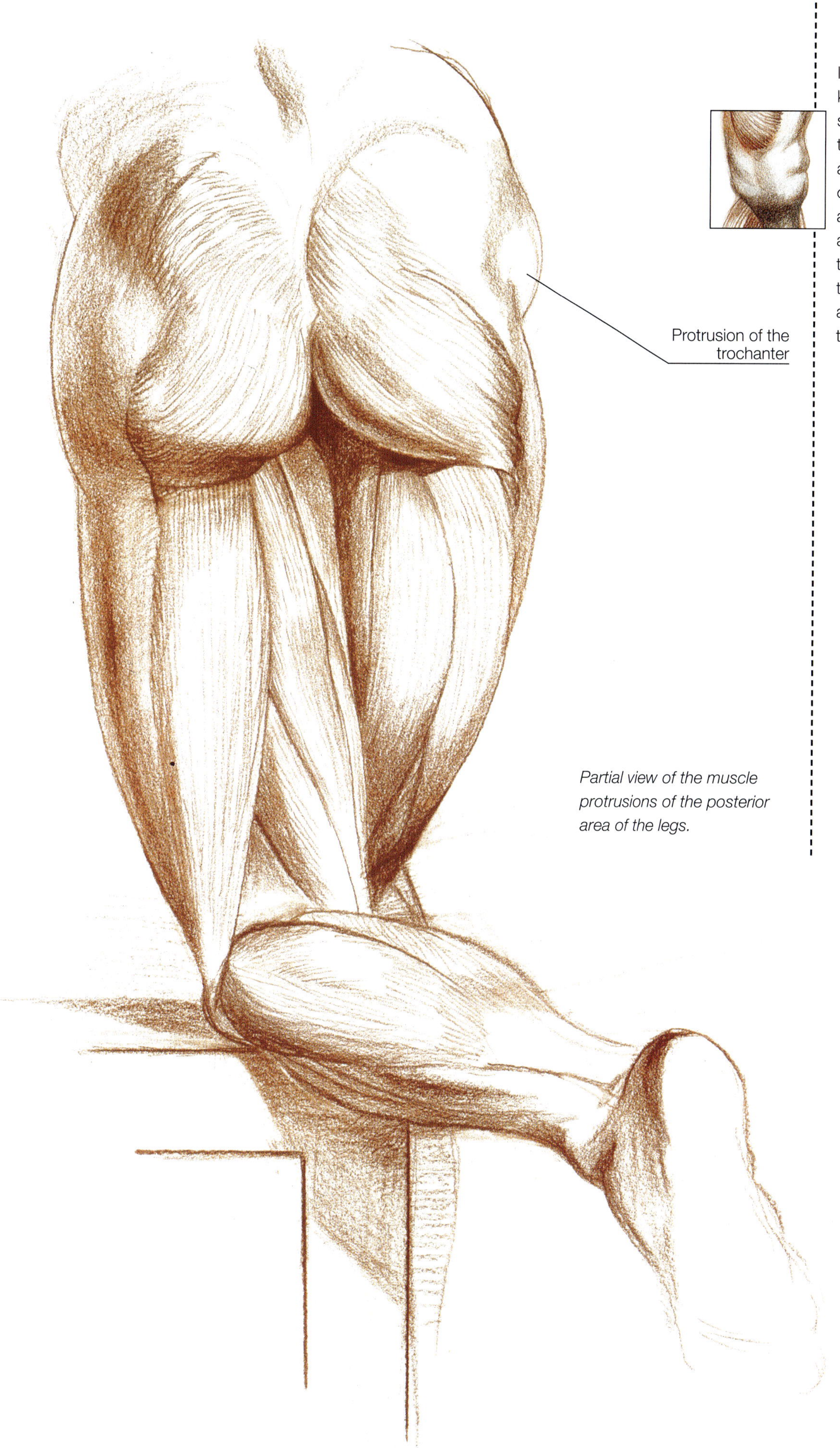

Partial view of the muscle protrusions of the posterior area of the legs.

In this view of the knee we can clearly see the protrusions of the patella (above) and of the wide head of the tibia. Both anatomical elements are covered with a tendon-like membrane that is common to all the articulations of the body.

Muscles of the Front of the Leg

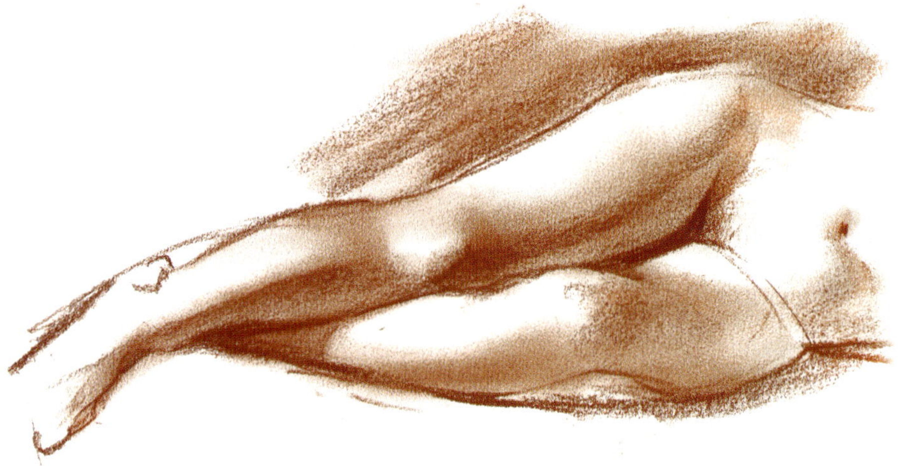

Here, we can identify the most distinctive muscle masses of the external region of the legs.

On the front of the leg, the broad mass of the quadriceps in the thigh, including the vastus lateralis and vastus medialis above the projection of the knee, is the most notable muscle. The protrusions of the muscles of the calf are also distinctive, as is the depression that marks the trajectory of the tibia from the base of the knee to the internal malleolus between the muscles of the tibialis anterior and gastrocnemius. In the drawing of the external contour, we can also see the shapes created by the adductor and sartorius muscles.

A. Bone diagram of the pose depicted in this drawing.
B. Muscle diagram of the drawing.

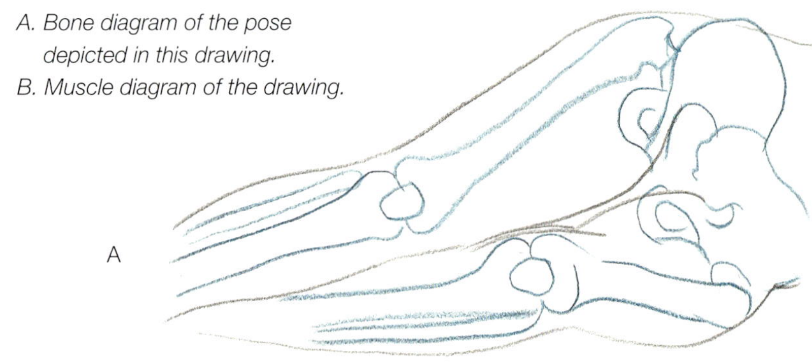

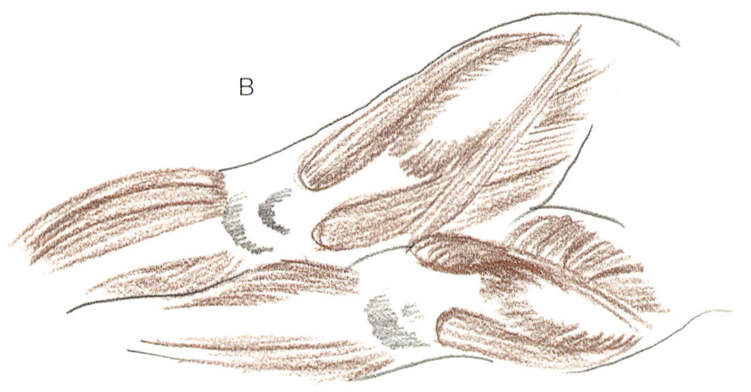

THE SARTORIUS

This is the longest muscle in the body. It is a thin, superficial muscle throughout its entire length, which wraps around the thigh. It originates in the iliac spine and wraps around the front of the thigh on its way down to the inside of the thigh and knee until it finally attaches to the superior inside part of the tibia.

The sartorius performs multiple actions on the hip and the knee, including flexing the thigh while bending the knee and rotating the thigh outward.

THE QUADRICEPS FEMORIS

Th quadriceps is the voluminous muscle that surrounds the femur. It is divided into four heads joined at its lower end by a powerful tendon inserted into the patella and the upper area of the tibia. The deepest head is the vastus intermedius muscle that surrounds the femur and is invisible under the skin. The vastus intermedius is surrounded and almost completely covered by the larger heads of the vastus lateralis and the vastus medialis, which form a sort of cover around the femur. The fourth head of the quadriceps is the voluminous rectus femoris, which occupies the center of the thigh and covers most of the vastus muscles. It extends from in front of the iliac spine down to the common tendon in the knee. The quadriceps extends the knee (the gesture for kicking with the toe) and participates in the rotation of the calf with the knee bent.

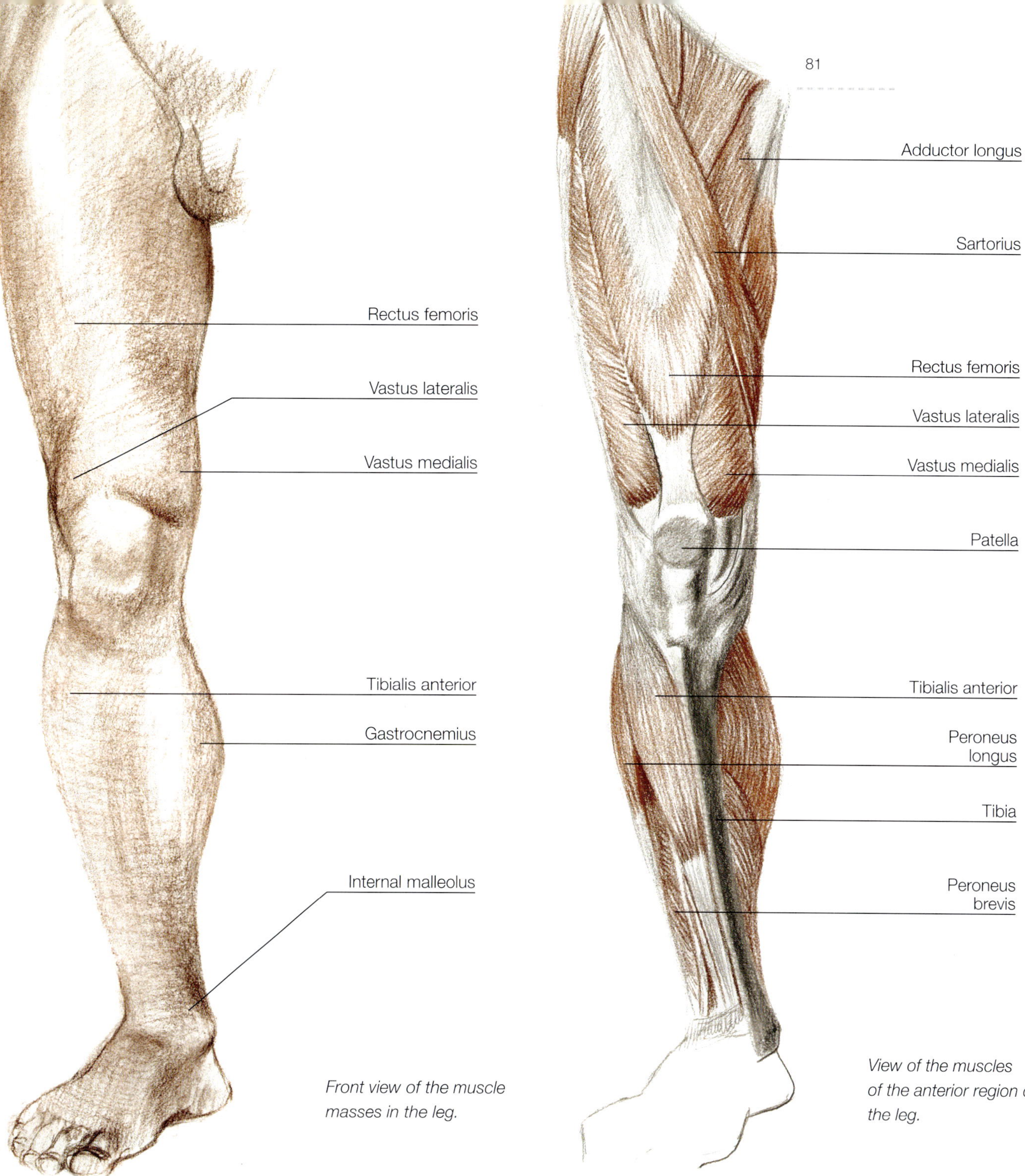

Front view of the muscle masses in the leg.

View of the muscles of the anterior region of the leg.

TIBIALIS ANTERIOR

This originates in the upper part of the external side of the tibia and descends along it to insert into the first metatarsal of the big toe in the foot. The protrusion of the tibialis anterior can be seen in the outline of the calf as a slight protrusion on its front side, between the lower part of the knee and the higher part of the top of the foot. It is an adductor muscle whose function is to elevate the inside edge of the foot.

THE TWO PERONEUS MUSCLES

In reality these muscles belong to the external side of the calf, but they are mentioned here because they are also seen in front view. The most superficial one is the peroneus longus (also known as the *fibularis longus*). It promotes the extension of the foot, making its external edge descend and points the toes downward and outward, as is seen in the steps of classical dance. The peroneus brevis (fibularis brevis) enables the abduction and external rotation of the foot.

General View of the Legs

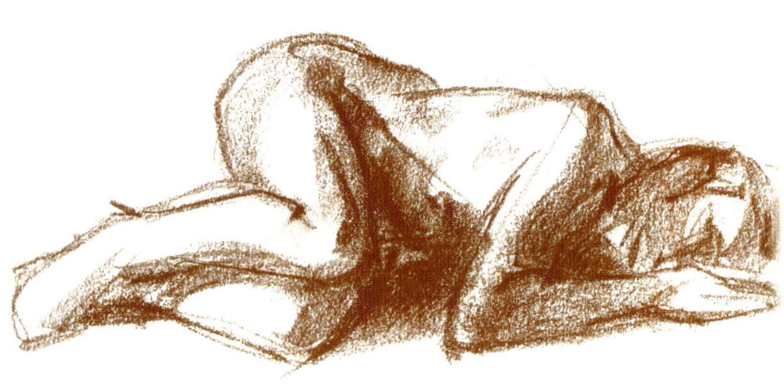

Bent knees can be problematic when drawing legs. Here, the difficulty has been resolved with proper shading, which emphasizes the change of plane that clarifies the articulation.

The illustrations shown on these pages are a summary of everything we have learned so far about the muscles of the legs. Each one of them depicts a movement and an outline for the legs, whether from the thigh or from the calf, and in them we can perceive the distribution of the most significant muscles as it pertains to the muscle masses of the legs. Normally, the artist approaches drawing the legs as a unit without differentiating the parts. However, for that unit to be coherent, it is important to know the volume and the "trajectory" of the most significant muscles. In brief, we can say that the essential muscles for the leg's outline are: the thigh, the gluteus maximus, the quadriceps and its heads, the rectus femoris, the vastus lateralis, and the vastus medialis, as well as the semitendinosus muscles and the biceps femoris on its posterior surface. On the calf, the muscles that always affect the volume are the gastrocnemius, the tibialis anterior, and the peroneus longus.

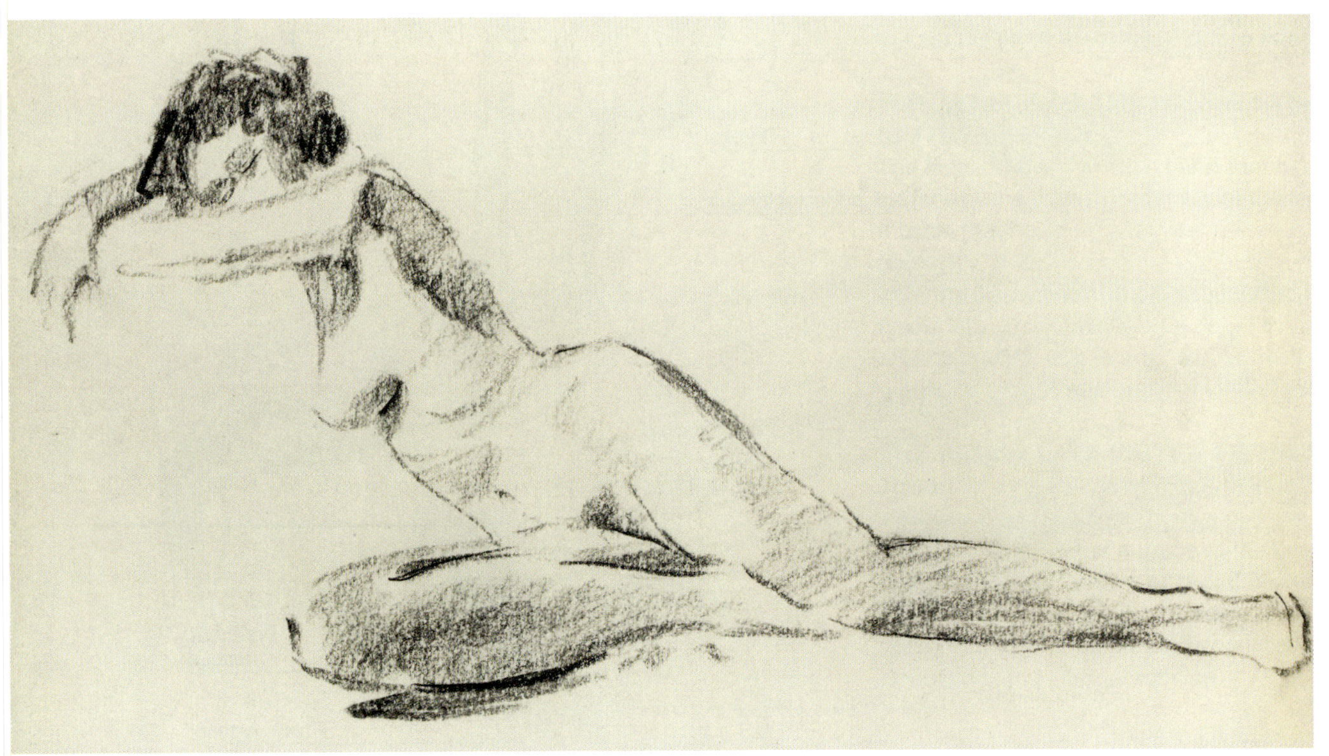

The flexed right leg of the figure is defined by the two main muscles in the calf that stand out and give it its characteristic spindle-like shape: the tibialis anterior and the gastrocnemius.

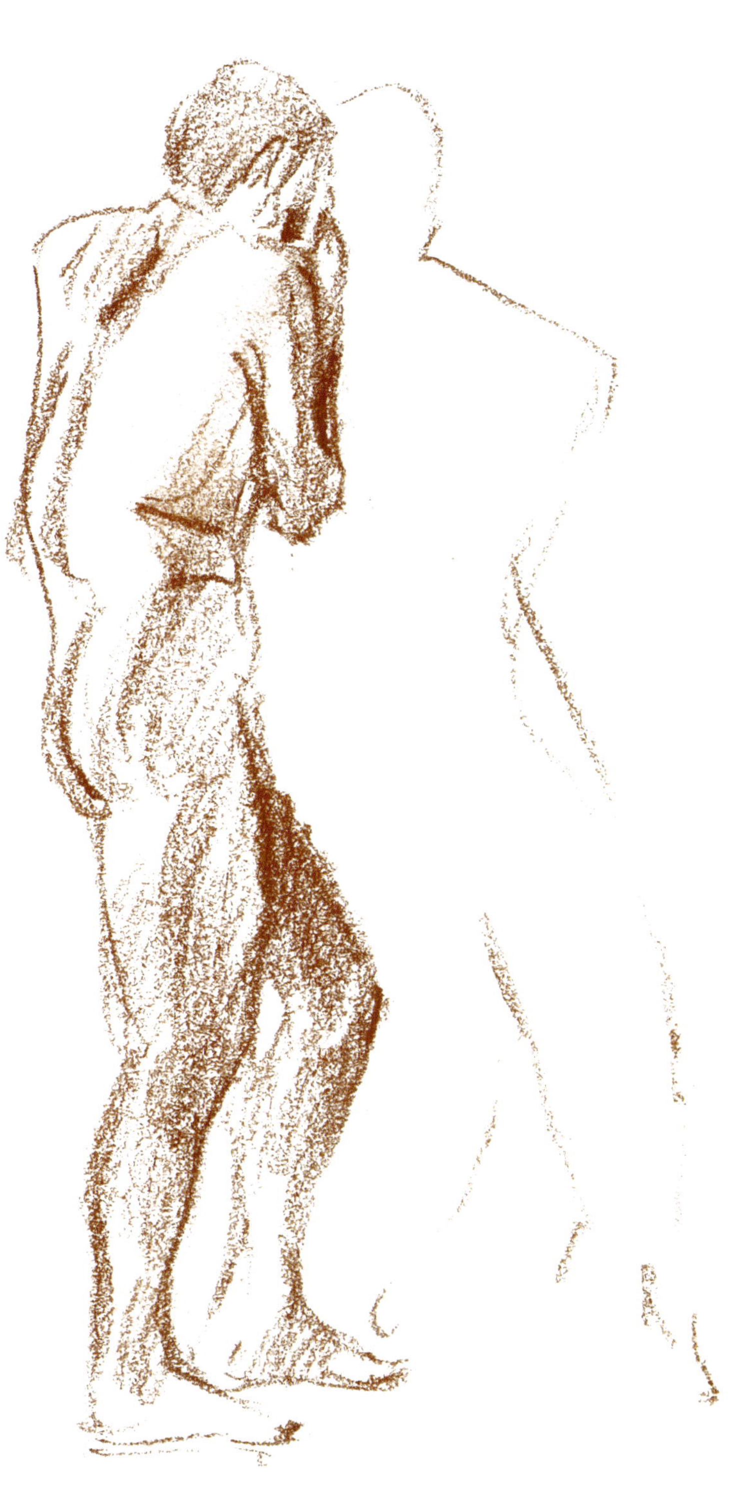

Notice the powerful volume of the thigh dominated on its anterior surface by the great mass of the rectus femoris and on its posterior surface by the masses of the semitendinosus and the biceps femoris.

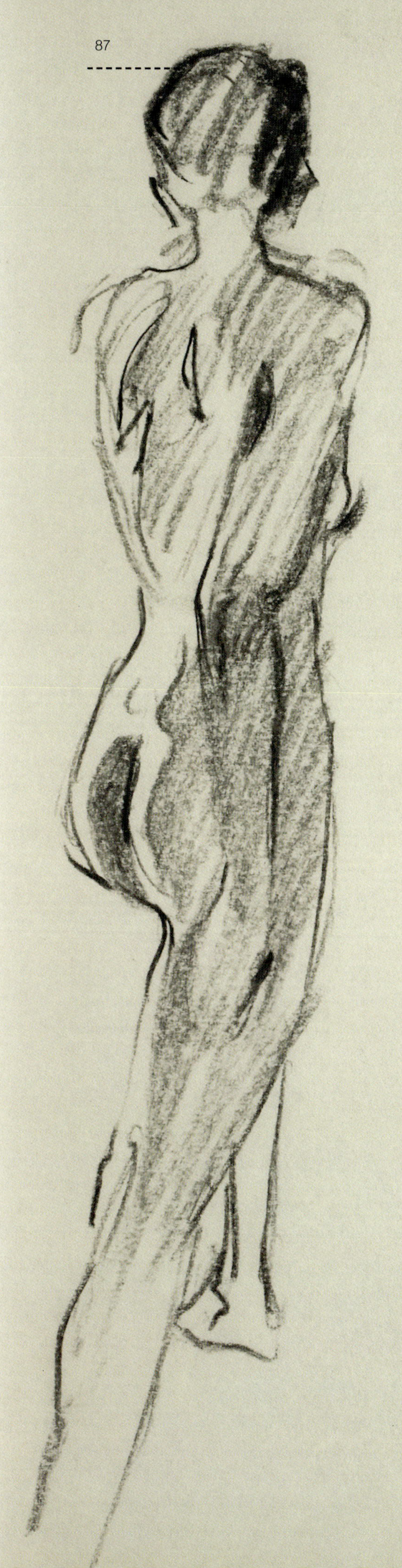

The glutei are one of the main anatomical references when drawing the legs, especially in the female figure. This sketch gives an accurate summary of their form and volume.

The Head, the Hands, and the Feet

"THE BEST THING IS TO DRAW MEN AND WOMEN FROM THE NUDE AND THUS FIX IN THE MEMORY BY CONSTANT EXERCISE THE MUSCLES OF THE TORSO, BACK, LEGS, ARMS, AND KNEES, KNOWING THE BONES UNDERNEATH."
Giorgio Vasari (1522-1574)

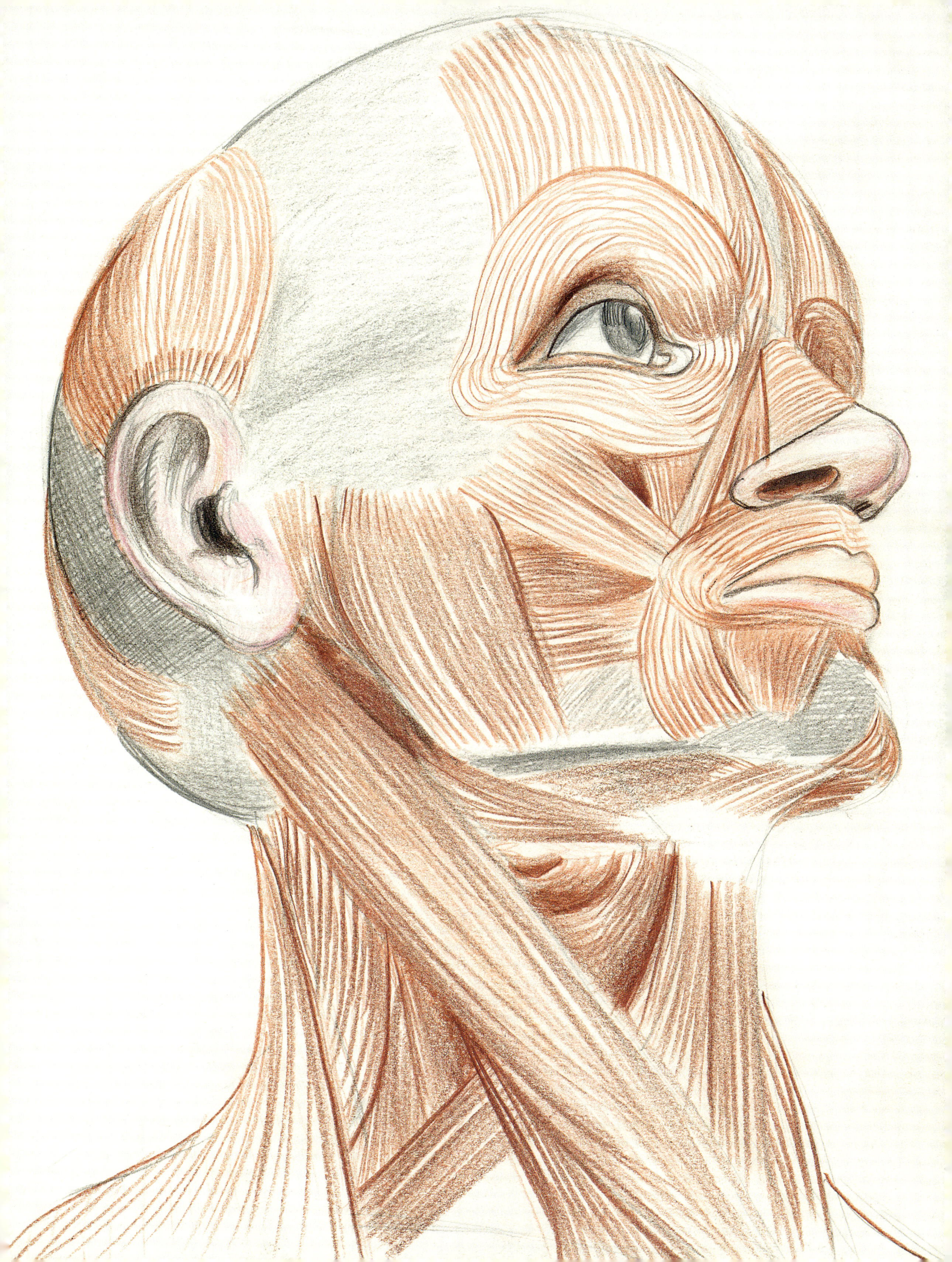

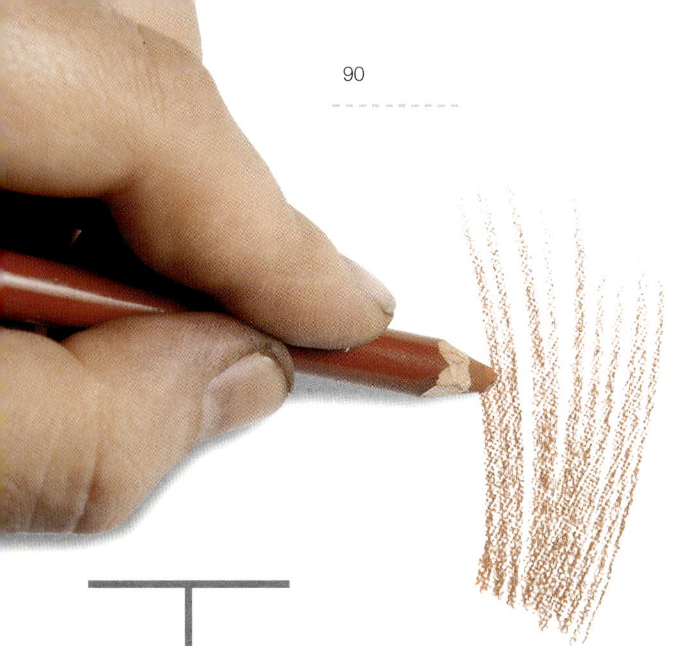

The Face and the Hands, Creators

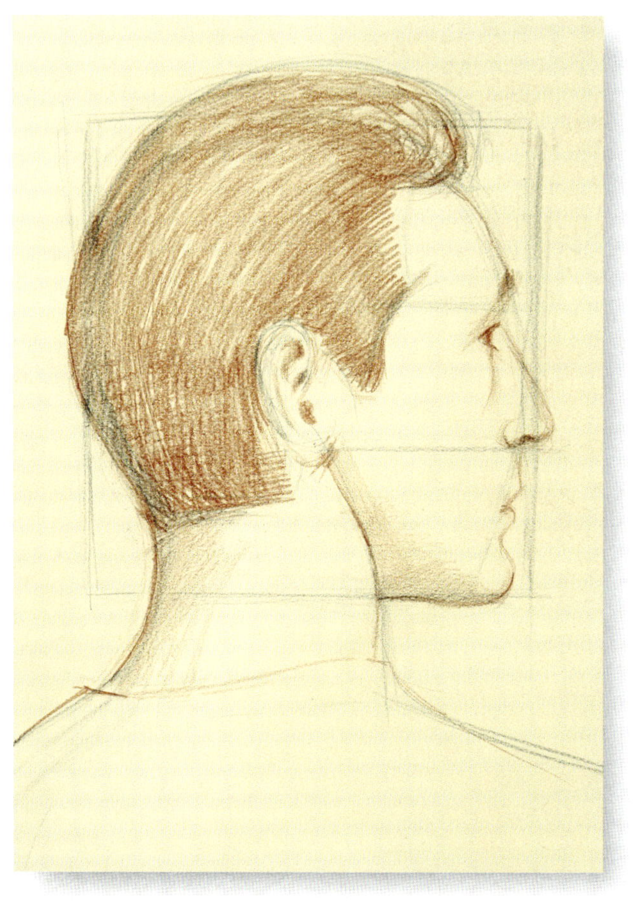

DAVID SANMIGUEL. REAR VIEW OF SERGI, 2000.
SANGUINE AND COLOR PENCIL ON OFF-WHITE PAPER

# of Expression.

Artists

from all periods

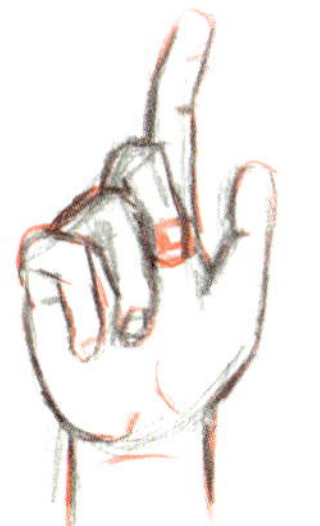

have not always scrupulously respected the natural proportions of the human head and its features, including the face. Those distortions are perceived as an artistic license in pursuit of an expressive objective rather than an error. We can say the same thing about the hands and the feet, which together with the face constitute the generators of human expression, and as such are sometimes defined beyond a specific canon of dimensions. However, those dimensions exist and will be presented in detail in the following pages.

The Cranium: Bone Configuration

The head presents various anatomical idiosyncrasies that set it apart from the rest of the body. Its bone configuration is that of an oval box, a volume surrounded by bone walls that are unlike the rest of the skeleton.

Its muscle configuration is also peculiar because it contains numerous flat muscles, most of which have skin attachments in addition to bone attachments.

In these pages, we will cover the most important bones and muscles, the ones whose presence or action can be perceived in the exterior profile of the head and the face.

CRANIAL BONES

The cranium is a container made of bone that sits atop the spinal column. The cranium walls are formed by eight broad and flat bones. Two of those bones come in pairs: the parietal and the temporal; and four do not: the occipital, the frontal, the sphenoid, and the ethmoid.

The occipital bone is located on the inferior side of the cranium's base, the frontal occupies the entire anterior side (the forehead), and the parietals are located on the superior right and left sides of the cranium, between the frontal and occipital, and are in contact with each other.

The temporal bones occupy the inferior right and left sides, below the parietal bones.

The ethmoid and sphenoid are bones that are largely internal and do not affect the external relief of the skull. All these bones are connected by sutures to form an ovoid shape container.

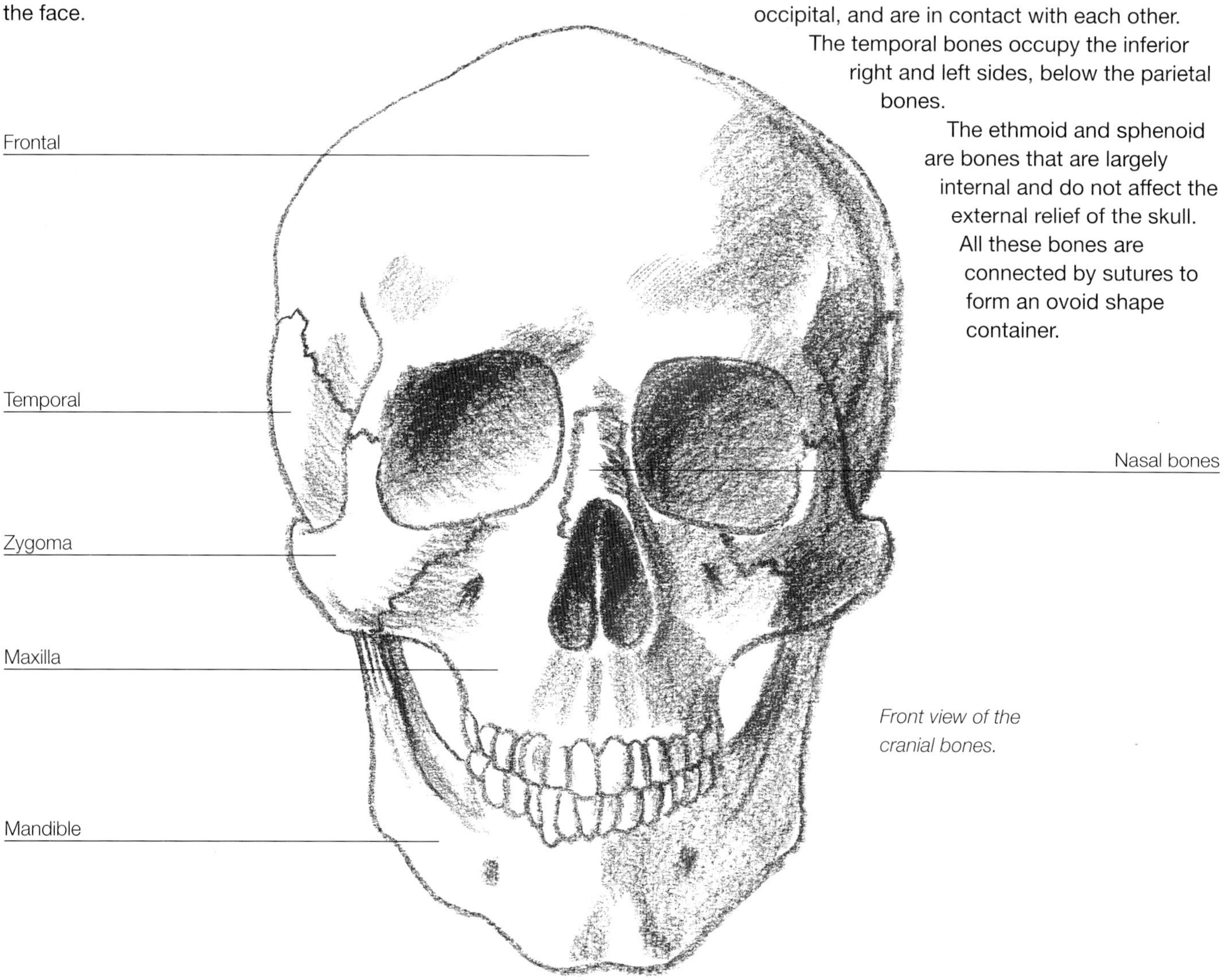

Frontal
Temporal
Zygoma
Maxilla
Mandible
Nasal bones

Front view of the cranial bones.

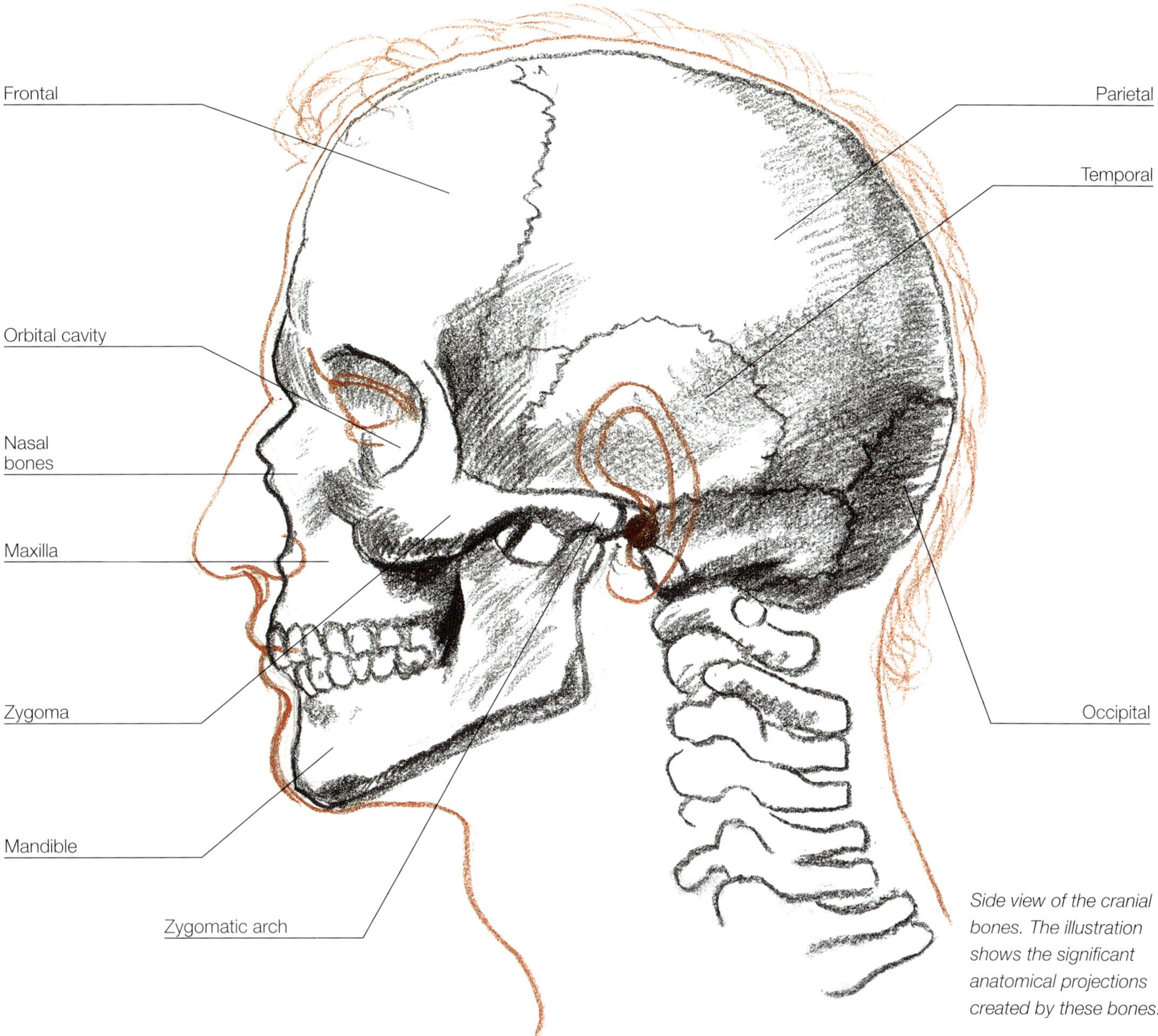

Side view of the cranial bones. The illustration shows the significant anatomical projections created by these bones.

BONES OF THE HEAD

The face is formed by two large bone pieces: the maxilla and the mandible. In turn, the maxilla is made up of various bones, of which only two pairs take part directly in the external profile of the face: the zygomata and the nasal bones. The maxilla and the mandible are the bones that surround and shape the mouth. The mandible is the only mobile bone in the cranium. The zygomata are the bones that shape the cheeks (as it extends from the front surface toward the ear, ending in the zygomatic arch) and the external area of the ocular orbitals. The nasal bones are small in size and identical in shape. They are connected along the midline, or symmetrical center of the face, and together form the bridge of the nose.

SKELETON AND APPEARANCE

Some of the bones mentioned are much more distinctive than others in the appearance of the face. For example, the zygomatic arch stands out notably with respect to the surface of the temporal bone, forming a depression in that area. This depression usually can be noticed clearly in thin or bony faces with a characteristic difference in the level of the surface located between the ear and the temple. Also, the zygoma becomes pronounced in shriveled up faces (especially on elderly people), in the area of the orbital and the cheeks. The nasal bones also determine dramatically the profile of the nose, and the same can be said of the mandible, whose lower edges and angles are visible in thin people.

Muscles
of the Head

among the muscles of the head two groups stand out: the mastication muscles, which attach to the bones and are located in the lateral areas of the head, and the cutaneous muscles, which attach to both the bones and the skin. The latter are responsible for the surface changes of the face, which alter the expression, while the former are responsible for chewing. The main chewing muscles are the temporalis and the masseter.

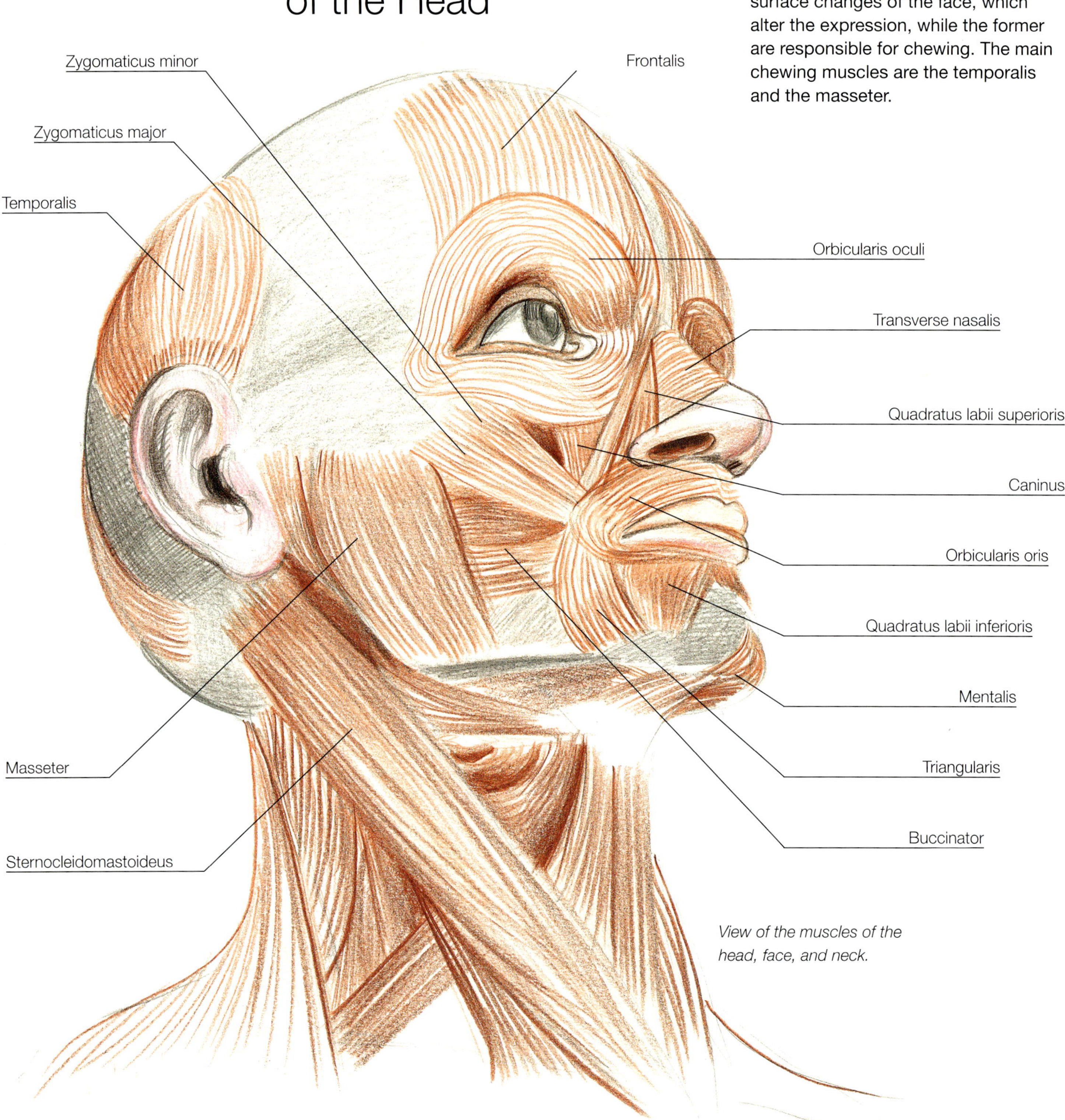

View of the muscles of the head, face, and neck.

TEMPORALIS
This is a fan-shaped muscle located in the temporal fossa, above the ear, and it completely covers the bone that bears its name. It is visible only during mastication.

MASSETER
This is a rectangular-shaped muscle located in the area of the cheek. Its function is to elevate the lower mandible. In thin people, the contraction of the masseter creates a protrusion on the side of the face that can be characteristic of the expression of anger, as in clenching teeth.

FRONTALIS
The epicranius covers the entire cranial dome. It consists of two flat muscles: the occipital and the frontalis (on the back of the head and the forehead, respectively), joined together by a broad tendinous fiber attached to the scalp. The frontalis is responsible for the transversal wrinkles of the forehead and the elevation of the eyebrows. It expresses attention, astonishment, and surprise.

ORBICULARIS OCULI
This is a flat and circular muscle that surrounds the ocular orbit and is responsible for moving the eyelids. In general, it participates in creating certain expressions when its movement is associated with that of other facial muscles (laughter, pain, crying, etc.).

ZYGOMATICUS MAJOR
This is an oblique elevator of the corners of the mouth and pulls them upward and back, creating wrinkles under the cheeks: It is the muscle of laughter.

ZYGOMATICUS MINOR
This is parallel to the zygomaticus major. Its contraction elevates the upper lip in a grimacing characteristic of crying or unpleasantness.

QUADRATUS LABII SUPERIORIS
This is one of a pair of muscles located in the groove that separates the nose from the cheeks. It pulls the upper lip upward when it contracts, widening and elevating the nostrils, giving the corners of the lips a downward and outward direction. It is the crying muscle.

CANINUS
This is located between the zygomaticus minor and the quadratus labii superioris. Its action is usually associated with the two anterior muscles and is responsible for expressions of sadness, unhappiness, or disgust.

TRANSVERSE NASALIS
Its contraction creates folds on both sides of the nose and tenses the cheeks. The expression associated is one of intense discontent or disgust.

ORBICULARIS ORIS
This surrounds the mouth and is responsible for the fleshiness of the lips. The lips project forward if only the external part contracts, producing to the characteristic action of kissing or sipping.

BUCCINATOR
This is the muscle that gives the cheeks their thickness and closes the cavity of the mouth laterally. It takes part in mastication and, especially, in the action of blowing, filling up the checks to push the air out.

MENTALIS
This lifts the lower lip when it contracts, creating a projection in the skin of the chin. This is the muscle of anger and of the dramatic expression of aggressive rage.

QUADRATUS LABII INFERIORIS
This draws the lip downward and a little sideways when it contracts. It creates an expression of anger or disgust.

TRIANGULARIS
This makes the corners of the mouth descend when it contracts, and together with the quadratus labii inferioris, it takes part in causing expressions of crying, sorrow, and sadness. If the contraction is too pronounced, the resulting expression is one of anger.

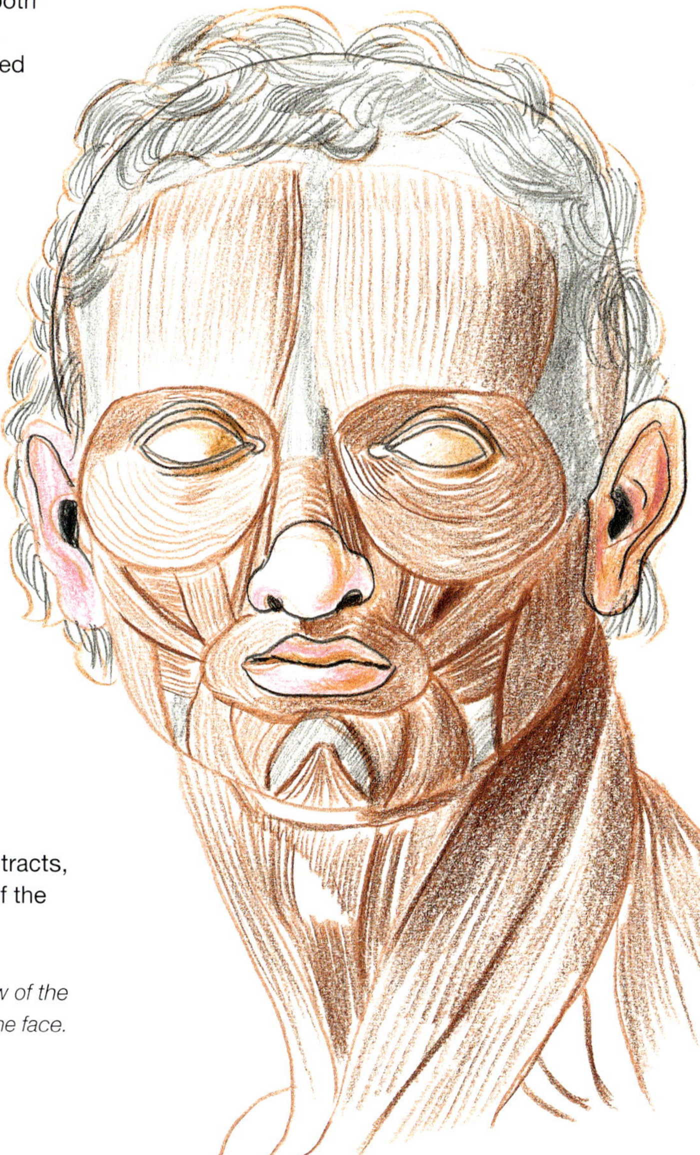

Frontal view of the muscles of the face.

Constructing and Drawing the Head

The practical method proposed here is suggested by the anatomy of the cranium itself, whose basic structure can be summarized as an ovoid shape over which we can partition or draw line references that correspond to the eyes, nose, and mouth (and more references if so desired). Also, it is helpful to draw the face's center line to define the placement of the nose and to draw the eyes proportionately. The only skill that the artist needs to have with this method is spatial imagination, or the ability to imagine the forms from different perspectives. With this basic knowledge the problems in drawing a head will be easily resolved.

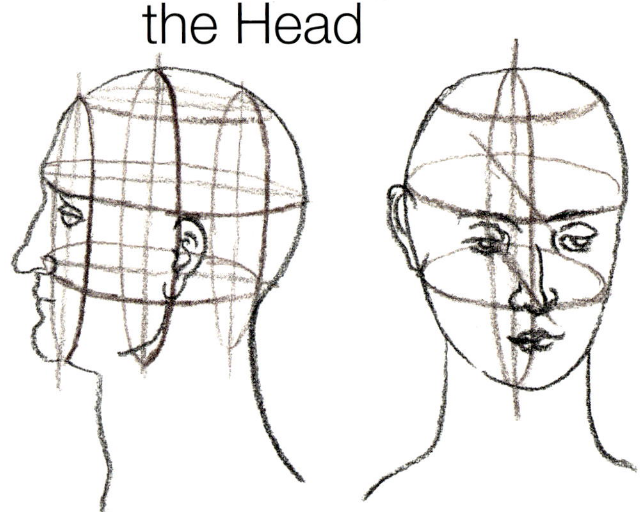

The main physical features can be defined with lines. These lines must follow the contours of the face and of the cranium as if they were drawn on an oval or egg-shaped object. This simple method makes drawing the head in any position easier.

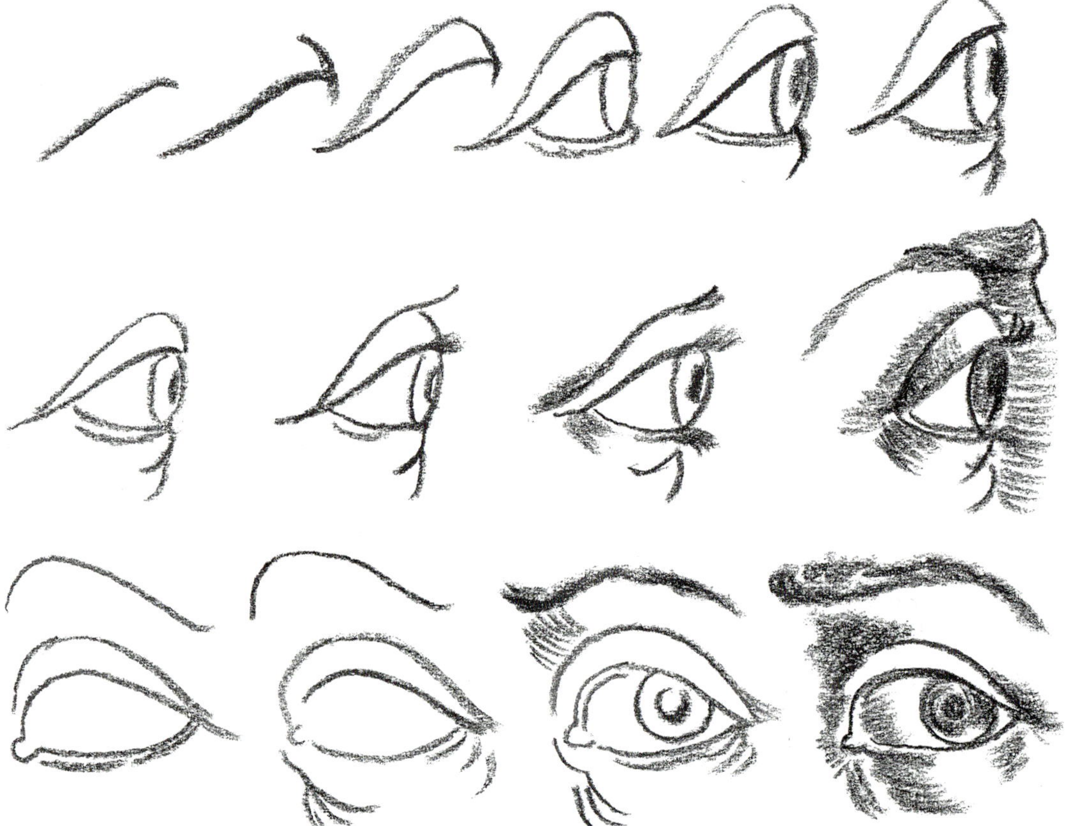

The eyes tend to be a problem for inexperienced artists. These diagrams show the approach for constructing the eyes through basic lines that, little by little, are enriched with shadows and details.

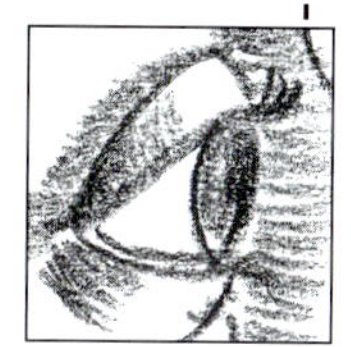

The shape of the eyes is determined by the eyelids. The artist must remember that the upper eyelid is wider than the lower one.

FORESHORTENING OF THE HEAD

This construction method is very helpful when the artist works from memory, without a model, especially if the head is being drawn from many different perspectives. Also, it is very helpful when drawing from a model (either a photograph or life) because it facilitates the organization of all the forms and makes it possible to situate the features in a coherent manner that conforms to the position of the head. Before drawing the face, it is essential to make sure that the foreshortening, or perspective, of the diagram is sufficiently correct (it cannot be completely exact, because it is usually drawn freehand). The errors of the diagram are visible only when we begin to draw the features. In the event of a grave mistake, it is preferable to redraw the initial diagram until it provides an accurate foundation.

DRAWING THE EYES

Drawing the eyes tends to be difficult for inexperienced people. It is very important to understand and to represent this volume correctly to avoid a deformed appearance. Seen in profile, the eye socket is mostly hidden behind the somewhat bulgy mass of the eyelids, which comes out further on the upper part than the lower. A very common mistake in drawing the frontal view of the eye is making the curvature of the upper lid exactly the same as the lower lid. It is also common to draw the eye in foreshortening as if it were a flat surface rather than curved.

Several examples of heads drawn without a model, working from diagrams drawn in different positions. The success of these drawings done from memory depends on the correct placement of the vertical and horizontal references drawn on an oval surface.

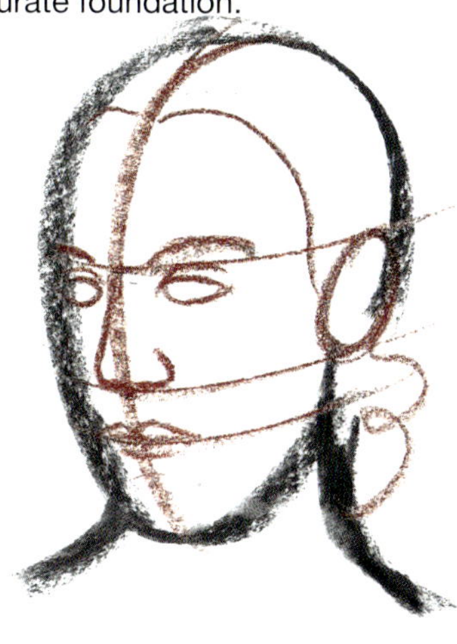

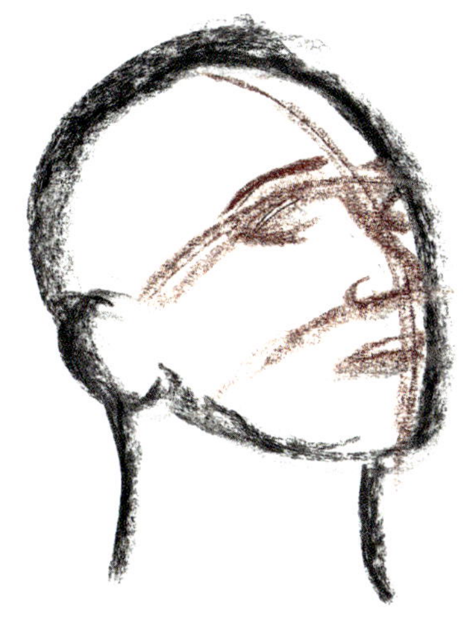

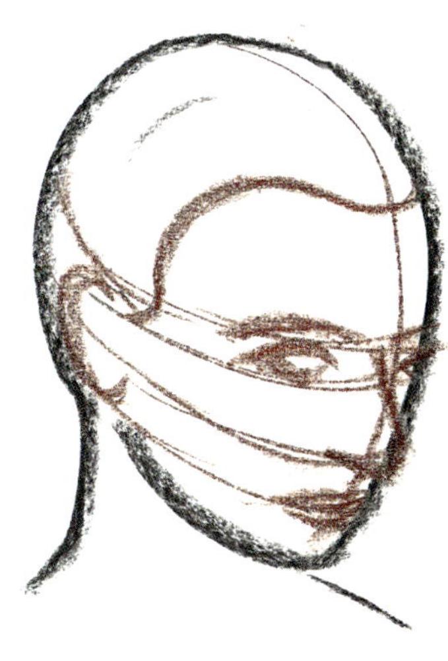

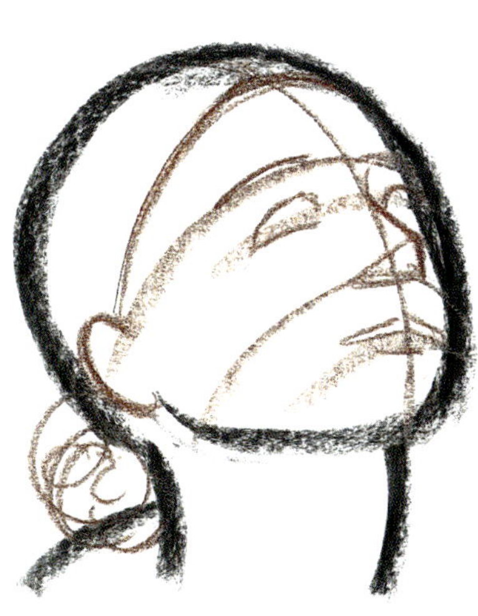

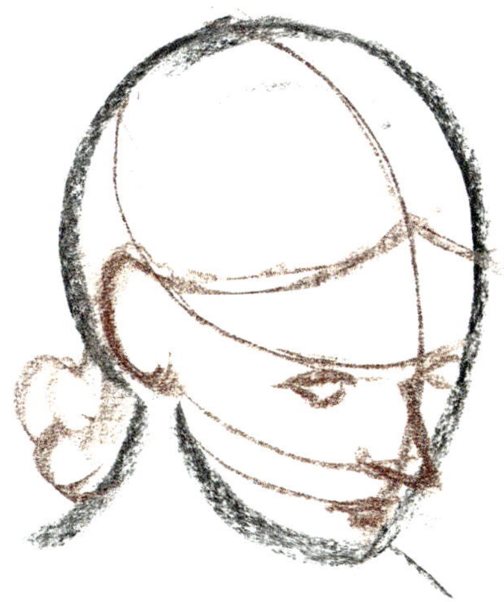

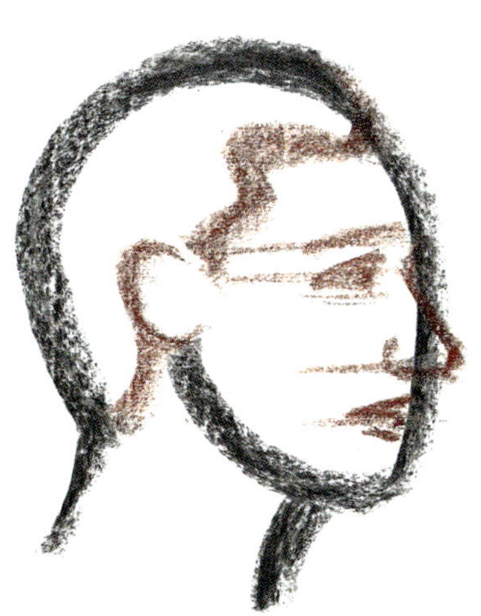

Drawing the Head: Portraits

The blocking in method explained and illustrated so far is not the only method available, but it is difficult to find another one that is more complete and simple at the same time. There are many methods for defining the head, almost as many as there are portrait artists. Most of them are abbreviated ways to define the correct position and proportions beginning with a few lines. In the following pages, we will show a process for drawing the head partly based on dividing it into modules, although it is more tentative than the one explained earlier because an experienced artist does not need as much preliminary preparation.

THE MODEL AND THE SKETCH

Ideally, each model should suggest the most appropriate composition approach for drawing it: more or less elaborate depending on the difficulty of the pose. However, this is not always the case, and most artists use a limited variety of diagrams whose usefulness has been demonstrated by continuous practice. The end objective of any blocking in method is to achieve a good drawing. In the end, the reference lines used could be a little off, but, if the position of the head is correct, the artist can make the necessary adjustments as he or she draws without having to start all over again.

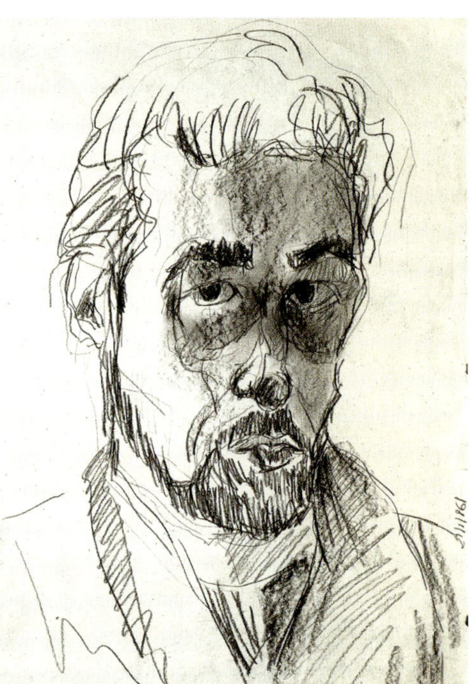

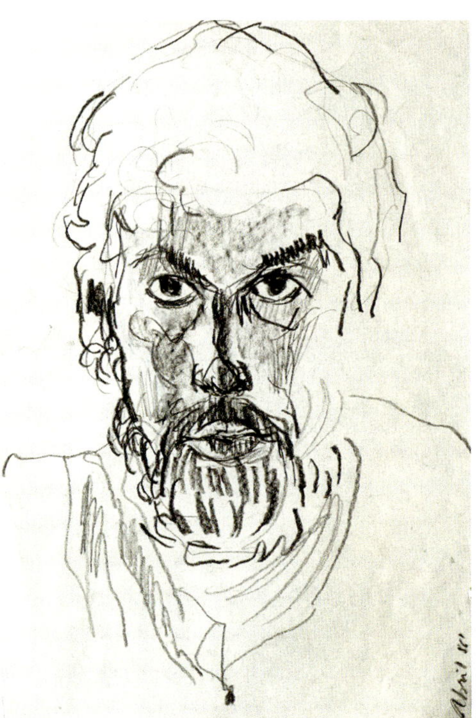

Preliminary sketches of the portrait developed in these pages. The graphic spontaneity discards a rigid approach in favor of expression over the strict adherence to facial proportions.

1

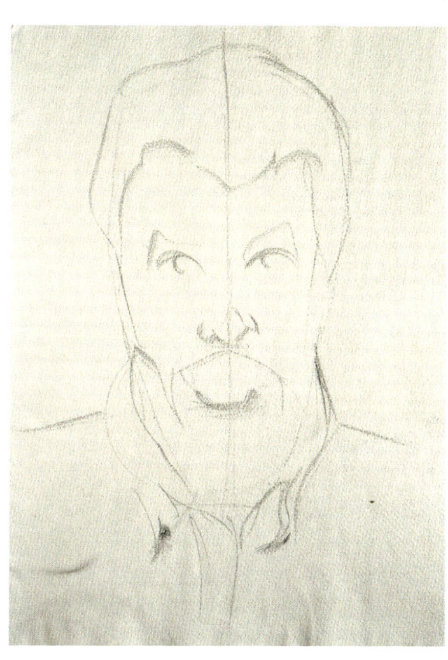

1. In this first stage of the drawing, we can see the distribution of the basic references of the facial features on both sides of the face's line of symmetry. Since this figure has a beard, the references to this feature are as important as the references of the facial features themselves.

2. Taking the proportional references as guides, the real profile and facial features can be drawn with confidence. The most characteristic profiles are drawn and shaded superficially with a stick of charcoal, respecting the basic, firmly established lines of the initial diagram.

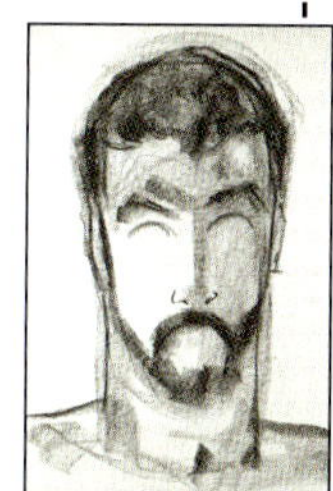

The sketch of the head does not necessarily have to be oval. For a frontal portrait, it is feasible to use an angular approach made of square shapes, like the ones in this figure.

3

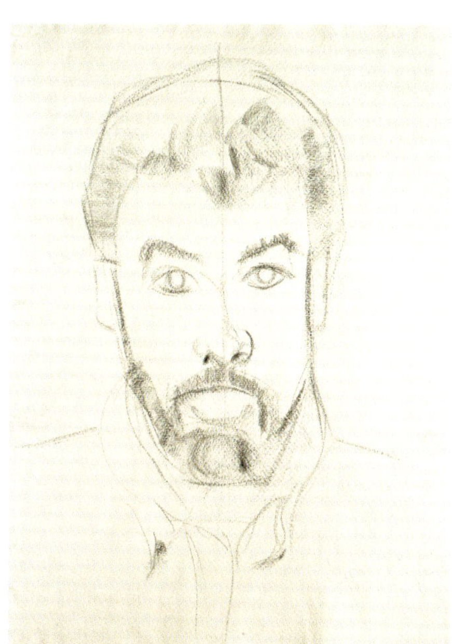

2

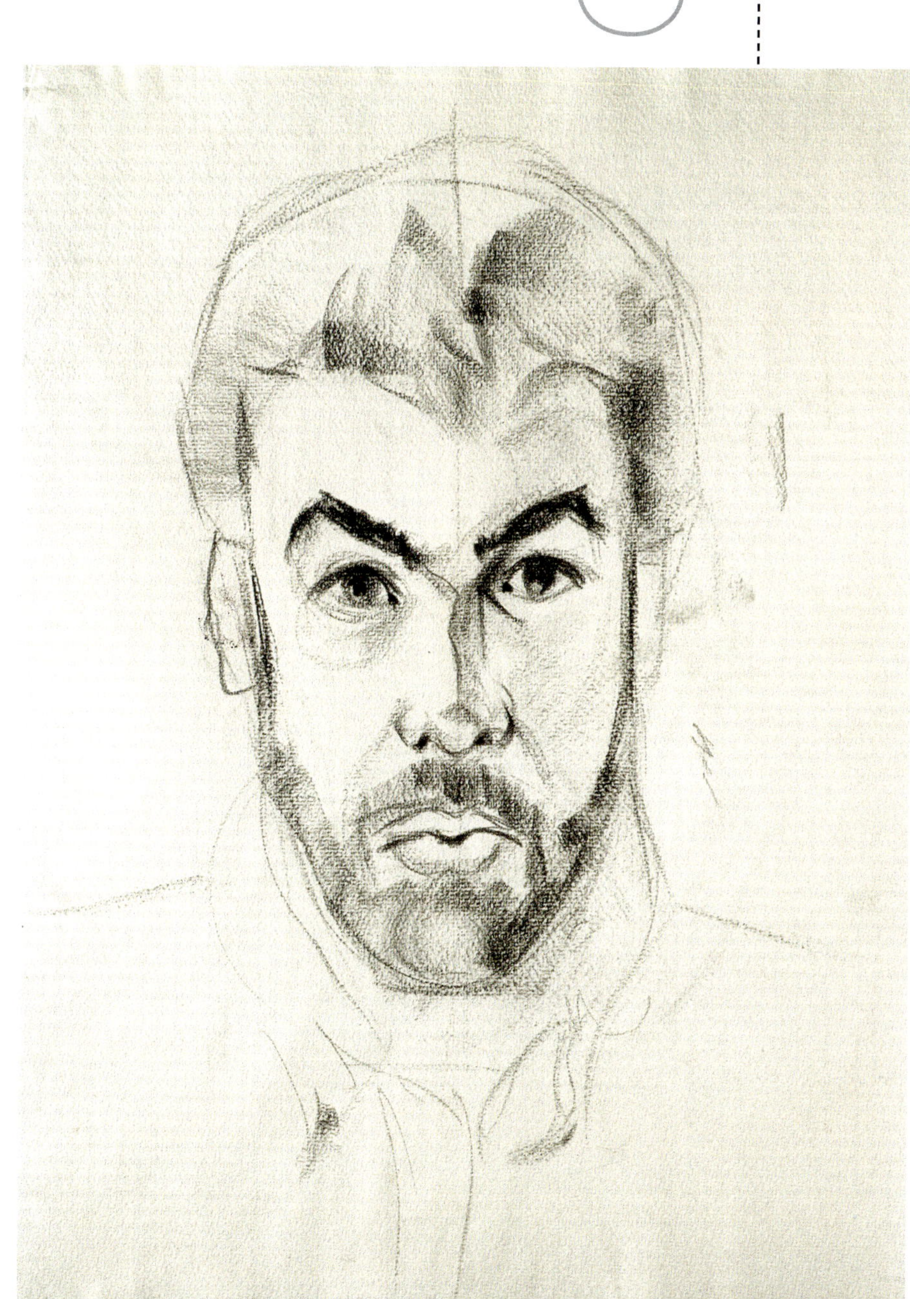

3. The final step consists of going over the profiles and the shading to emphasize them. The appearance is achieved from the beginning, and the process progresses to consolidate that initial appearance. Drawing by Lluís Armengol.

Anatomy and Drawing Hands

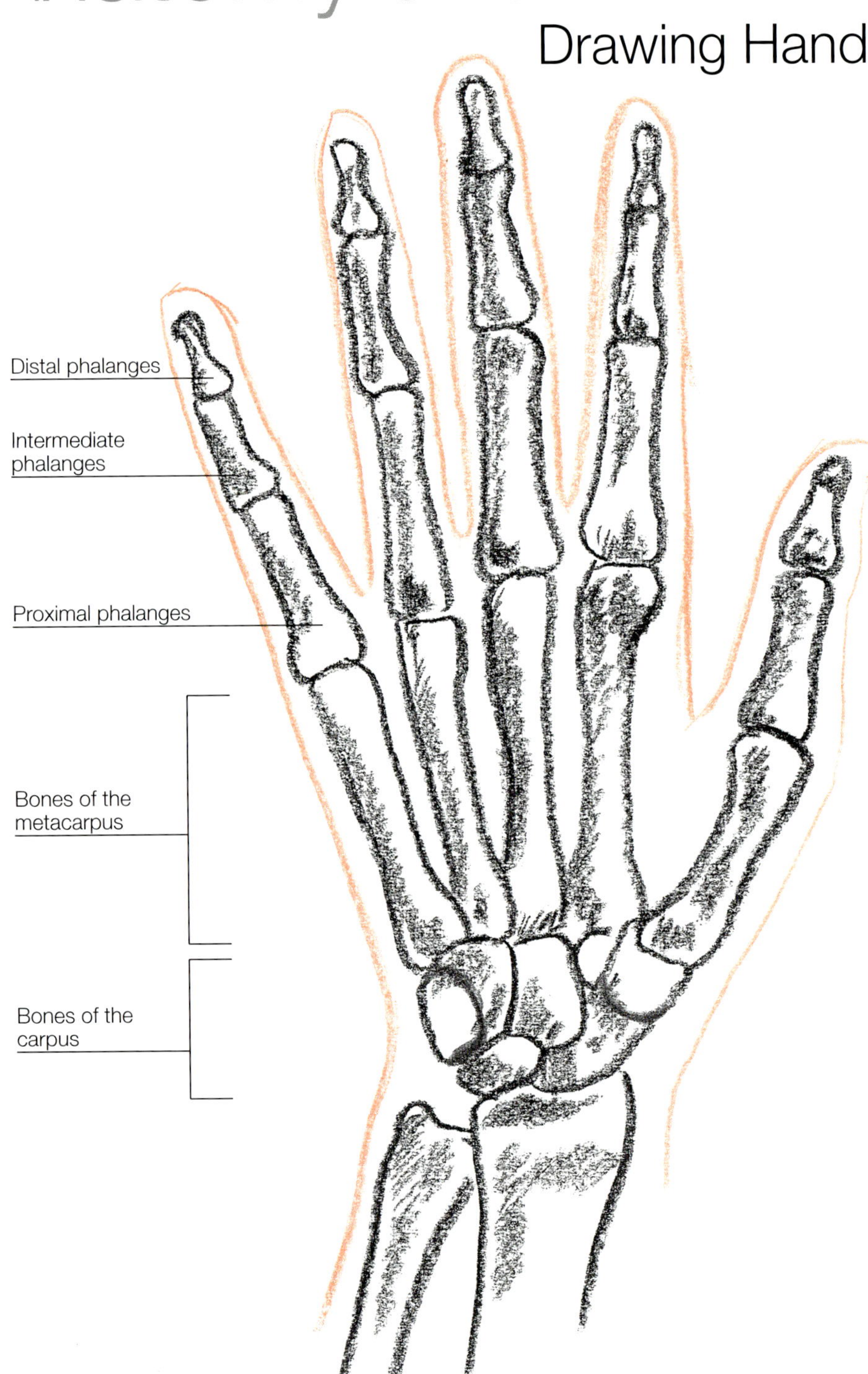

The hands are the most articulated parts of the entire body. In-depth knowledge of the muscles and tendons located here is not vital to understanding their outward appearance; therefore, we will only study their bone structure. It consists of three parts: the wrist, or the carpus, the palm, or metacarpus, and the fingers, or phalanges.

THE CARPUS

This is formed by eight small bones, compact and irregular in shape and located in two rows: an upper row, which corresponds to the articulations of the wrist with the bones of the forearm, and a lower row, for the articulation of the wrist with the bones of the metacarpus. Beginning at the thumb, the bones of the upper row are the scaphoid, the lunate, the triquetral, and the pisiform. The lower row is formed by the trapezium, the trapezoid, the capitate, and the hamate.

THE METACARPUS

This is formed by five long, although small in size, bones called the metacarpal bones. They extend from the carpus to the phalanges. The metacarpal bones are numbered from one to five, beginning with the thumb. These bones have different lengths; the longest of them is the second metacarpal (index finger) and the shortest and broadest is the first one (the thumb).

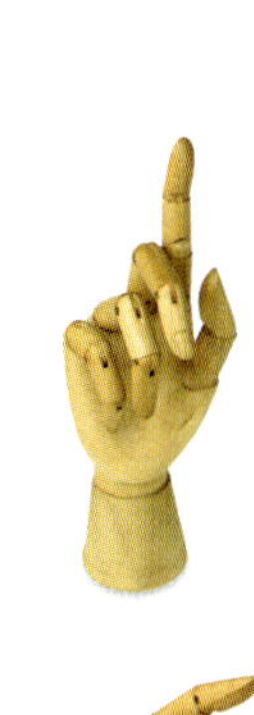
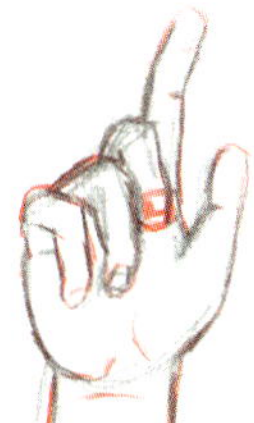
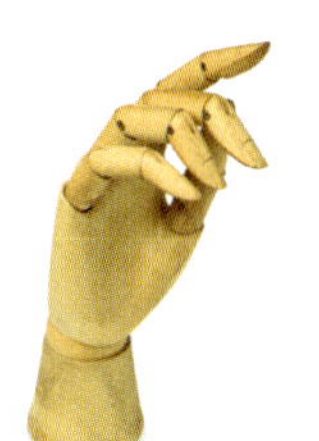
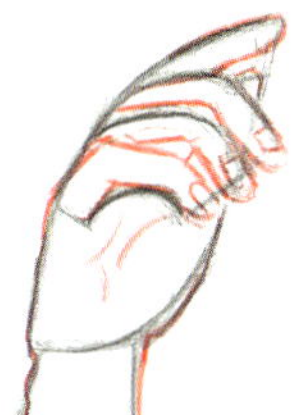
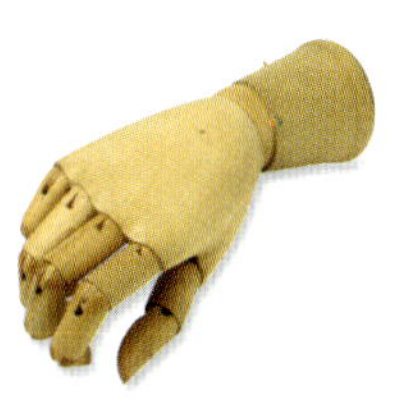
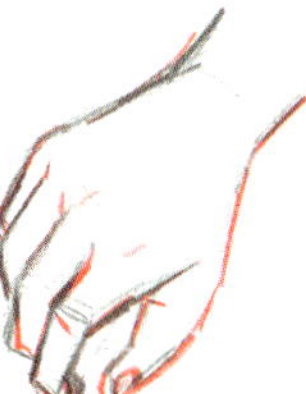
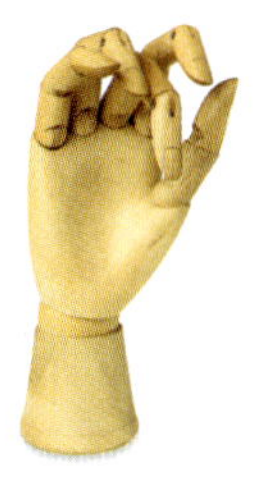
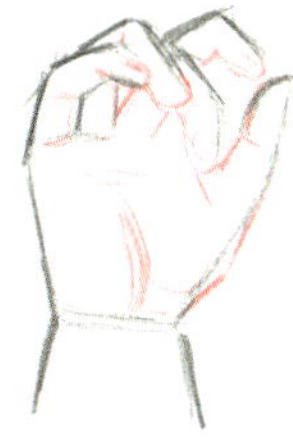

PHALANGES

These bones are long, but small in size and articulated on each end. The name of the first, which is closest to the palm, is the proximal phalanx, the second is the intermediate phalanx, and third, the tip of the finger, is the distal phalanx. These three phalanges become progressively shorter, with the third phalanges being the smallest. The thumb has only two phalanges and lacks the third, or distal, phalanx.

PROPORTIONS OF THE HANDS AND DRAWING THEM

Due to its range of motion and varied articulations, the hand constitutes a subject matter in its own right. It is the part of the body that offers the greatest number of positions. In these pages, we are going to present a few drawings of hands made from an articulated wooden hand model, which provides a model similar to the previous diagrams, but is three-dimensional. This articulated hand can adopt many of the poses of a real hand. By drawing it with all its joints, one can easily understand the basic underlying structure of an anatomical drawing of this difficult body part.

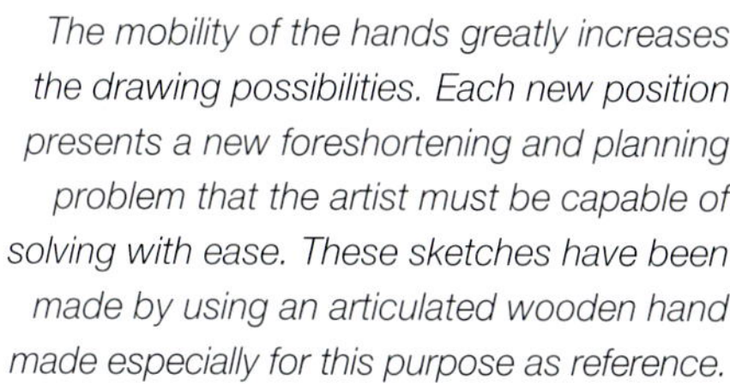

The mobility of the hands greatly increases the drawing possibilities. Each new position presents a new foreshortening and planning problem that the artist must be capable of solving with ease. These sketches have been made by using an articulated wooden hand made especially for this purpose as reference.

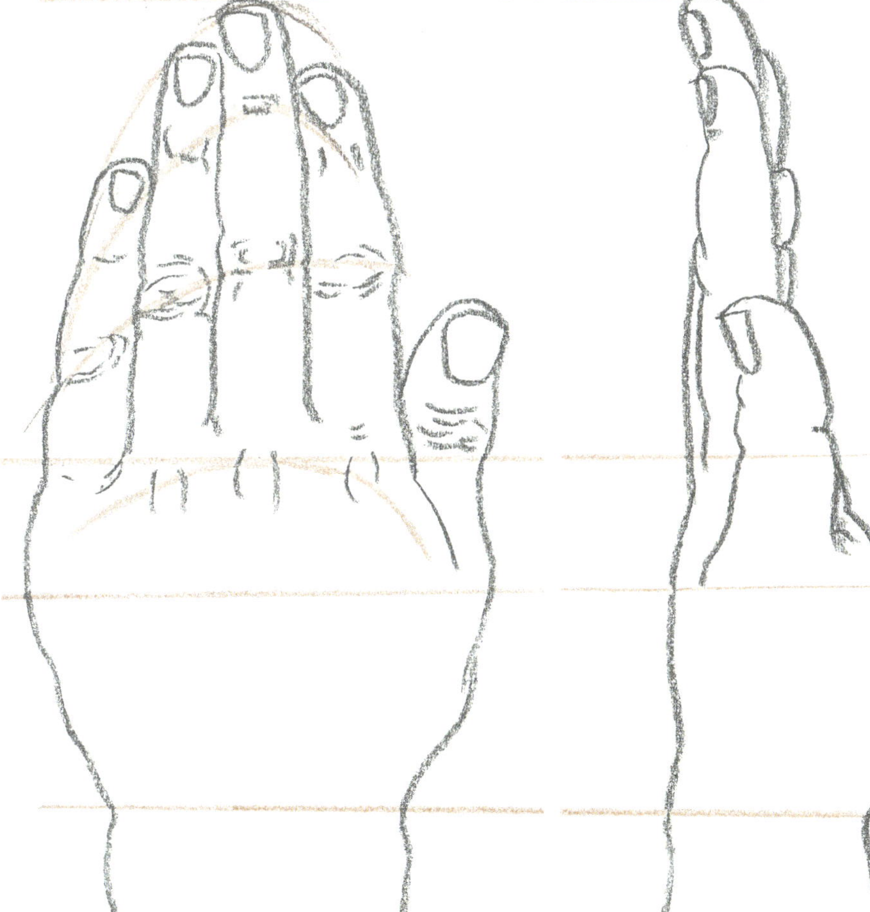

Rear and side views of the hand. The center line of the hand is located along the middle finger's knuckles. The knuckles of the back of the hand and the intermediate and distal phalanges are located along arches of different arcs.

Anatomy and Drawing Feet

Although the feet are a part of the anatomy that is equivalent to the hands, they have significant differences as a result of their function. Their bone structures are similar, but they are arranged differently. The bones of the feet are divided into three bone areas: bones of the tarsus, of the metatarsus, and of the toes. The first group corresponds to the bones of the carpus or wrist, the second with the bones of the metacarpus, and the third with the phalanges of the toes.

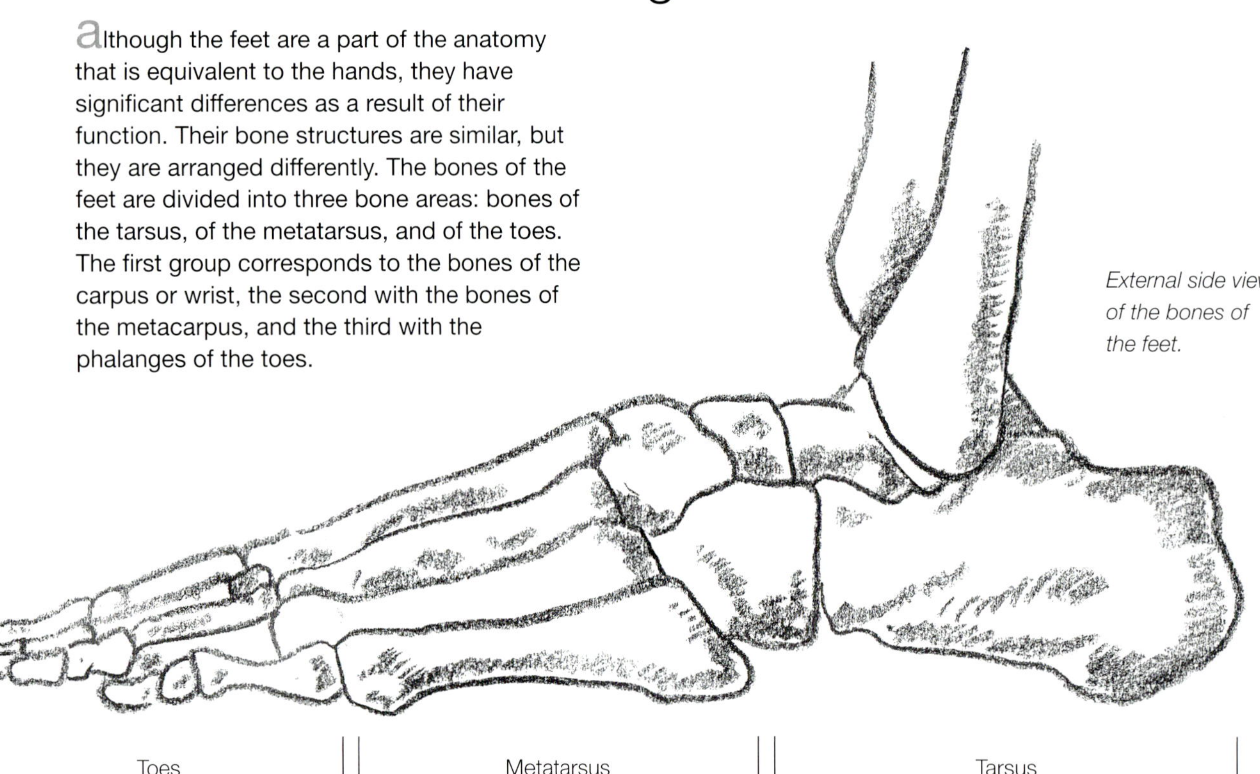

External side view of the bones of the feet.

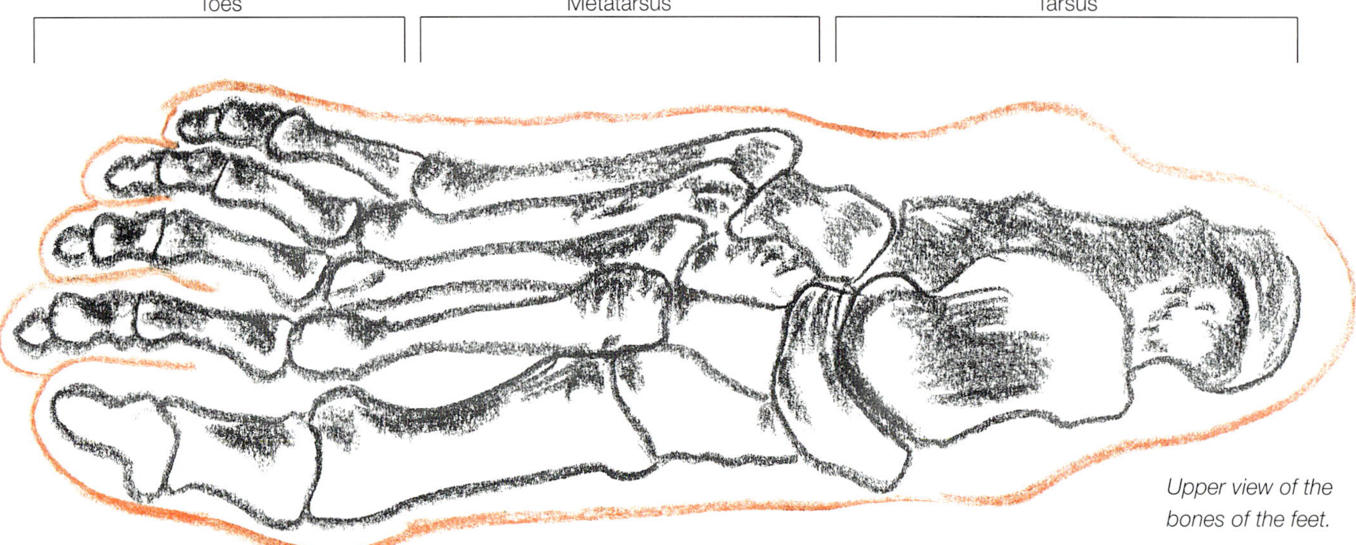

Upper view of the bones of the feet.

THE TARSUS

This is a group of bones that occupies almost half of the foot and that supports the weight of the body. It is formed by seven short, articulated, and strong bones, which, like the bones of the carpus, are divided into two groups. The posterior group is formed by two superimposed bones: the talus (also known as the astragalus) and the calcaneus. The anterior group is composed of five bones: the navicular, the cuboid, and the three cuneiform bones.

THE METATARSUS

This is the group of bones that corresponds to the metacarpus in the hand. It is made up of five parallel bones that form a slightly curved fan shape and cover the arch on the sole of the foot. The first metatarsal bone (from the big toe) is quite a bit thicker than the rest. It differs from the metacarpus in the thumb in that it cannot oppose the rest of the toes, and therefore has much less mobility.

THE TOES

Like the fingers in the hand, the toes have three phalanges, with the exception of the big toe, which has only two. They are also known as proximal (first), intermediate (second), and distal (third).

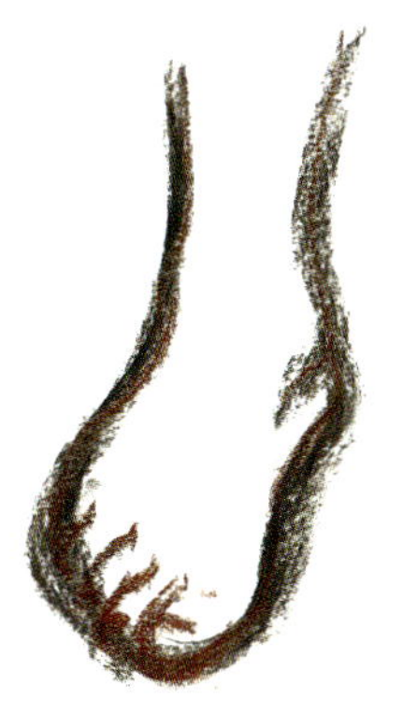

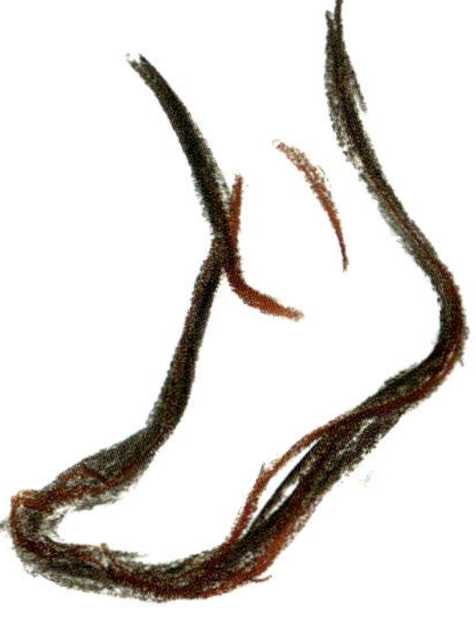

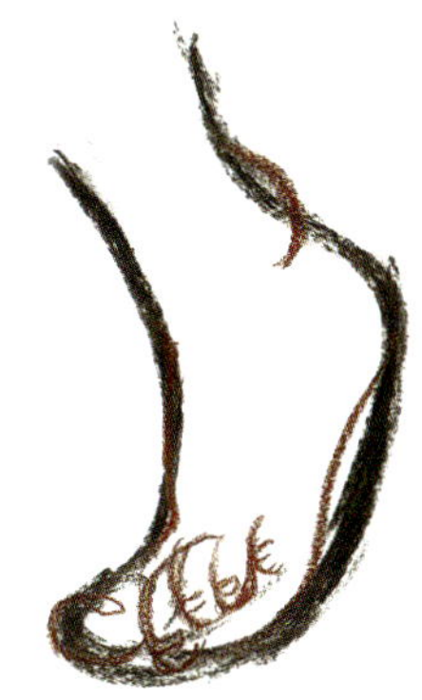

The toes occupy the anterior third portion of the foot. They are not parallel with respect to the axis of the foot seen lengthwise, but are slightly at an angle with an inclination toward the exterior side of the foot.

Drawings of feet made from very simple sketches. They require special attention because the feet are a part of the body that is almost always shown in foreshortening.

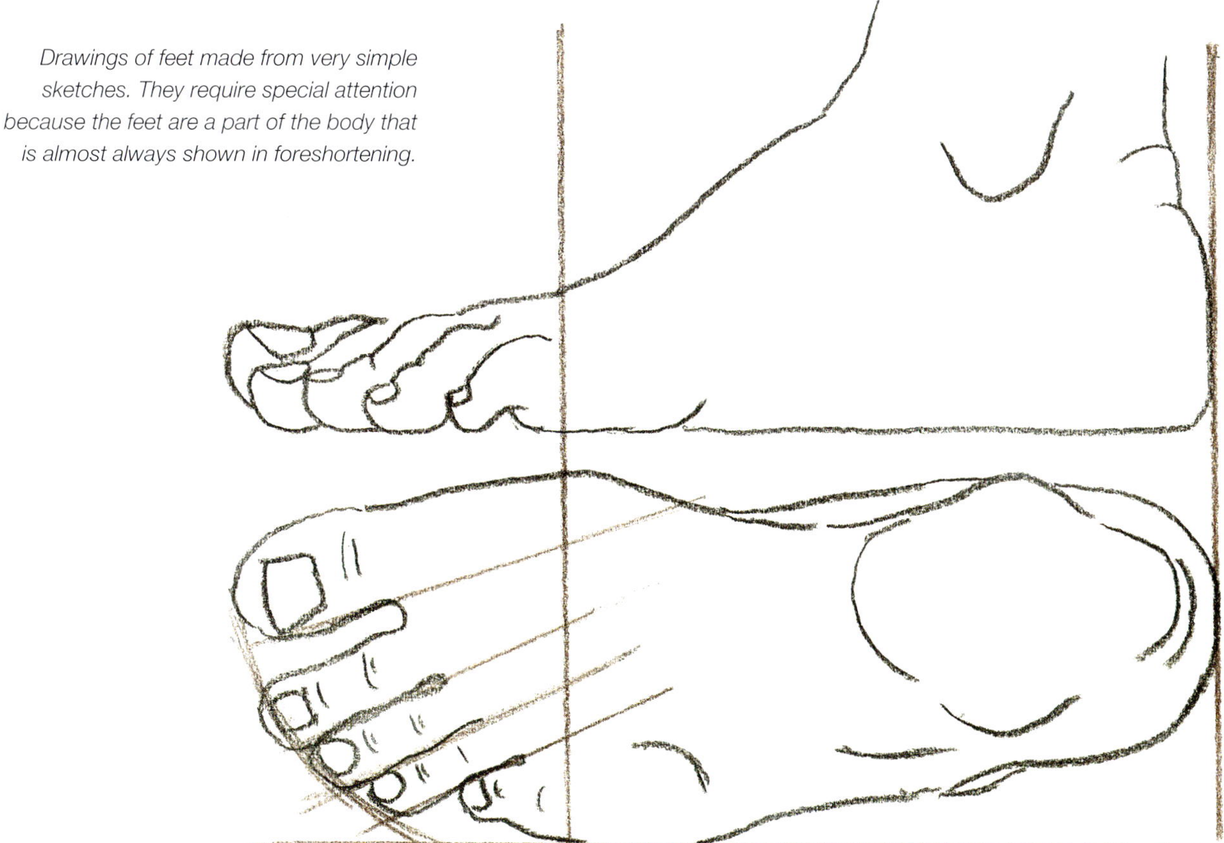

Anatomy and Drawing

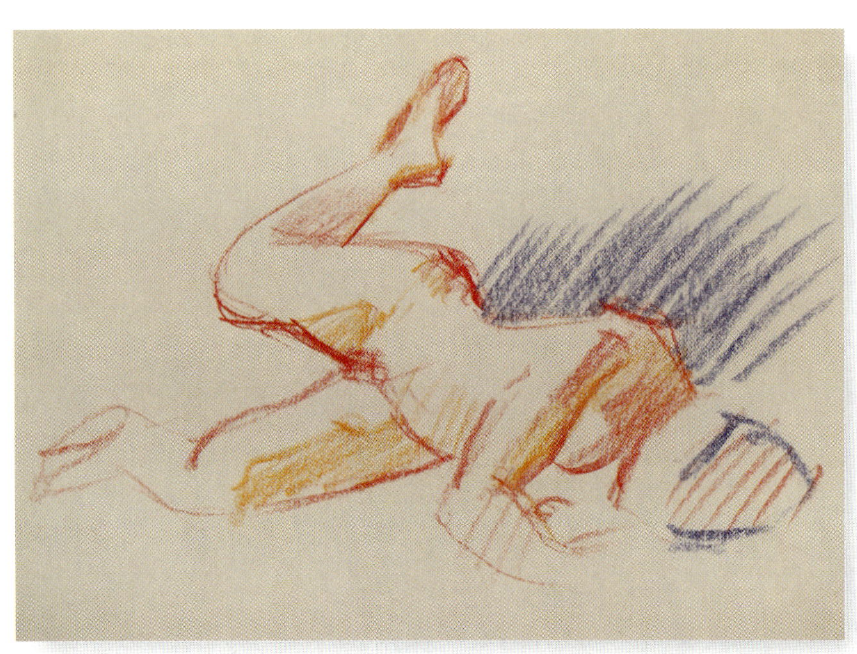

ÓSCAR SANCHÍS. LIFE SKETCH, 2006.
COLOR PENCILS ON PAPER

the Figure.

Anatomy is not an artistic goal in itself

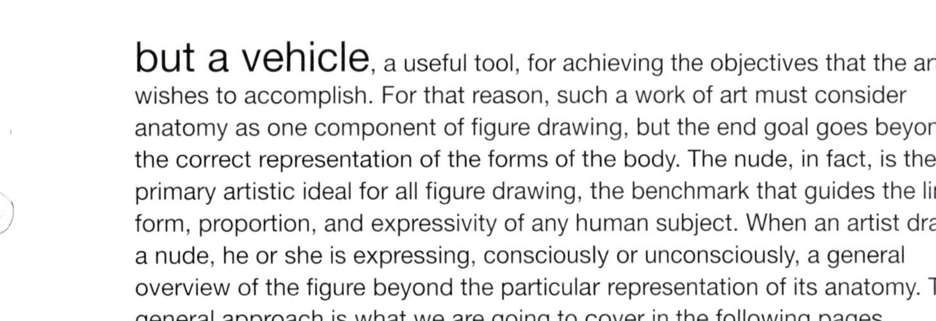

but a vehicle, a useful tool, for achieving the objectives that the artist wishes to accomplish. For that reason, such a work of art must consider anatomy as one component of figure drawing, but the end goal goes beyond the correct representation of the forms of the body. The nude, in fact, is the primary artistic ideal for all figure drawing, the benchmark that guides the line, form, proportion, and expressivity of any human subject. When an artist draws a nude, he or she is expressing, consciously or unconsciously, a general overview of the figure beyond the particular representation of its anatomy. That general approach is what we are going to cover in the following pages.

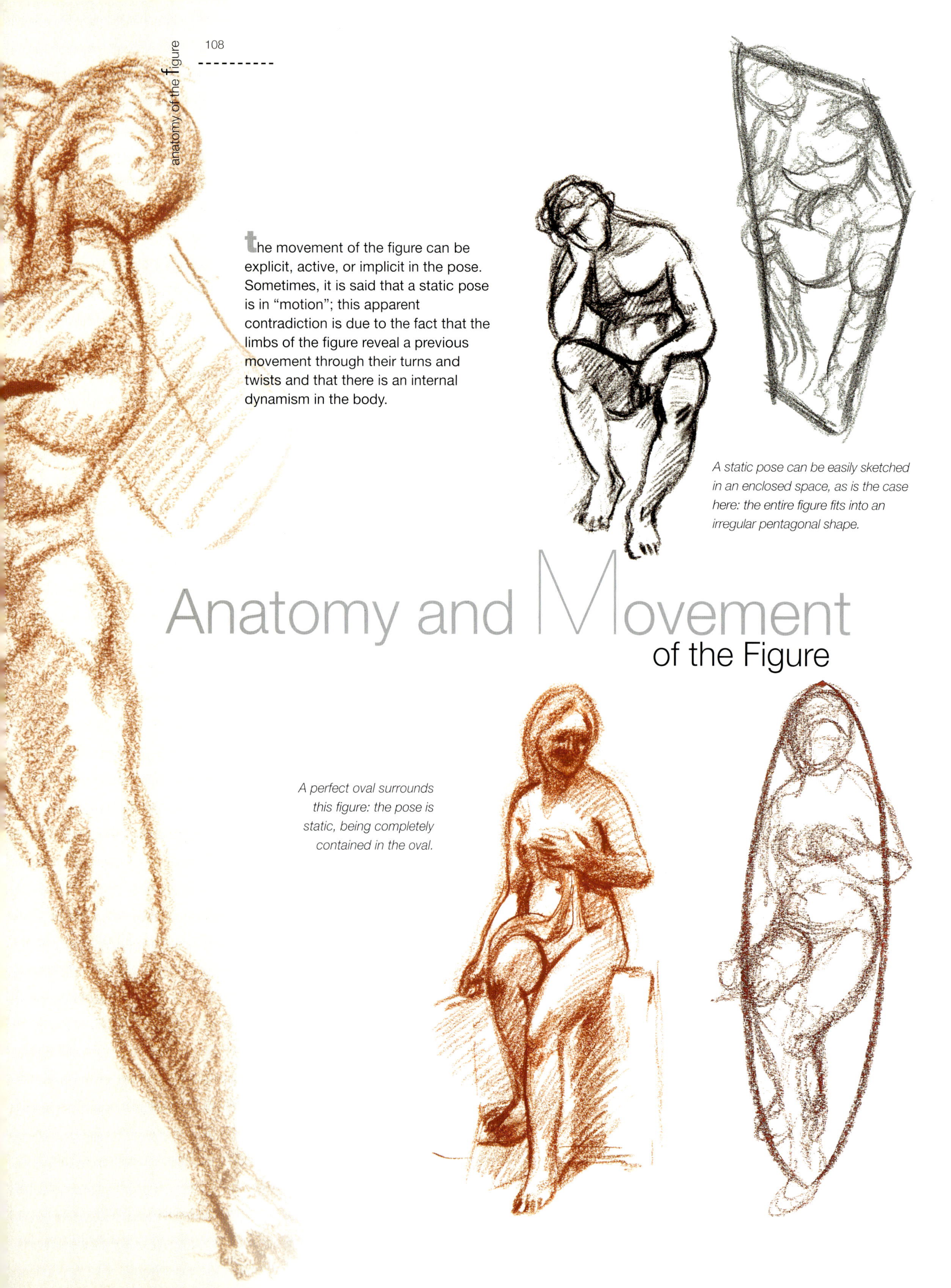

Anatomy and Movement of the Figure

The movement of the figure can be explicit, active, or implicit in the pose. Sometimes, it is said that a static pose is in "motion"; this apparent contradiction is due to the fact that the limbs of the figure reveal a previous movement through their turns and twists and that there is an internal dynamism in the body.

A static pose can be easily sketched in an enclosed space, as is the case here: the entire figure fits into an irregular pentagonal shape.

A perfect oval surrounds this figure: the pose is static, being completely contained in the oval.

STATIC POSE AND FIGURE IN MOTION

If we think of the human figure as a series of parts that fit well together (this is how an artist should always view a figure), a figure in motion is one where some of these parts are more individualized with respect to the others based on position and trajectory. The static pose, on the other hand, is one where the overall structure is the commanding force, which imposes itself over each of the parts, creating the impression of a single whole.

Static poses can be sketched within a form that captures the body mass, allowing no parts to fall outside of it (an oval, a rectangle, a triangle; they can be regular or irregular shapes, but must be enclosed). The diagram of a dynamic pose necessarily comprises more elements, more shapes to achieve the line of the form and placement of the limbs.

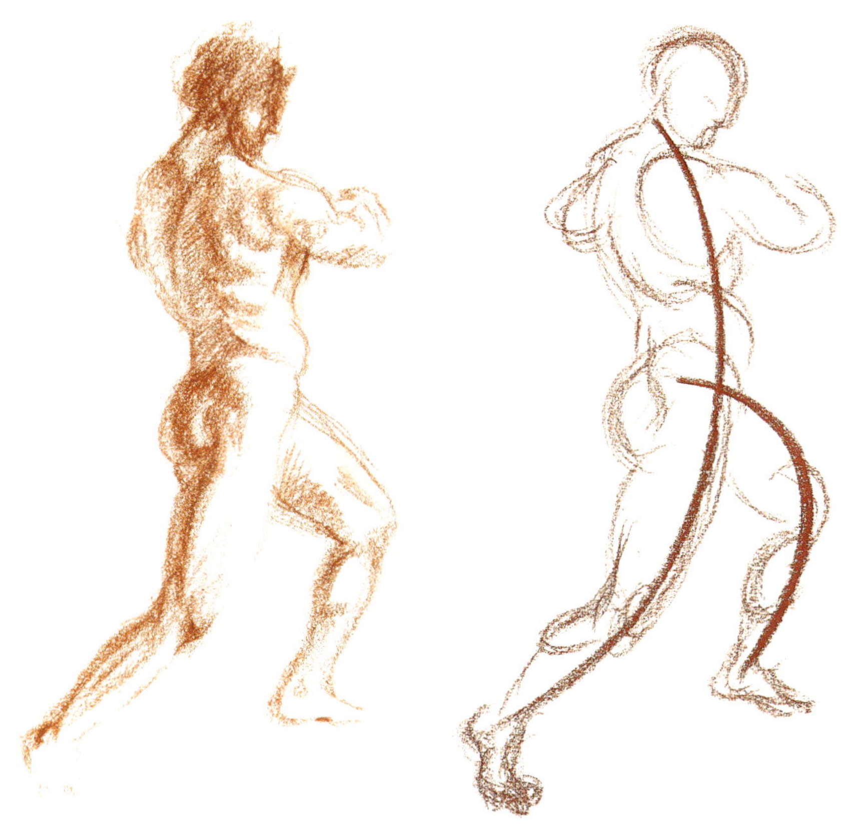

An explicit movement cannot be enclosed within a simple form; rather, it extends beyond the apparent limits, projecting outside of its space.

EXPLICIT MOVEMENTS

This is the movement represented just at the moment when it happens, no sooner or later. In these poses (and in all poses in general), the movement must be justified, meaning the position of the arms and the legs must be coherent with a specific action or movement, and not simply arranged indiscriminately by the artist. If the movement is coherent, it is because it corresponds to a natural action to which the positions of the limbs are logical results.

It is important for this movement to correspond to a natural gesture; otherwise, the artificial or fake look of the movement will be obvious.

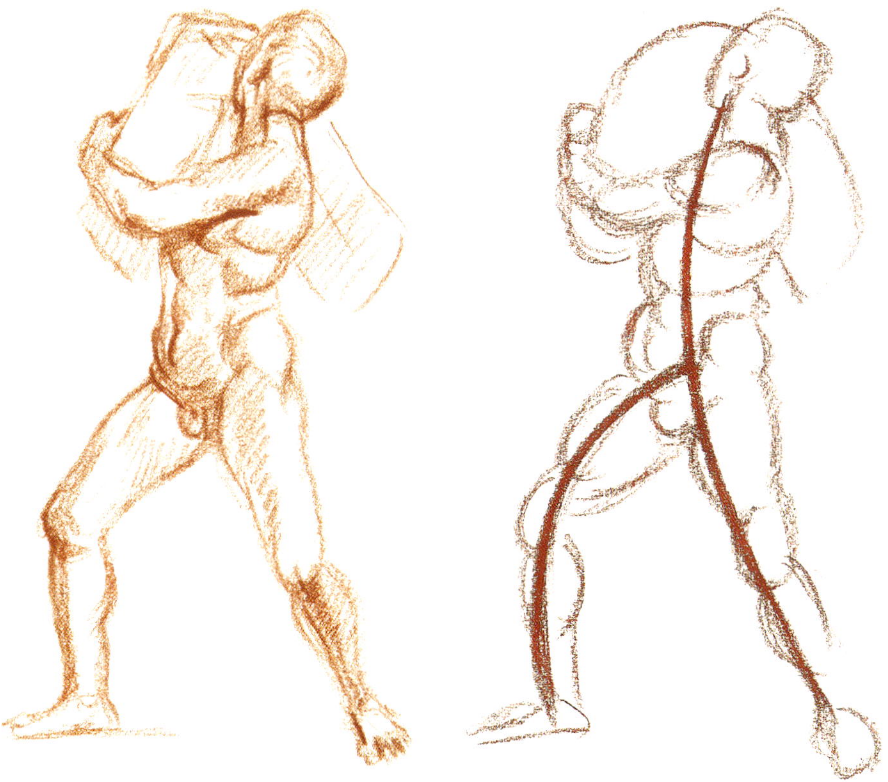

The diagram next to the figure shows the lines of movement: tense arches that project the figure beyond its confines and anticipate the next movement of the limbs.

Process of Drawing a Moving Figure

This is an interesting pose: a figure in the act of walking, which represents a dynamic pose. It is not true that these poses are more difficult than static poses. It may appear so at first sight because the limbs of the figure are in motion, that suggested movement we discussed in previous pages. The raised arm is a movement in itself, as is the position of the head. Such a drawing requires the same attention and understanding of the form as any other; the only difference is that here we interpret movements and gestures that draw special attention to the points of support of the body, which are the ones that provide balance and stability to the figure.

1

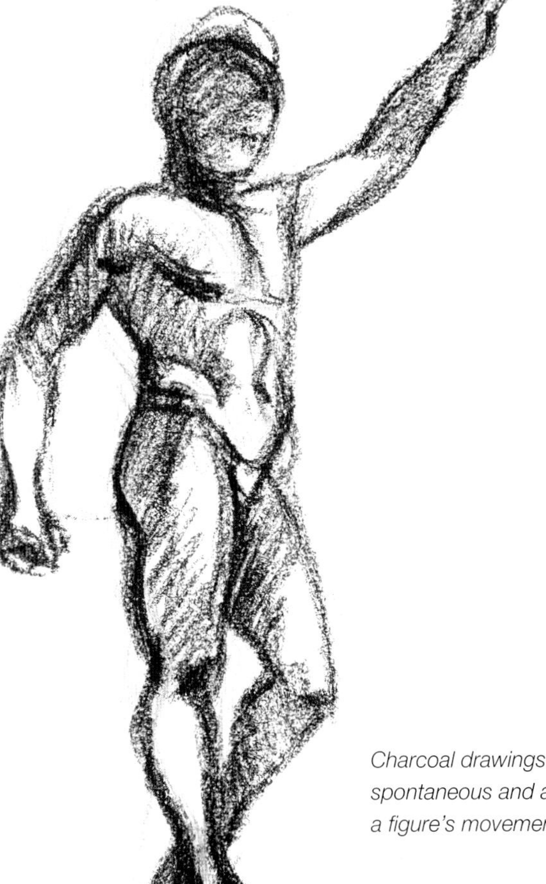

Charcoal drawings are especially spontaneous and always suit the essence of a figure's movement very well.

1. The sketch of the pose is drawn with very free and spontaneous lines, trying to capture the gesture by trial and error until we find the one that reflects the articulation of the movement.

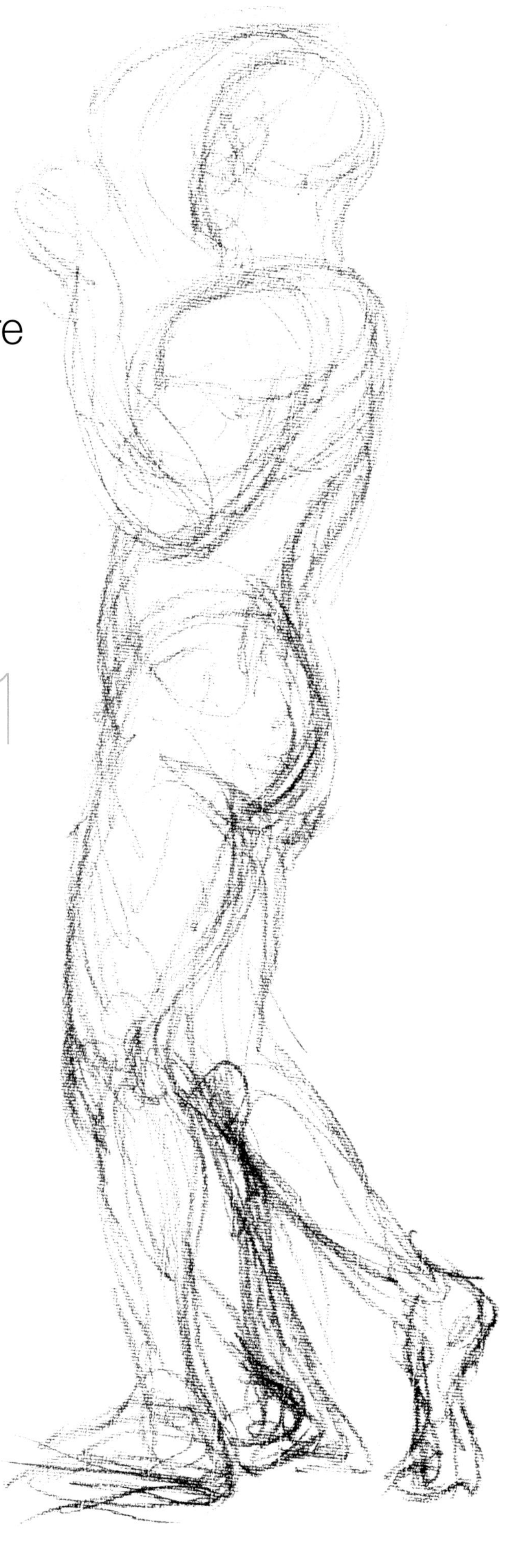

PROCESS WITH CHARCOAL

Charcoal adapts better than other drawing media to the expression of movement. The line is easy and quick, thick or thin, depending on how the stick is handled, and shading can be applied quickly because the lines can be blended with the fingers or with a rag. The process begins with tentative lines that define the contours gradually without marking them too much until the end of the process. This is characteristic of the representation of movement: It is important to avoid drawing outlines that are rigorous and very defined, which would make the figure appear encased within an outline.

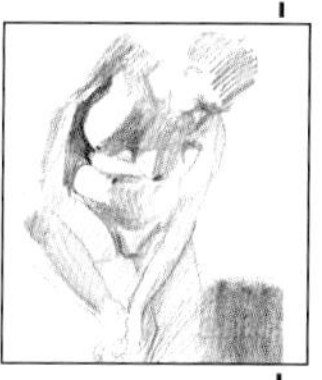

Movement is much better expressed when the outlines of the figure are not completely defined with dark lines. The form must flow and suggest the mobility of the limbs.

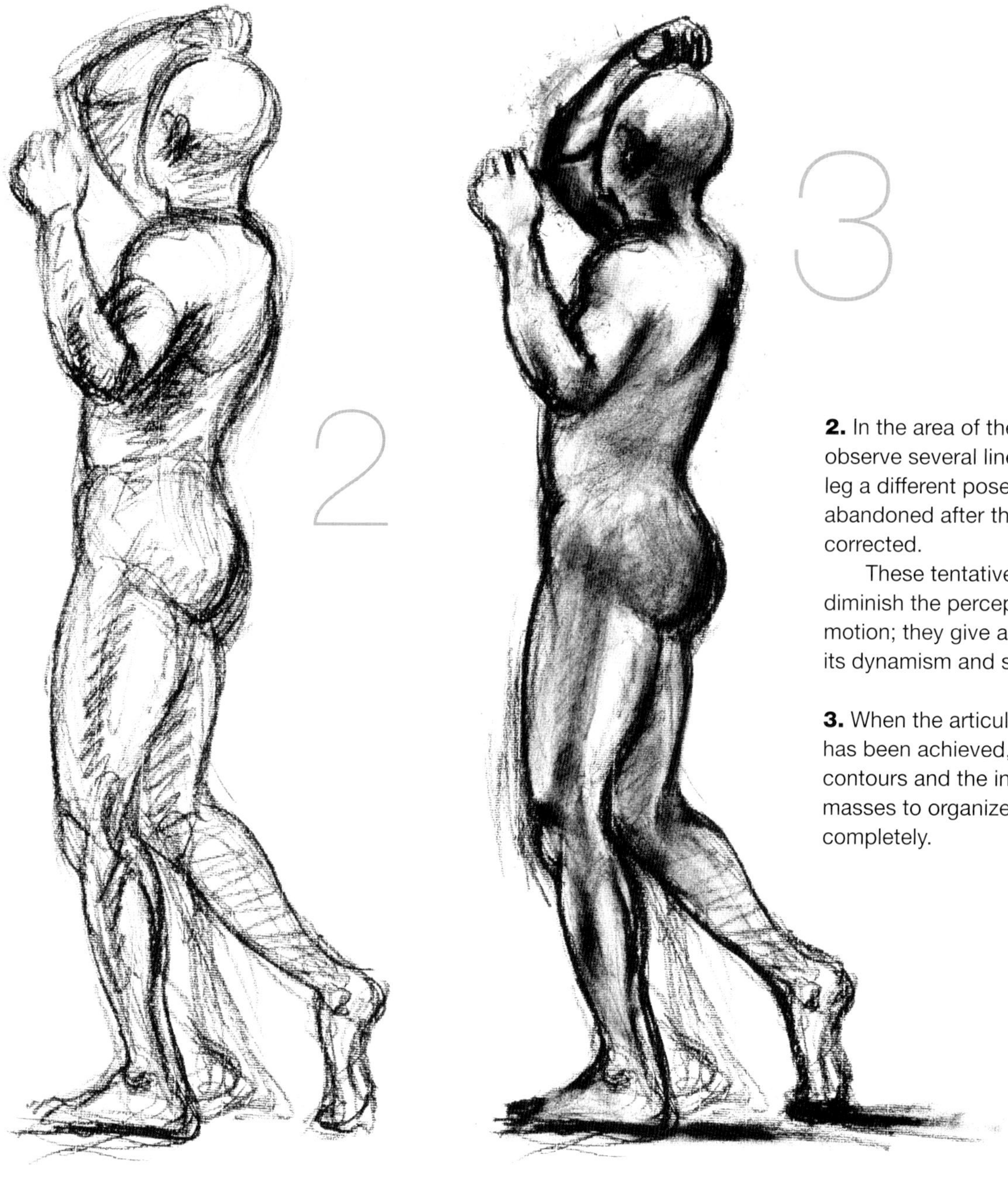

2

3

2. In the area of the calves we can observe several lines that gave the leg a different pose, but that were abandoned after their position was corrected.

These tentative lines do not diminish the perception of figures in motion; they give an added value to its dynamism and spontaneity.

3. When the articulation of the pose has been achieved, we go over its contours and the internal shading of its masses to organize its anatomy more completely.

Phases of Movement:
Walking and Running

a drawing is a static representation, but it can suggest dynamism if it accounts for the movement of the figure. In the following diagrams, we show the basic sequence for a human figure walking and running obtained by using a wooden articulated mannequin as a model. This is a resource that is available to anyone and that is very helpful for studying movement. By making different sketches of this mannequin, the artist can memorize the basic poses for the figure walking and running.

WALKING

It is interesting to observe that the position of the torso and the head stays almost unchanged through each of the walking phases and that the legs appear completely extended only when the weight of the figure falls on either one of them. The arms maintain a relaxed position, somewhat flexed, and only the shoulders depict forward and backward movements.

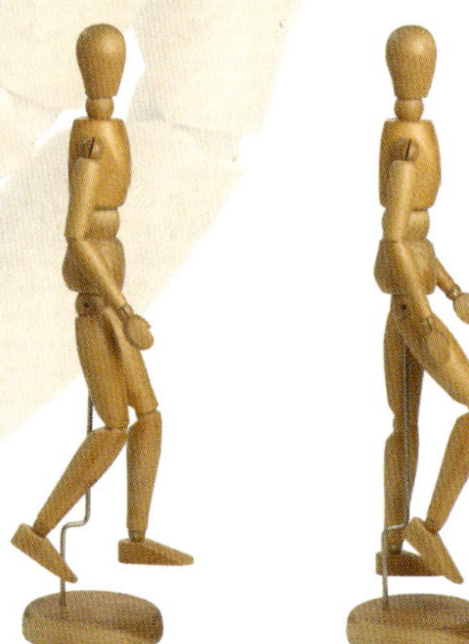
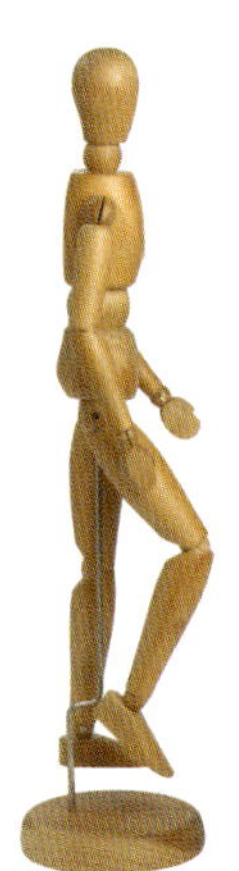
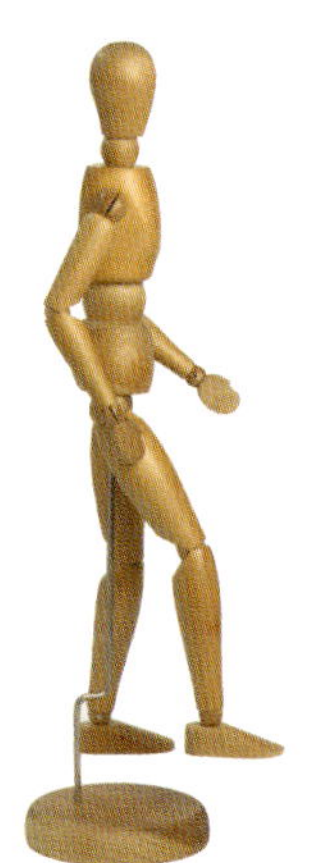
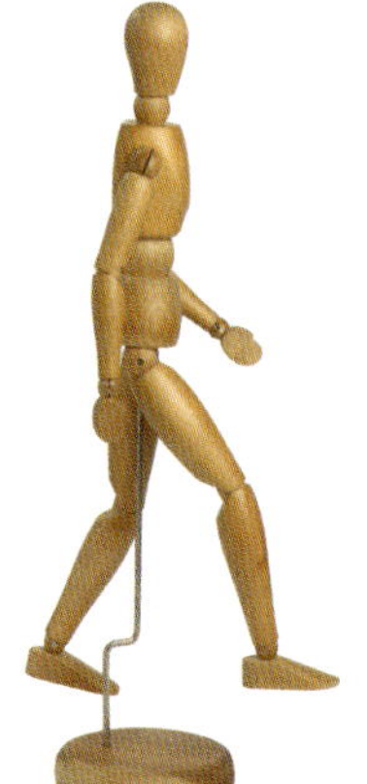
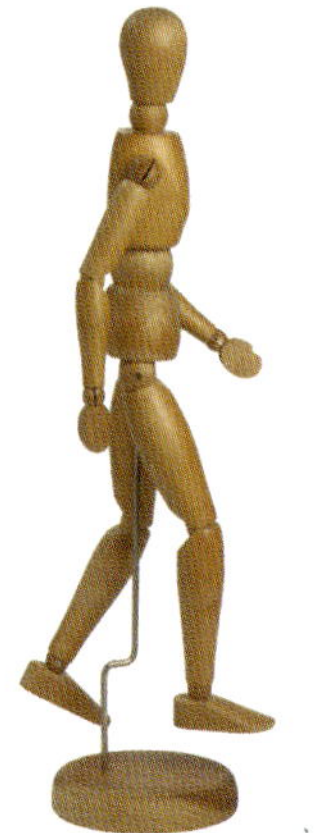
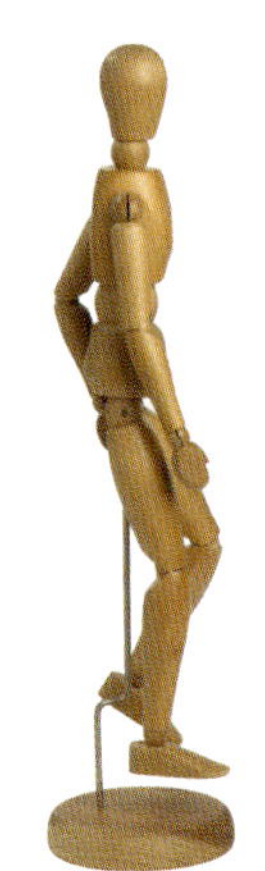
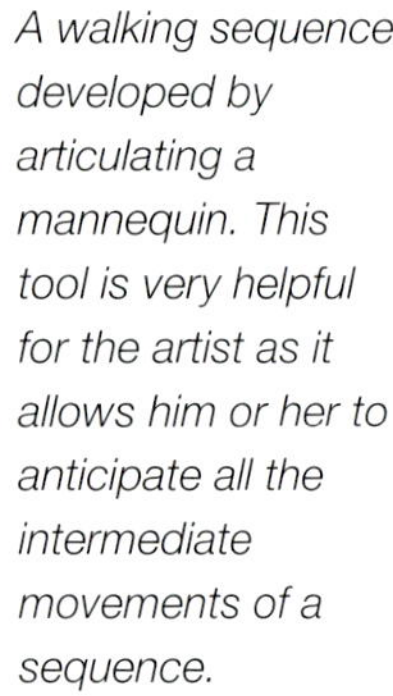

A walking sequence developed by articulating a mannequin. This tool is very helpful for the artist as it allows him or her to anticipate all the intermediate movements of a sequence.

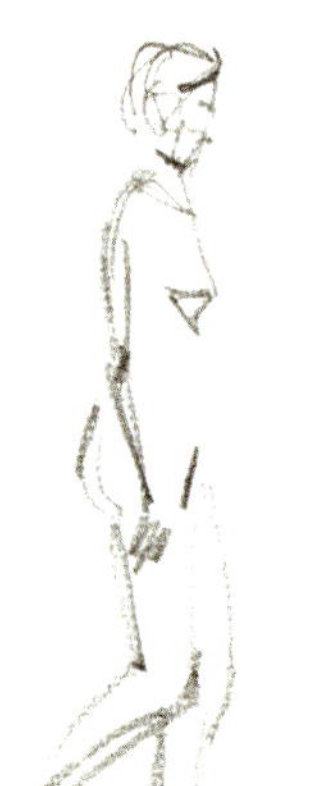
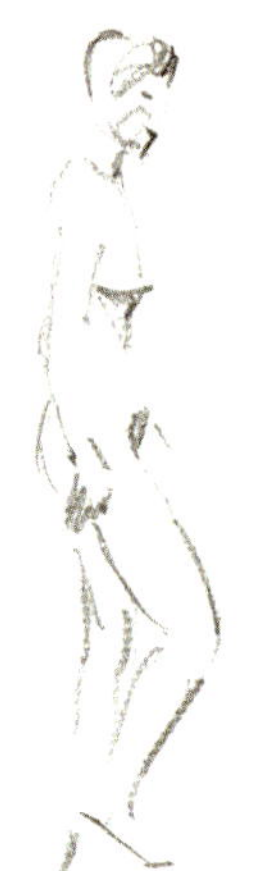
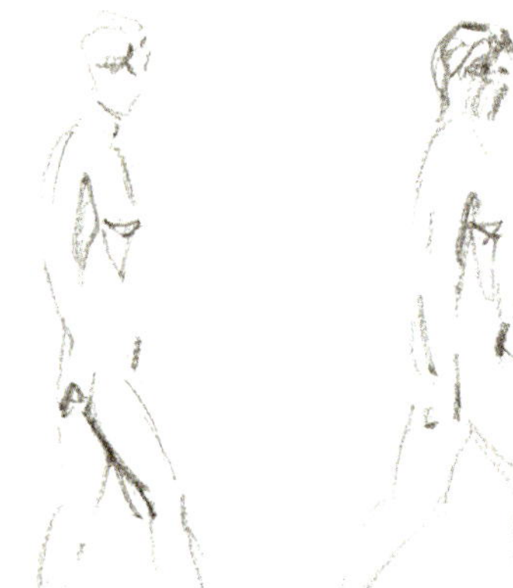
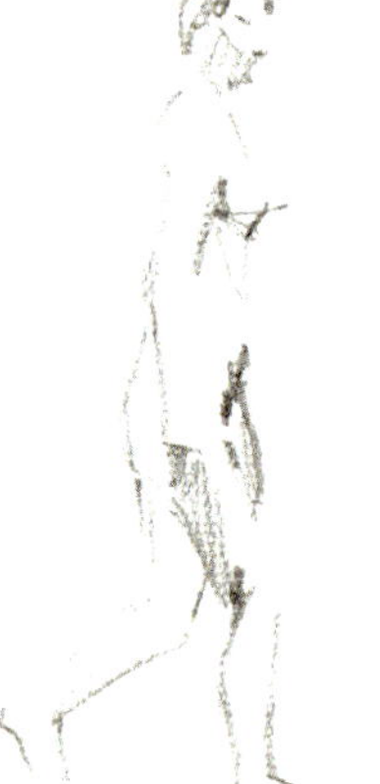
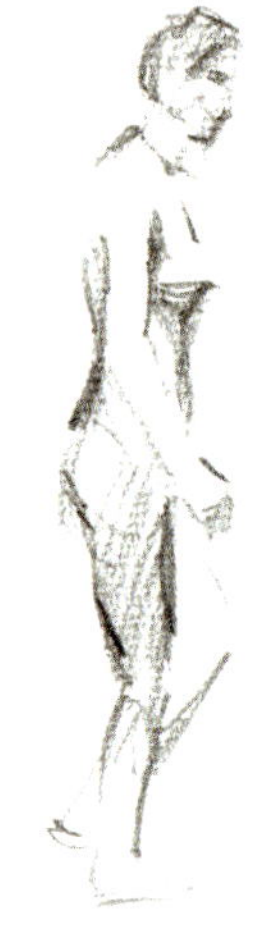

Drawings made by interpreting the position of the articulated mannequin in a walking sequence.

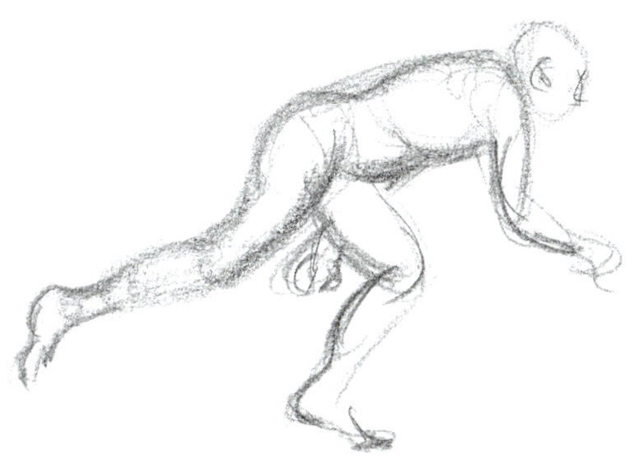

The expression of movement is a matter of articulation rather than exact representation. The details always get in the way, and the emphasis should be on the important lines of the figure.

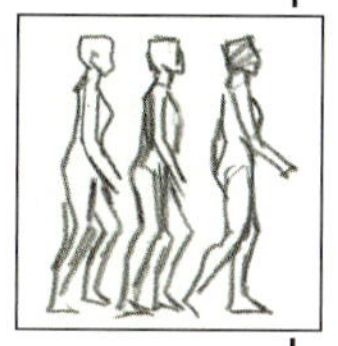

A few simple straight lines that express the direction of the limbs are enough to convey the movement of the figure. Movement is always better represented with the simplest methods.

RUNNING

Running implies a series of movements that are completely different from those for walking. The only thing in common with it is the rhythmic relationship of forward and backward movements of arms and legs. During running, the torso is usually at an angle and the center of gravity of the figure moves forward. One could say that a figure running is always falling forward and avoiding that fall with the quick advancement of the legs.

In the drawings illustrated here showing the sequence of running we can see how the torso leans forward. This angle is more pronounced just before the foot located farther out makes contact with the floor and more upright just before the foot located behind comes off the floor. The arms are more flexed than during walking, and the forward and backward motion of the shoulders becomes more visible.

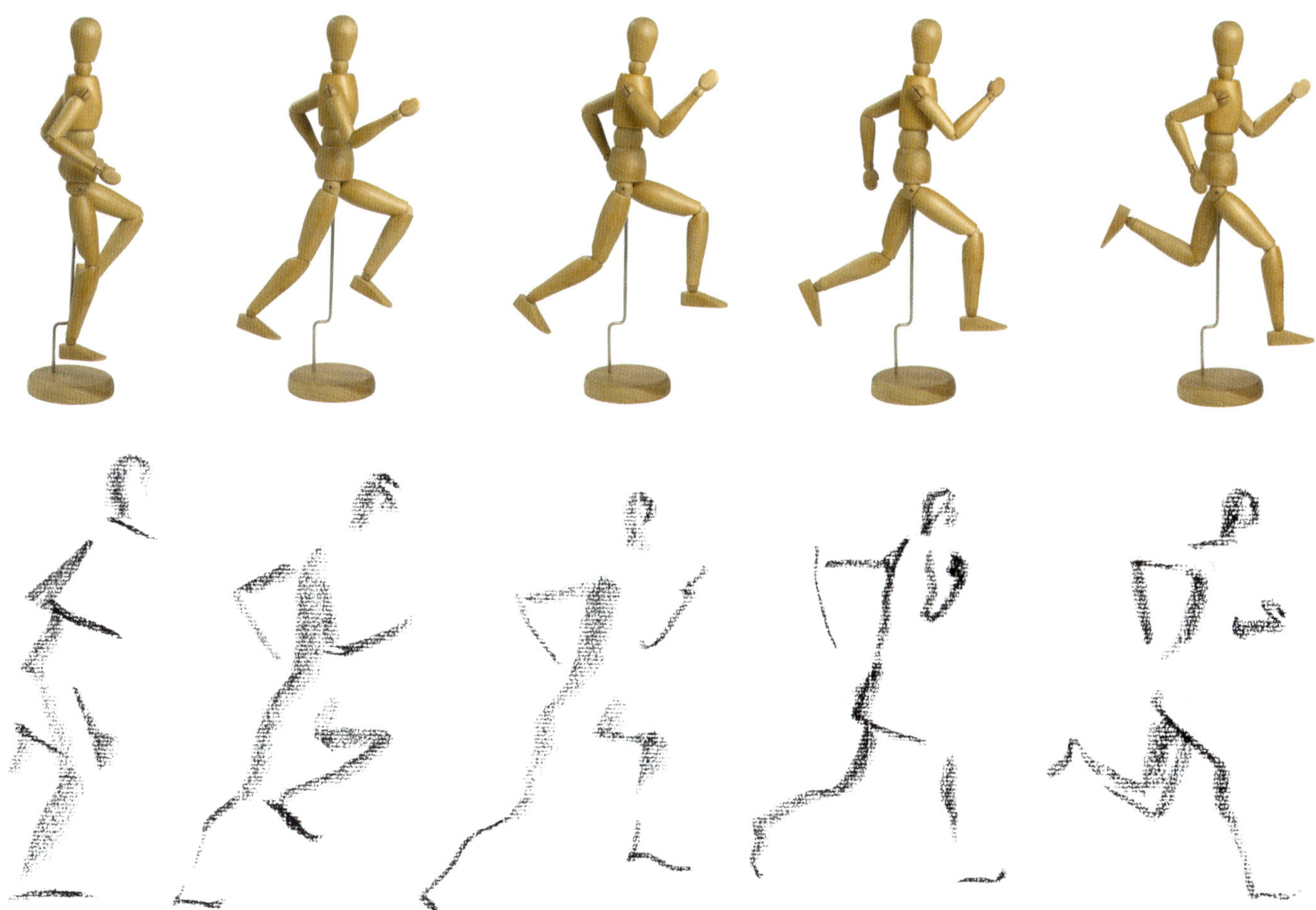

The legs are flexed much more when running than walking, to the point that the calf can elevate the foot almost to the level of the glutei. During the contact with the floor, the leg remains flexed, and it appears completely extended only just before or after initiating or losing this contact.

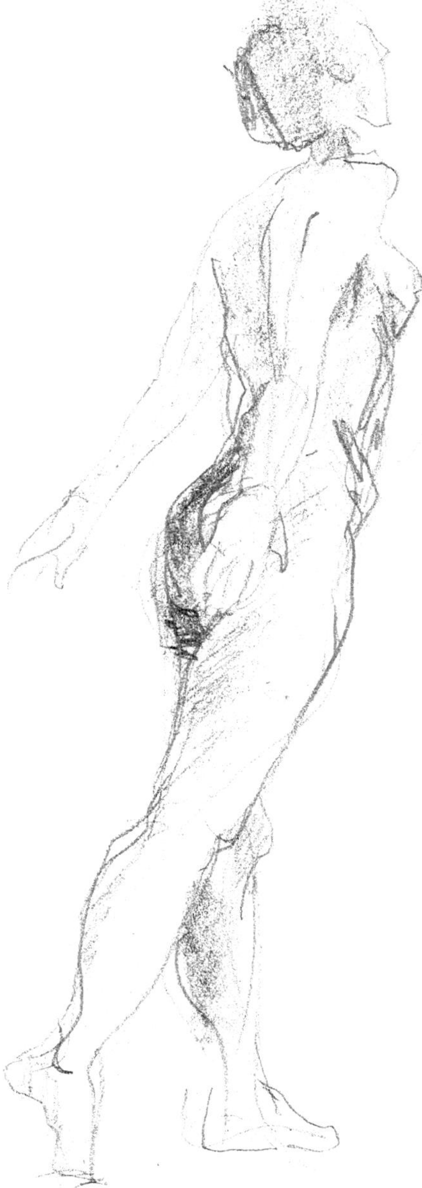

Media for Drawing
the Anatomy of the Figure

The pencil is a flexible and very versatile medium; it can be used for details and intricate studies as well as for free and spontaneous lines. Drawing by Muntsa Calbó.

The procedure and the technique used for drawing figures are vitally important to the final result. The same figure will differ not only in its technical aspects (color, approach, and finish), but also in the feeling and expressivity conveyed to the viewer according to the tools chosen and how they are used. Some media are warmer than others, or more spontaneous, flexible, or intimate. Any drawing medium has its own expressivity, which is inevitably transferred to the subject matter. This is why it is so important for the artist to know the various media well: For each figure drawing, the artist must be able to choose the approach that best responds to his or her intentions and what he or she wishes to express. A figure that is in full movement is not the same as a portrait or an interior scene or a group of figures outdoors; each subject calls for a specific treatment among the various options that are shown in the following pages.

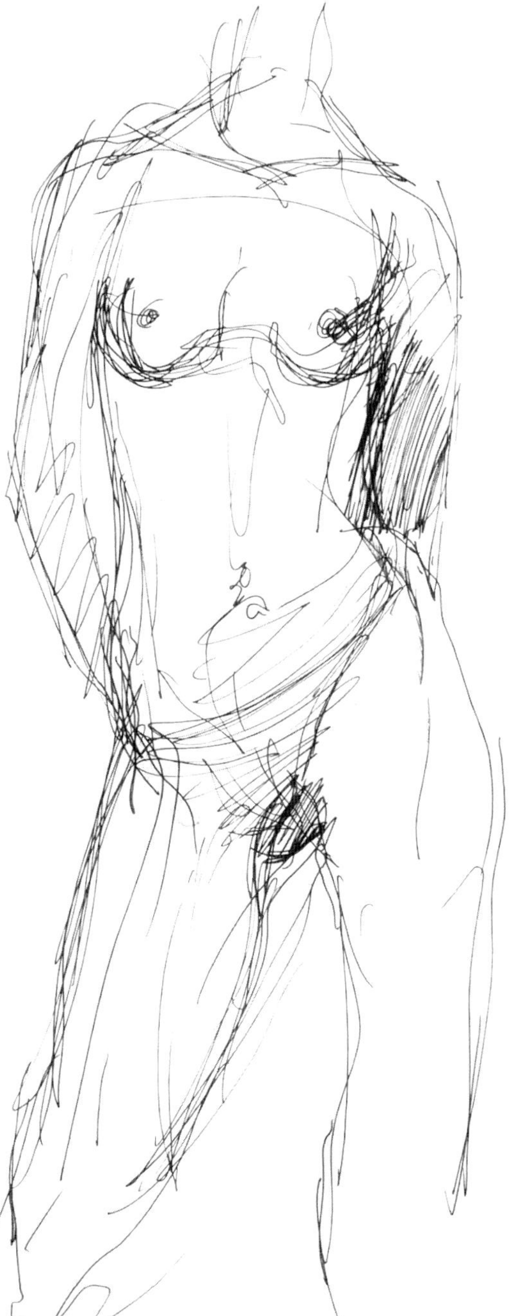

Drawing made with a marker. As in all the ink media, the defining characteristic is always the strong and free line that can be very detailed but also create a loose open form. Drawing by Ramon Vayreda.

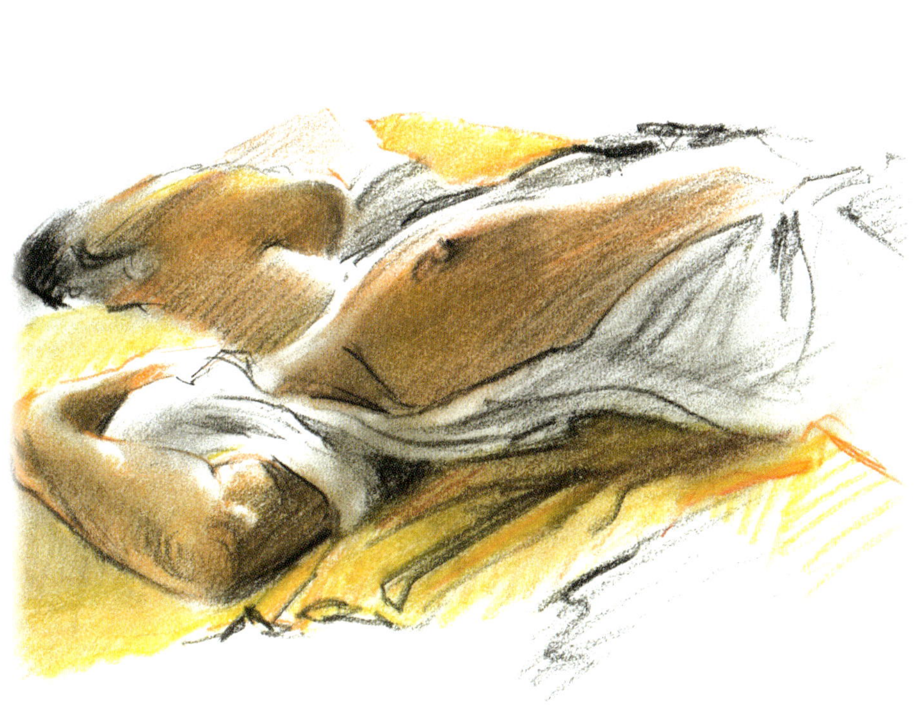

Color chalks and pastels in general offer a wide range of possibilities emphasizing warmth and the delicate development of shading. Work by Óscar Sanchís.

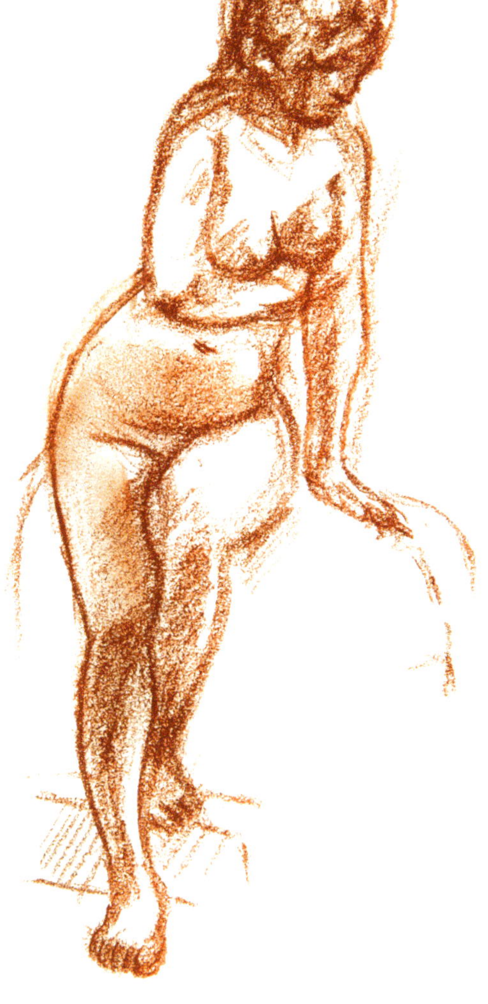

Sanguine is particularly warm. It adapts very well to the forms of female nudes. Drawing by David Sanmiguel.

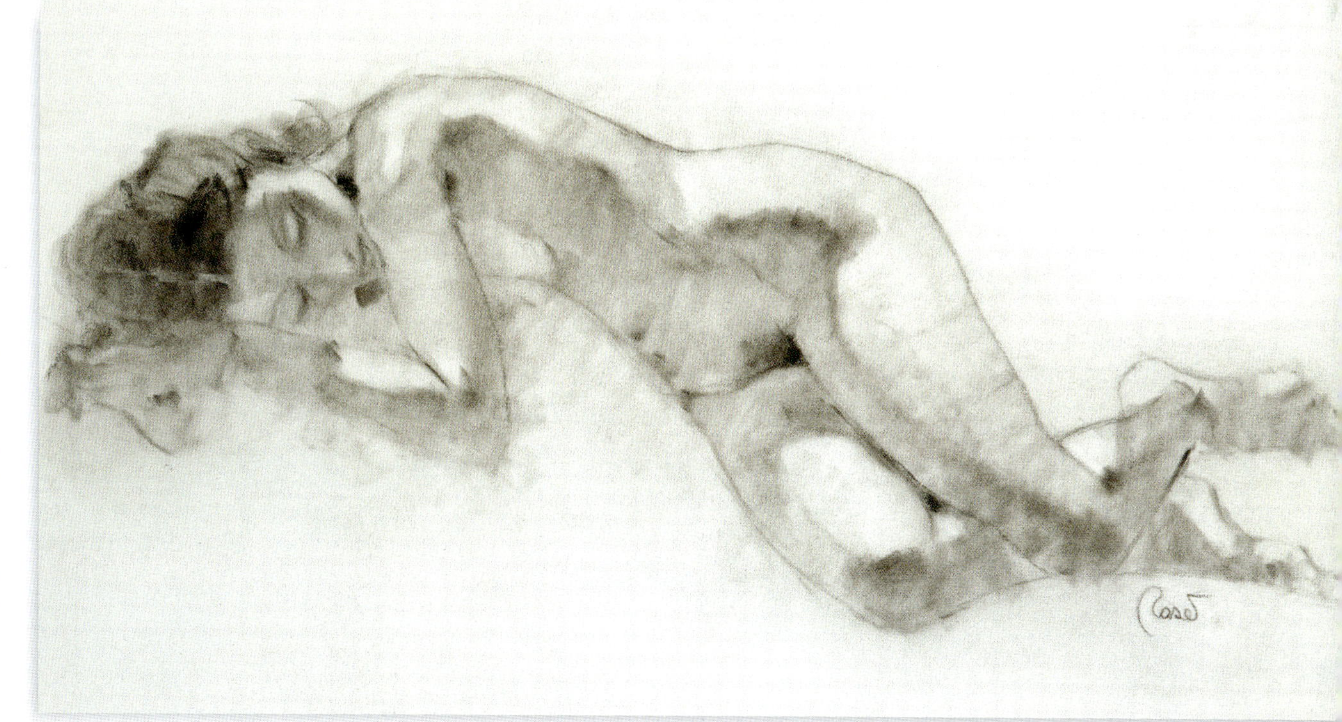

Charcoal is a very versatile medium. Figures drawn in this medium convey special warmth and a sensuality that is the result of soft shading and diffused edges. Work by Joan Raset.

Drawing Anatomy with a Pencil

This is the simplest and most direct of all the drawing media. A pencil is a thin graphite bar inside a wood casing. There are still people who refer to it as "pencil lead" because when graphite was discovered in the sixteenth century it was incorrectly believed to be that metal. Artists usually draw with soft leads, which produce a very dark and intense line; hard leads are used for very delicate lines. There are also thick leads without wood casings (graphite bars) that are used for sketching and for large pieces.

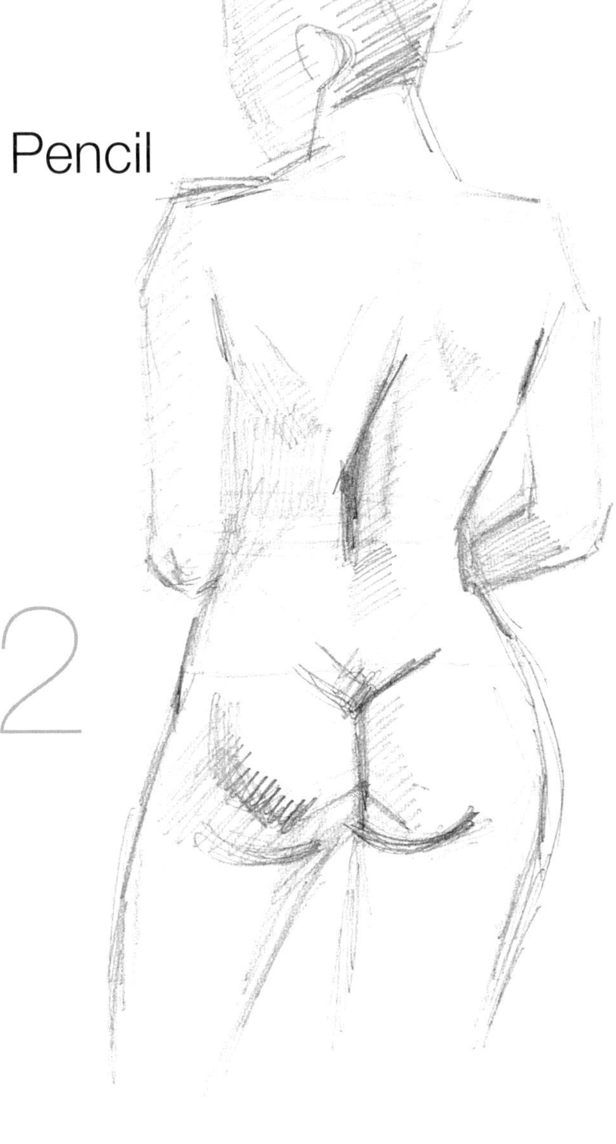

2

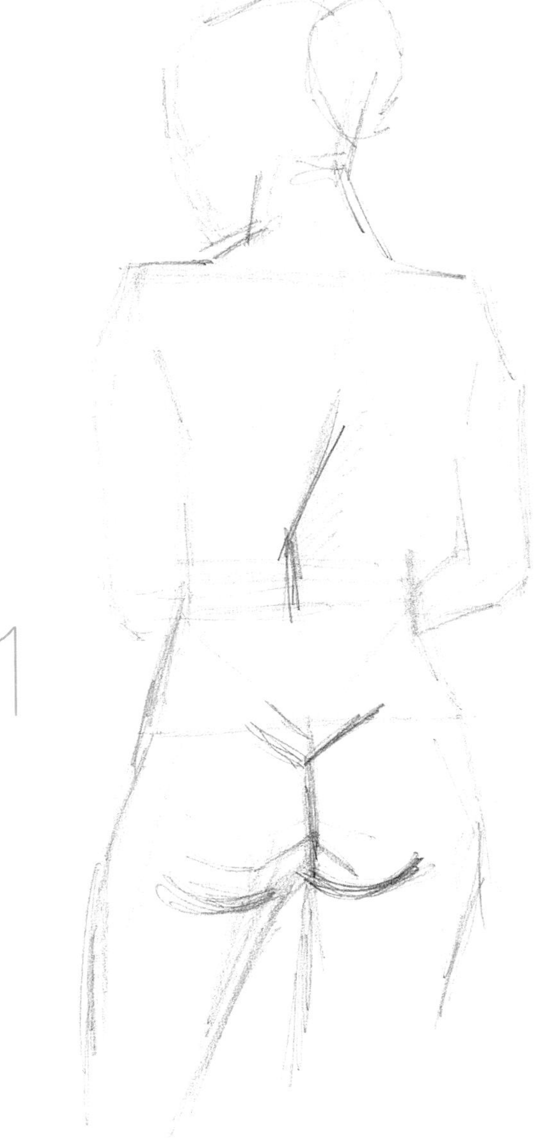

1

1. Hard pencils are useful for the first phases of a drawing, when the lines are sketchy and the artist is looking for the overall form rather than the real contour of the figure's anatomy.

2. The transition from the sketchy forms to the anatomical details and intricacies can be done with pencils that are a little bit softer, but without applying very heavy lines.

INTENSITY VARIATIONS
Working with pencils of differing hardness makes it possible to control the intensity of the drawing, which enriches the uniform gray tone of the graphite tip. Hard pencils make very thin and soft lines, which are ideal for small details and for more delicate shading. Soft leads can be used to reinforce the most important features of the figure and its most shaded areas with lines and shading that stand out sharply against the white of the paper. It is also possible to obtain a wide range of intensities simply by working with a single lead, applying more or less pressure and adjusting the angle of contact with the paper.

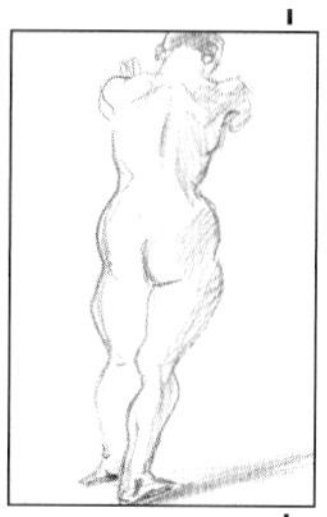

Shading with a pencil can be created by using parallel and crisscrossing lines, or blending them with the finger. The softer the pencil, the darker the shading will be when working in this manner.

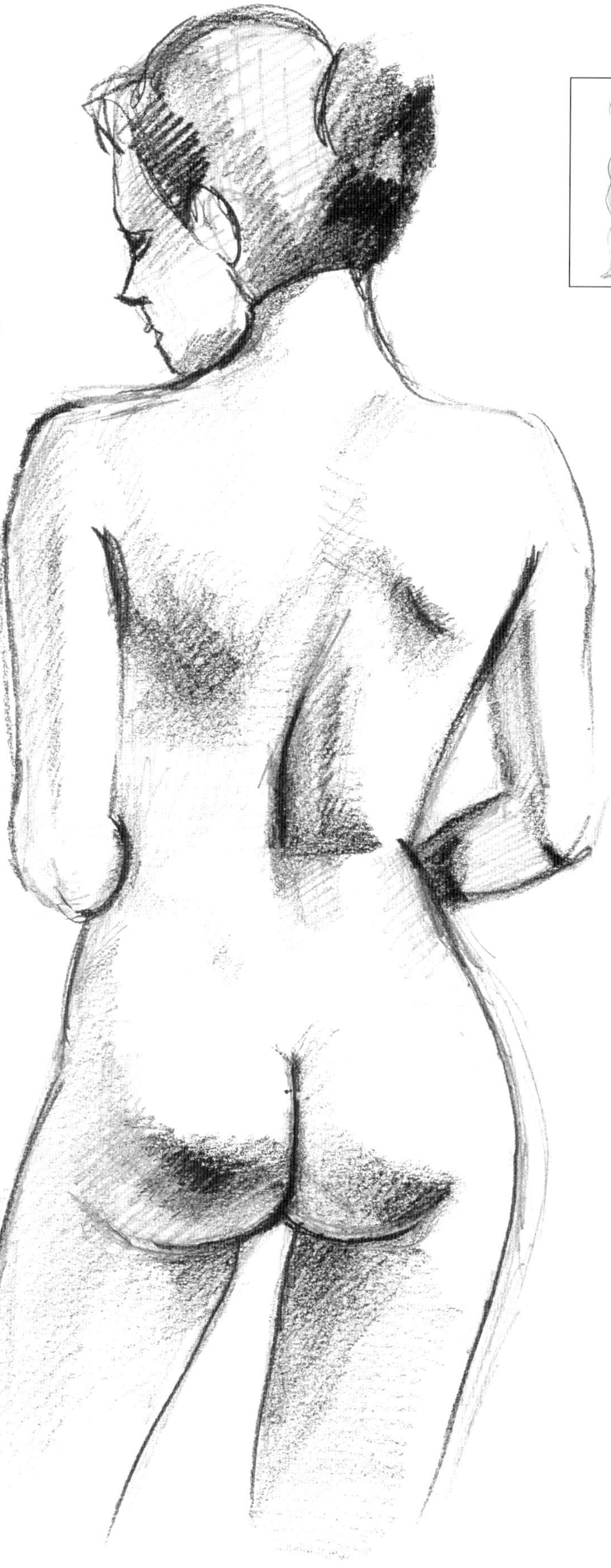

3. Soft pencils make deeper and darker lines than hard ones and are suitable for sketching or, as in this case, to add the last touches to a very detailed anatomical drawing.

3

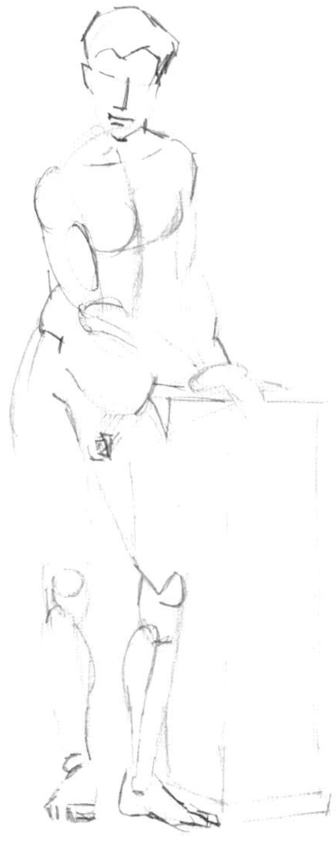

Using soft pencils that make dark lines from the beginning can be very interesting if the artist is skilled at drawing and the desired effect is light and spontaneous.

The Figure with Chalk and Pastels

Pastels are very soft and are made of dry pigments lightly bound with gum arabic, which allows the color to adhere to the paper. Chalks are smaller square bars that are quite a bit harder than pastels. Traditionally, this name was given to the small white, black, sepia, and sanguine bars used since the Renaissance to make colored drawings whose foundation was tonal contrast rather than color. Many artists use both mediums in the same piece: Extensive areas of color are applied with pastels, while chalk is used to define the contours and the linear details of the work. Pastels are basically a colorist medium that is applied very liberally and that can be softened and blended as in the more impressionist techniques, which are based on bursts of pure color.

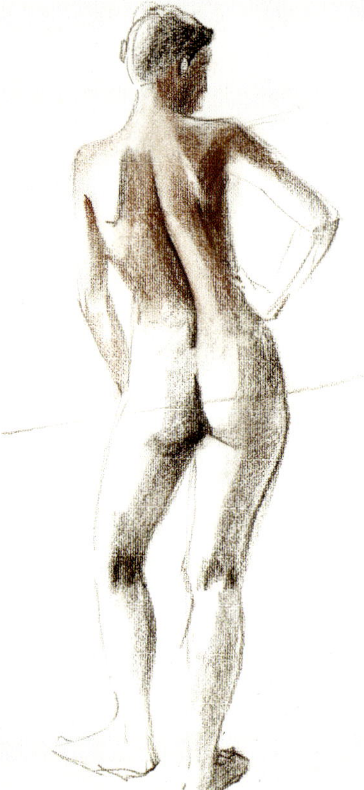

1. The initial drawing takes into account the factors related to the joints and to the anatomical contours of the figure. It is a simple and fluid drawing that leaves room to work with the colors.

2. Since chalks have good covering power, colors can be superimposed, concealing the previous color completely. However, there is a possibility for the superimposed color to get a little bit muddied in the process; for that reason it is better to begin with dark colors followed by the light ones, which will be enriched by the possible “soiling.”

SHADING
Chalks (and pastels and charcoals) can be used either to make lines or for shading, depending on whether the stick is applied with the tip or applied to the paper with the flat side. Shading can also be used for drawing. Shading expresses the areas and the values of the shadows, which create the figure's mass. The smaller and more abundant the shading, the more precise will be the modeling. With this technique, the use of the line will not be as necessary to reveal the form. In addition, shading with chalk can be diffused and blended together, enhancing the efficiency of this medium.

Most pastel artists, especially the ones who practice figure drawing, use color papers that go well with the overall tone of the piece. It is logical to choose warm pastels (light greens, pinks, sienna, light mauve, light ochre, etc.) that complement the flesh tones of the figure.

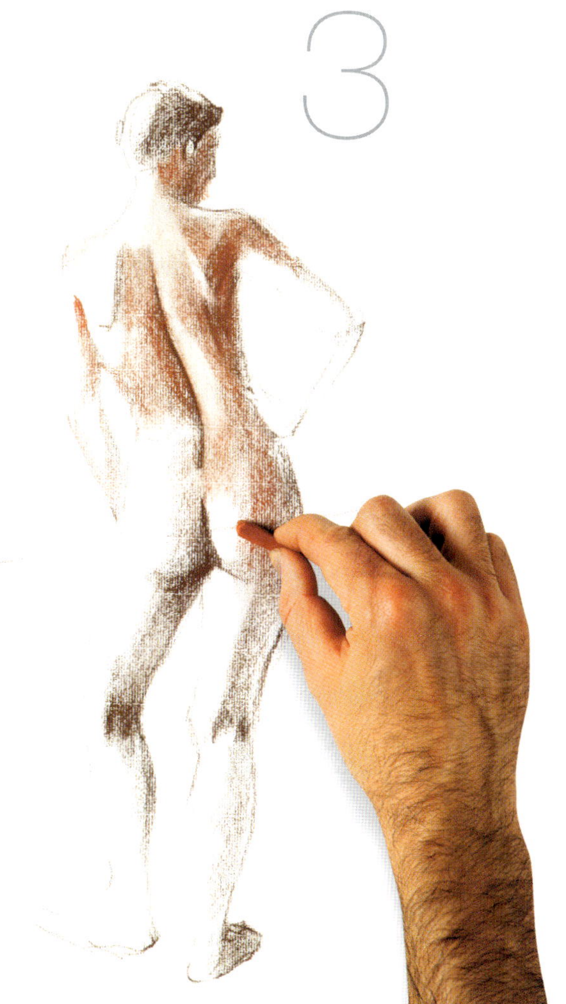

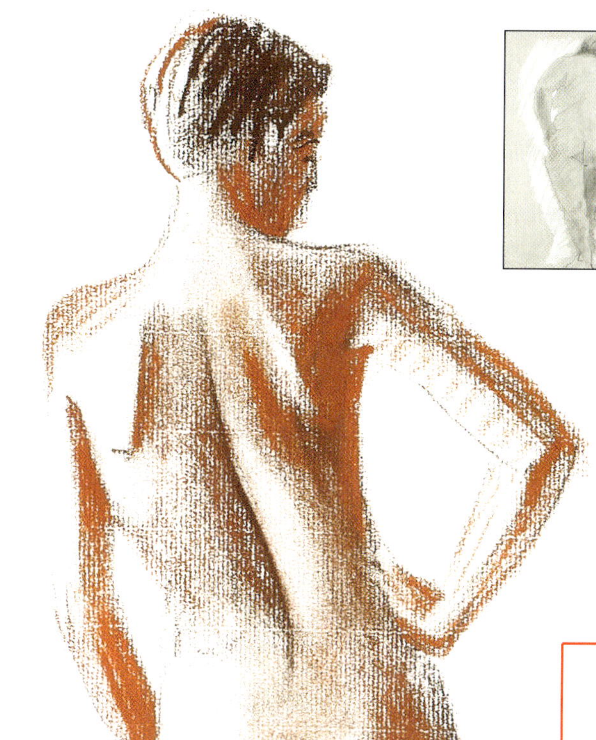

3. Sanguine color is applied over sepia color. The sanguine bar is placed flat on the paper to create large shaded areas that give the artist the option of diffusing them wherever he or she wises to have darker and more compact colors.

4. Modeling with chalk is characterized by its softness and warmth. This is a very suitable medium for drawing anatomy, although it does not allow as many details as other mediums.

Sketching the Figure

Quick sketches are the basis for the study of the human figure. Every piece begins with one or several quick sketches. A quick sketch could be the beginning of the final piece, or it could be a step in the process; but in any case, the importance of sketches is paramount because they are the firm foundation over which the work is developed. Because they are easy to handle and to carry, pencils, charcoal, sanguine, and nib pens are the most common mediums for working outdoors. A pocket sketchbook can be taken anywhere, and it is always ready to use in any situation. The paper should not be thin or smooth; slight surface texture highlights the lines and provides special warmth to the finish.

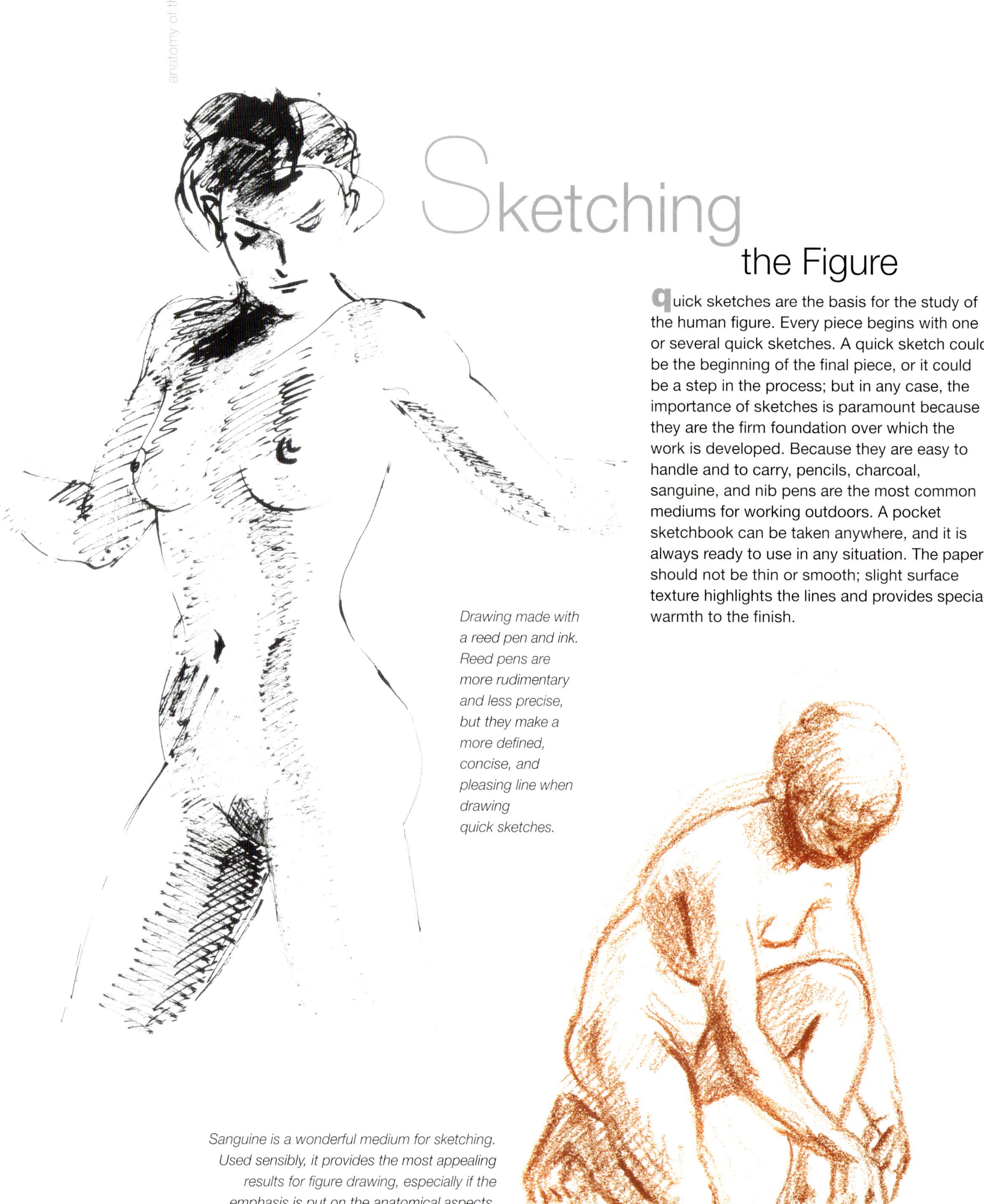

Drawing made with a reed pen and ink. Reed pens are more rudimentary and less precise, but they make a more defined, concise, and pleasing line when drawing quick sketches.

Sanguine is a wonderful medium for sketching. Used sensibly, it provides the most appealing results for figure drawing, especially if the emphasis is put on the anatomical aspects.

LIGHT AND SHADOWS

Shading in sketches should always be light and never overdone. It is important to look for synthesis between light and shadows to construct the figure with the essential elements. Excessive emphasis on shaded areas is a problem typical of inexperienced artists that makes drawings confusing.

INK SKETCHES

The immediacy of the nib or reed pen and the brush has no equal. These drawing tools make it possible to express movement, light, and atmosphere with minimal use of resources and with results that qualify as sketches but also as finished pieces in their own right. Additionally, it is one of the best exercises for the artist. It develops hand dexterity and the ability to observe and retain—the ability to see and understand—the form almost instantaneously in order to transfer it to the paper immediately.

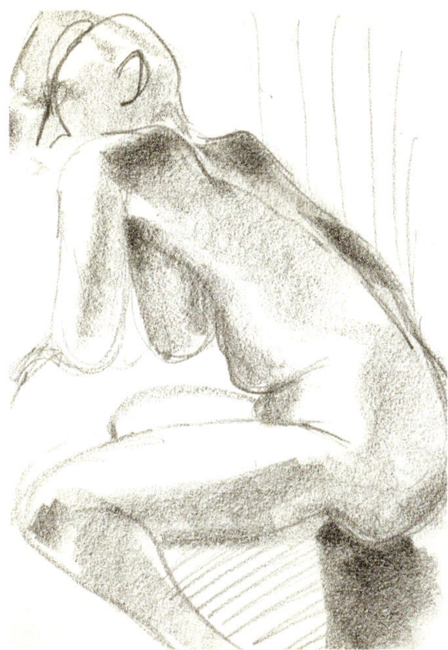

Graphite bars make it possible to cover large shaded areas very quickly. This way, the anatomy can be resolved in synthesis and with a few lines.

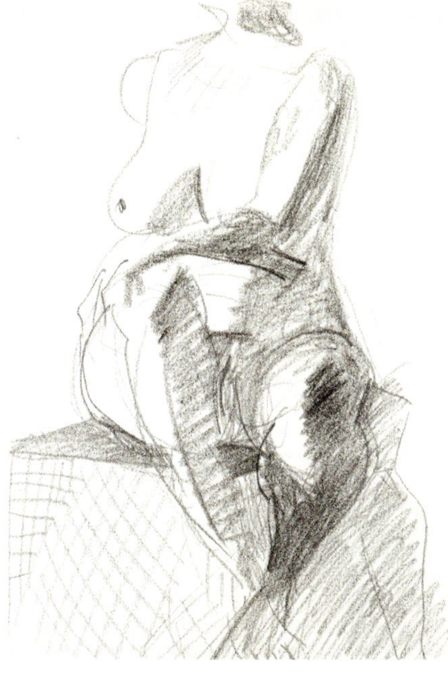

A conventional pencil can be used to make lines and hatching for shading quickly. These complement the chiaroscuro treatment; they control the density of the lines and provide good tonal gradation.

Chalks and pastels do not provide the immediacy of reed pens and pencils, but they make drawing certain details of the figure easier, leaving the rest in a sketched state.

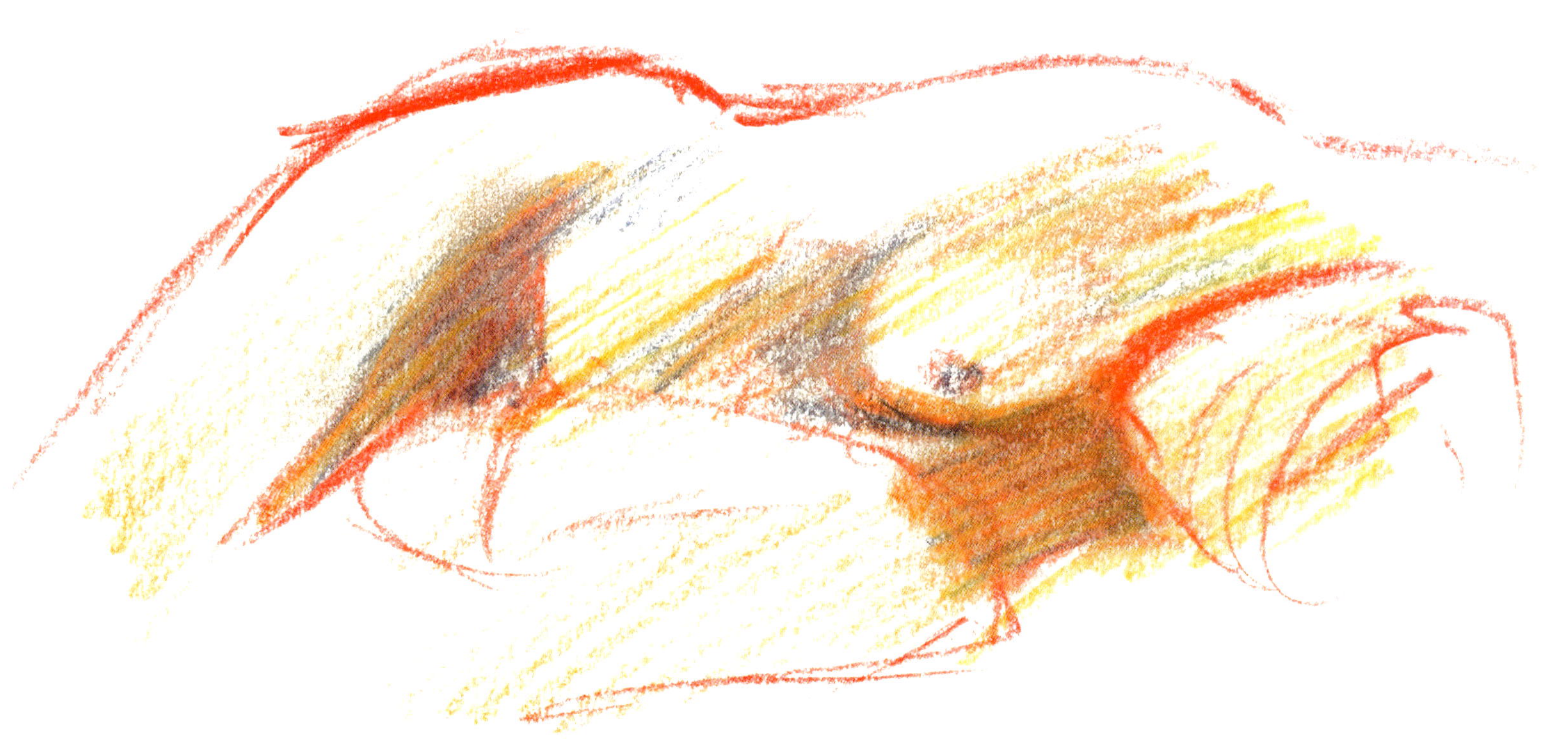

Synthesis:
The Essential Drawing

Delacroix used to say that a good artist is capable of capturing the motion of a body falling from the fifth floor. Maybe this famous French painter exaggerated a little, but the idea of his comment is very true: the greater the ability of an artist to represent the motion of an instant, the greater the ability to synthesize. To represent the figure in synthesis is to understand the overall anatomical features that take place in the pose in question and to give an abbreviated and precise rendition of them. The practice of synthesis drawing consists of drawing poses in a very short time (a maximum of 20 or 30 seconds) using very few lines, only the ones needed to express the pose visually. Going a step further would require reducing that lapse of time to make "snippets" or frozen movements perceived in an instant. All these studies must be very quick and cannot be corrected or erased.

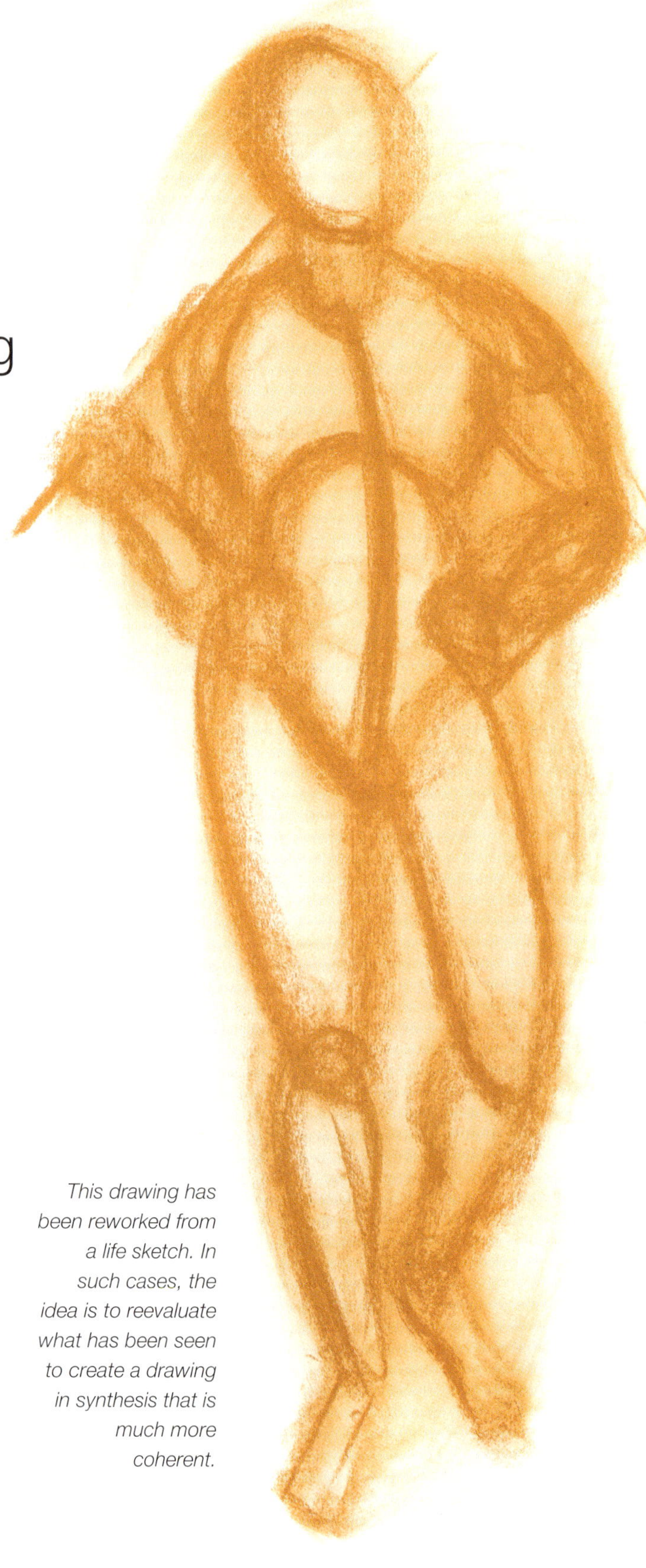

This drawing has been reworked from a life sketch. In such cases, the idea is to reevaluate what has been seen to create a drawing in synthesis that is much more coherent.

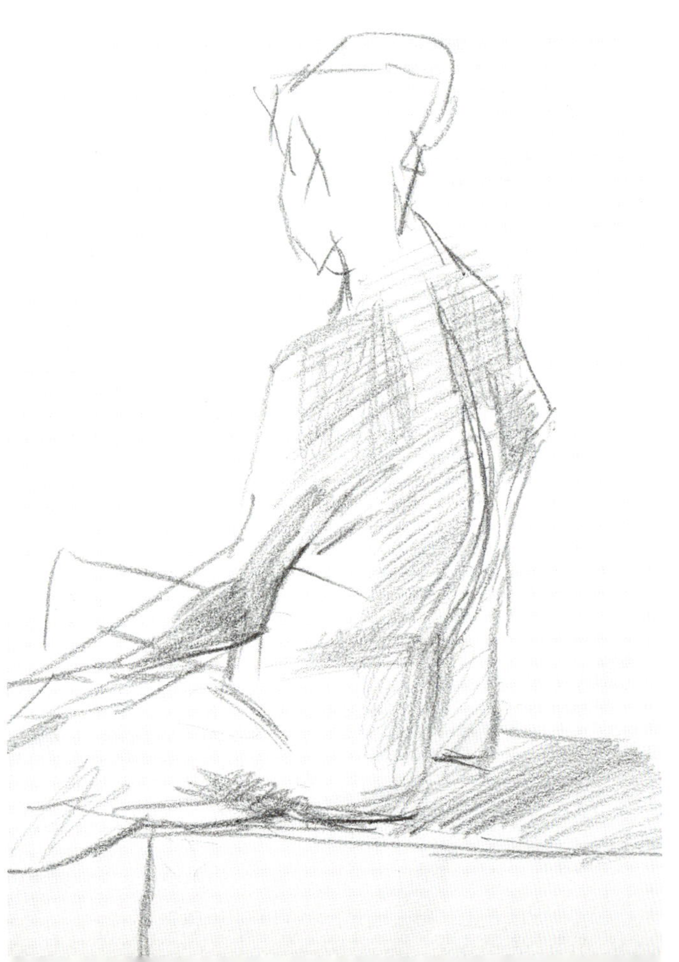

This back has been drawn in synthesis, but the artist has not disregarded its anatomy. Synthesis drawing is not a disfiguration but a simplification of the process to make it easier to understand.

QUICK SKETCHES

It is a good idea to have small sketchbooks or loose sheets of paper handy at all times to make quick sketches to resolve a difficult body position or the movement of the back, a facial expression, and so forth. Sketches can be just a few simple lines that could prove to be very useful. Many times, just four lines drawn in an instant and almost unconsciously can suggest original possibilities to the artist. Never throw away those sketches (at least for a reasonable period of time and as long as the artist is convinced of their usefulness). Quick sketches can be full-body sketches or partial ones and can be made before the definitive piece or during the process of drawing it.

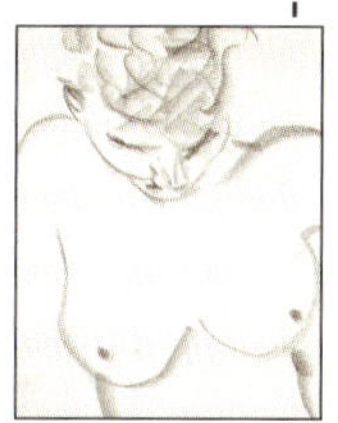

Synthesis forces us to disregard the unnecessary. Even drawings made without taking the eyes off the model and without checking the lines can include solutions in synthesis that the artist would have never thought of any other way.

The idea that must drive the mind of the artist when he or she is working in synthesis is the overall figure seen as a piece of simple architecture made of organic parts.

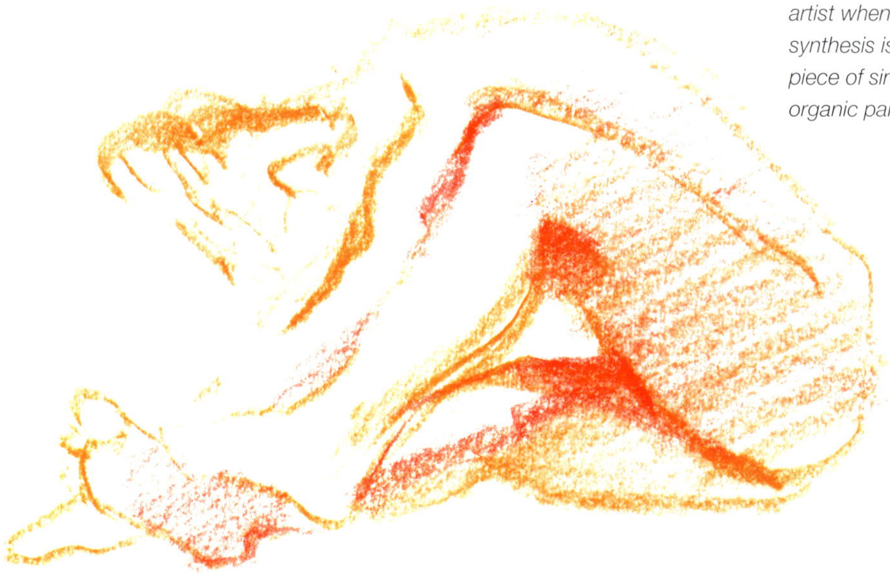

Sometimes, trial and error lines and mistakes are inevitable in sketches made in synthesis, but these lines are very helpful during the process because they suggest new solutions.

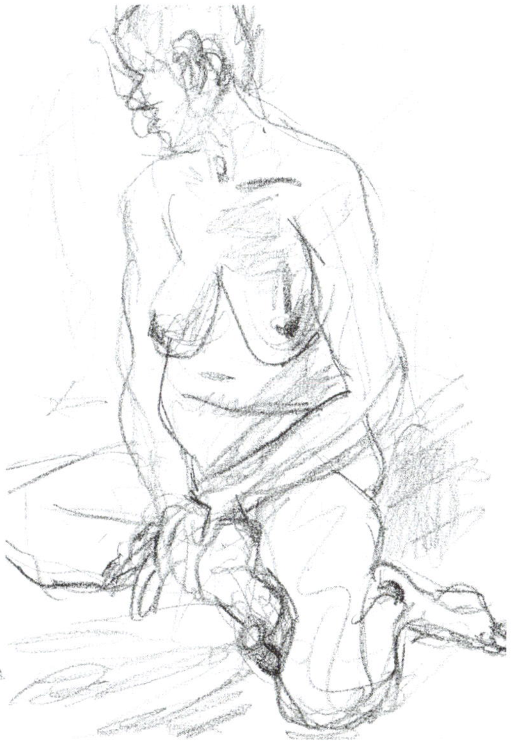

The outline can be the vehicle for the synthesis when the line only represents the aspects of the anatomy that are different, disregarding the transitions between them.

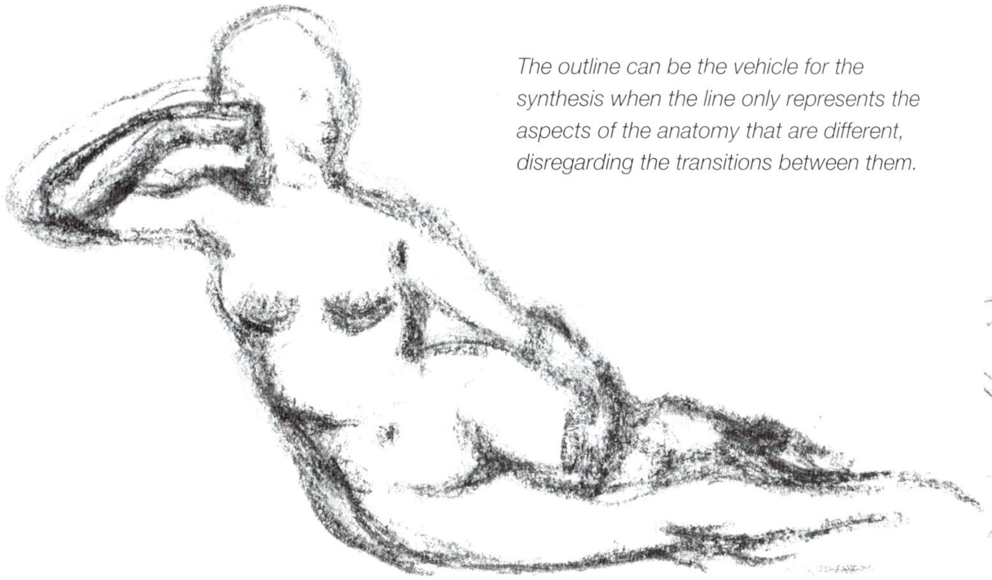

foreshortening is seeing the body or a part of the body in perspective. During the Renaissance and Baroque periods many artists showed their knowledge of anatomy by filling their compositions with foreshortened figures in the most varied (and even forced) positions. Any subject matter justified the inclusion of multiple contorted figures that gave a new figurative dimension to human anatomy. Tintoretto and Rubens were two of the great masters who used foreshortening to create dramatic effects.

Foreshortening: The Figure in Perspective

DRAWING IN FORESHORTENING
Drawing a figure in foreshortening requires a certain degree of practice and knowledge of the basic forms of the anatomy, because every foreshortening is an interpretation in perspective of such forms. Every figure always presents a part in foreshortening: the face, an arm, a hand, etc. But these are foreshortenings of little significance that hardly alter the "normal" perception of the anatomy. When a figure is seen from above or at eye level, some part of its body is shown without a doubt from an unusual viewpoint; therefore, the forms of the anatomy must be interpreted in a different way, trying to understand the logic of its perspective. Foreshortening is one of the typical technical aspects of learning figure drawing and painting. Aside from its academic interest, foreshortening can be an outstanding art tool if it is used with skill, and above all, without pretense. It is extremely important to draw very many sketches to achieve convincing foreshortenings.

Foreshortening can create truly fantastic drawings of the anatomy. This is very interesting because they can create surprising anatomical representations of the human body from angles that are not normally seen.

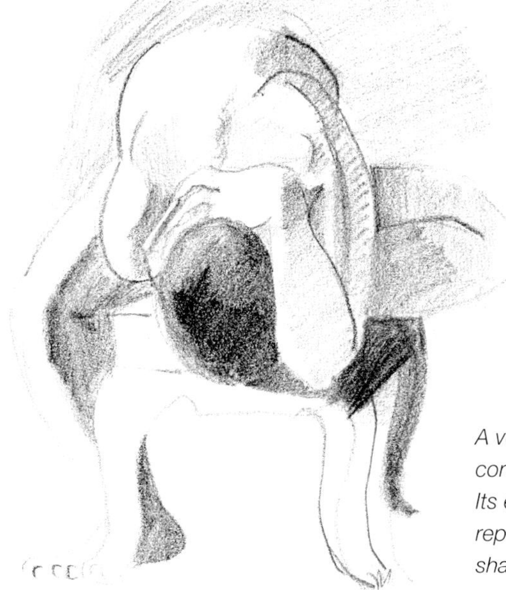

A very complete foreshortening, but not as complicated as it may appear at first sight. Its execution is based on the strict representation of the play of light and shadow inspired by the pose.

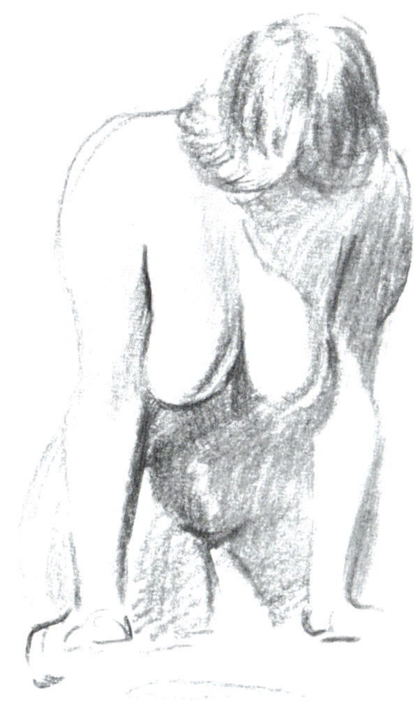

In this figure only the head is foreshortened; however, this is sufficient to create additional interest in the representation of the pose.

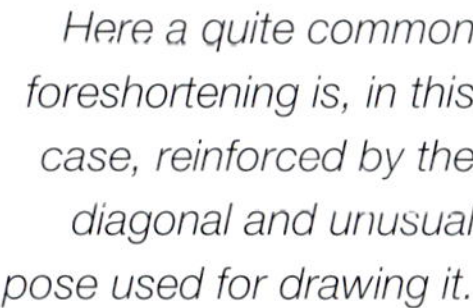

Here a quite common foreshortening is, in this case, reinforced by the diagonal and unusual pose used for drawing it.

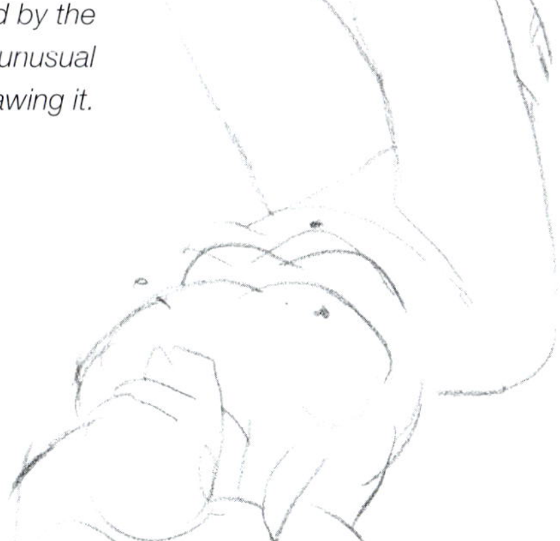

Reclining figures provide a good opportunity for practicing foreshortening. In this case, the entire torso and head are subjected to this type of perspective.

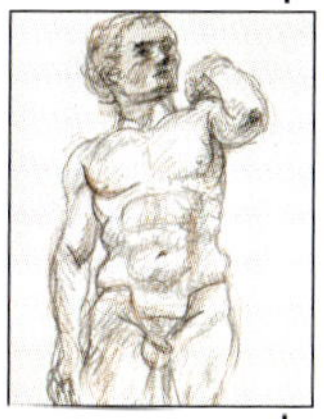

In almost all the poses some part of the figure is always foreshortened. It can be the arm (as is the case here), the head, the leg, and so forth. Foreshortening is practically unavoidable.

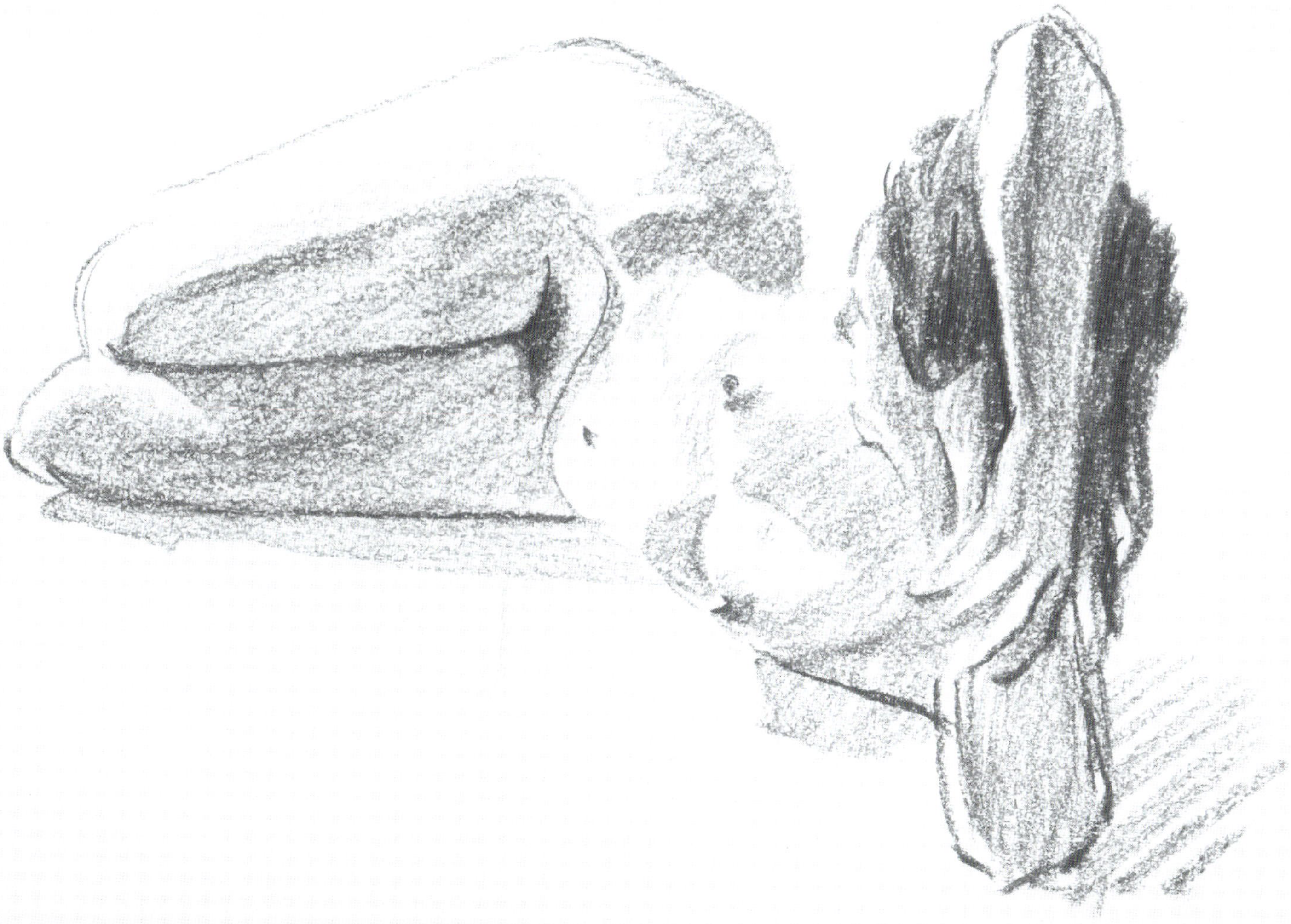

Step by Step

"ALTHOUGH ONE SHOULD ALWAYS STUDY THE METHOD OF A GREAT ARTIST, ONE SHOULD NEVER IMITATE HIS MANNER. THE MANNER OF AN ARTIST IS ESSENTIALLY INDIVIDUAL, THE METHOD OF AN ARTIST IS ABSOLUTELY UNIVERSAL. THE FIRST IS PERSONALITY, WHICH NO ONE SHOULD COPY; THE SECOND IS PERFECTION, WHICH ALL SHOULD AIM AT."

Oscar Wilde (1854-1900)

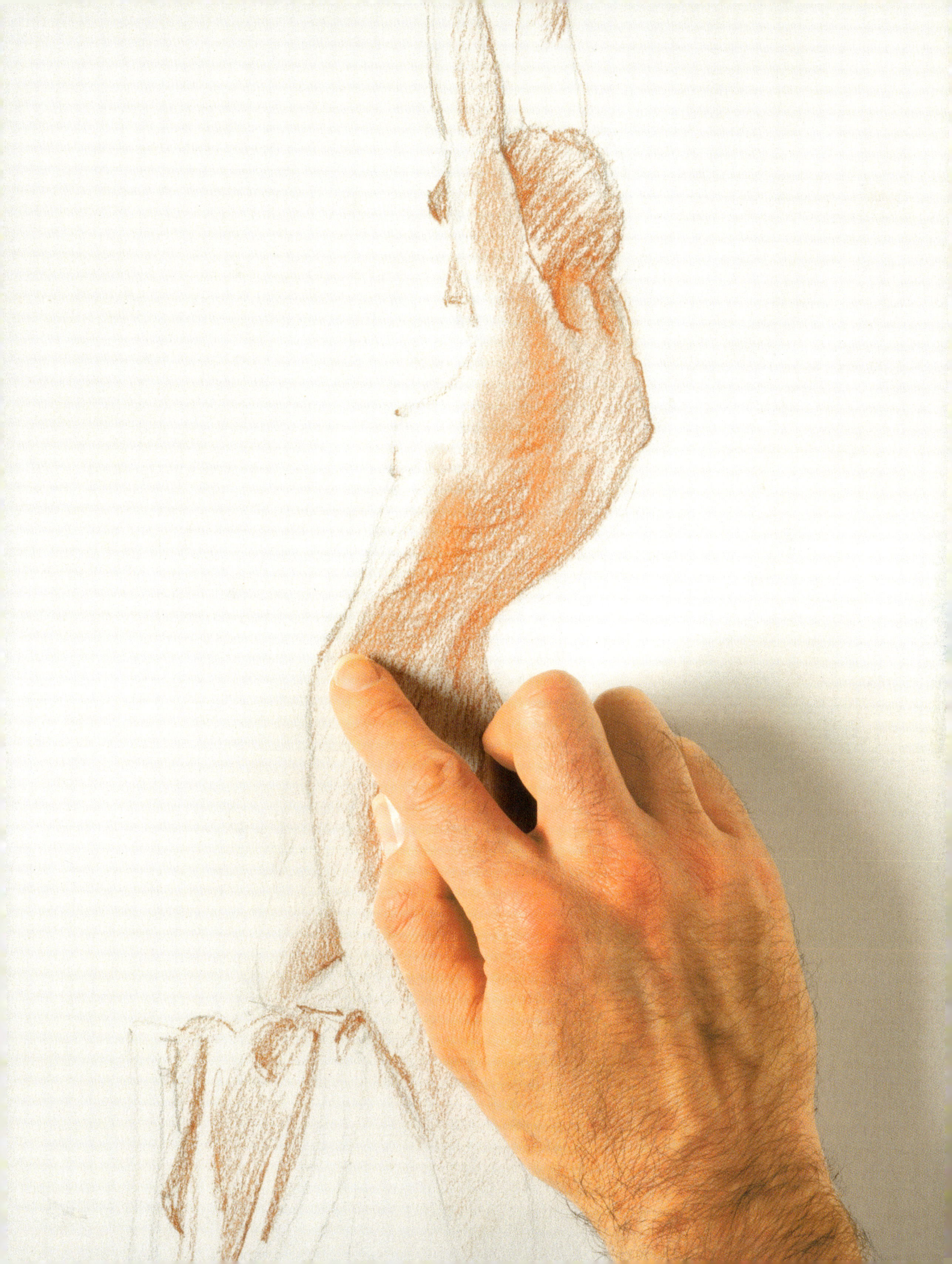

Woman's Back
with Charcoal and Sanguine

Charcoal is a drawing medium that is traditionally used in art schools to study figure anatomy. In this exercise the artist, David Sanmiguel, will combine charcoal and sanguine to create a warmer and deeper tone. Almost as important as these two mediums will be an eraser with which the artist will "open" areas of light within the areas of gray shading. Also, a cotton rag is very important to blend the lines and to apply a method of constructing the figure that was studied in the first part of this book.

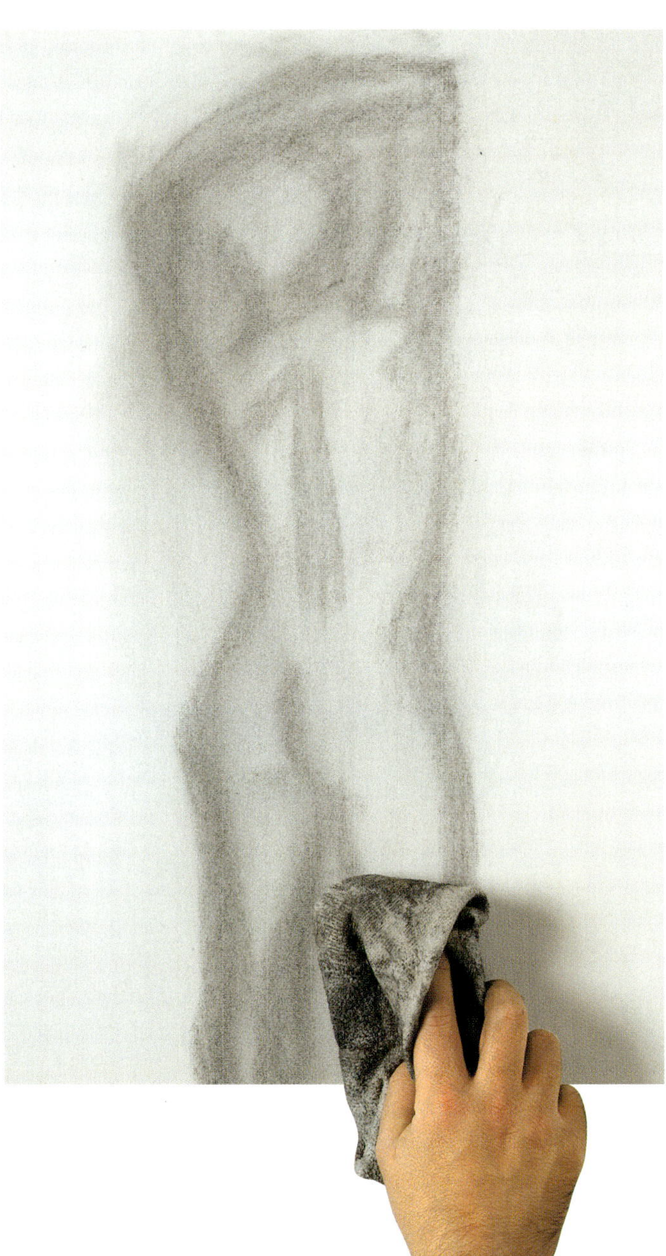

2

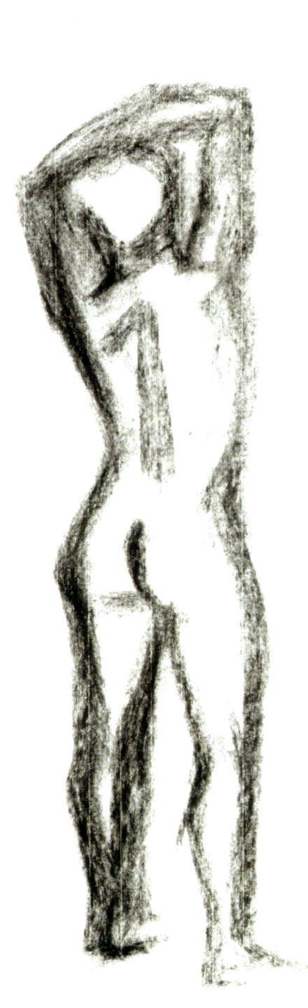

1

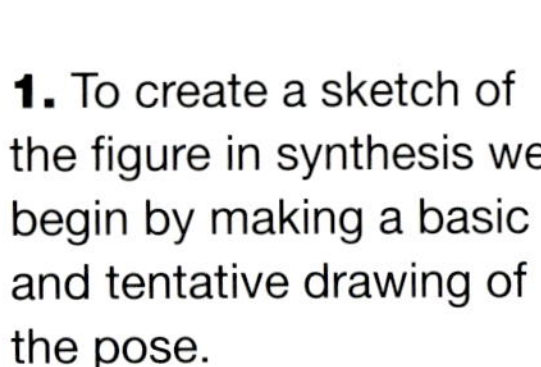

1. To create a sketch of the figure in synthesis we begin by making a basic and tentative drawing of the pose.

2. Next, we rub the drawing completely with a clean cottonrag. The traces of the charcoal lines will help reconstruct the contours of the anatomy with greater precision.

3

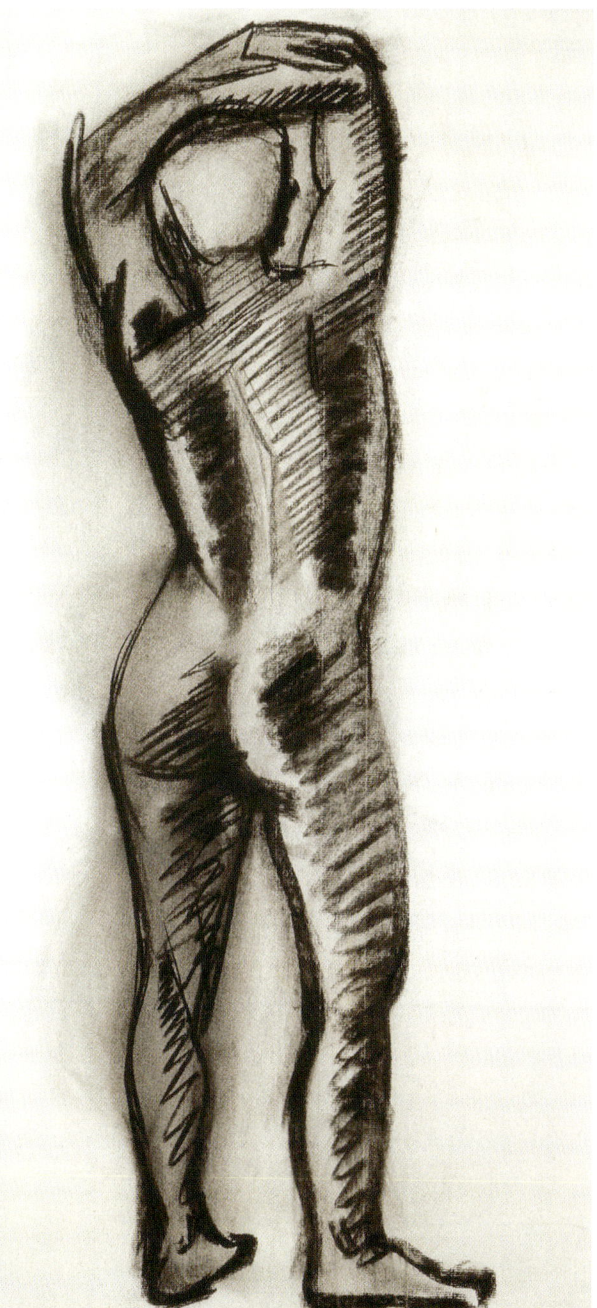

3. This exercise requires drawing the anatomical figures in synthesis. From the beginning, the volume can be created from the synthesis of previously drawn lines. The shading is concise and very vigorous, and it is resolved with areas of maximum light and areas of maximum shade using very vigorous and lively charcoal lines.

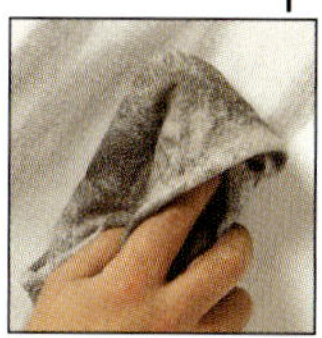

A cotton rag is an irreplaceable item when working with charcoal. It is used for erasing and blending lines, and also for wiping the hands.

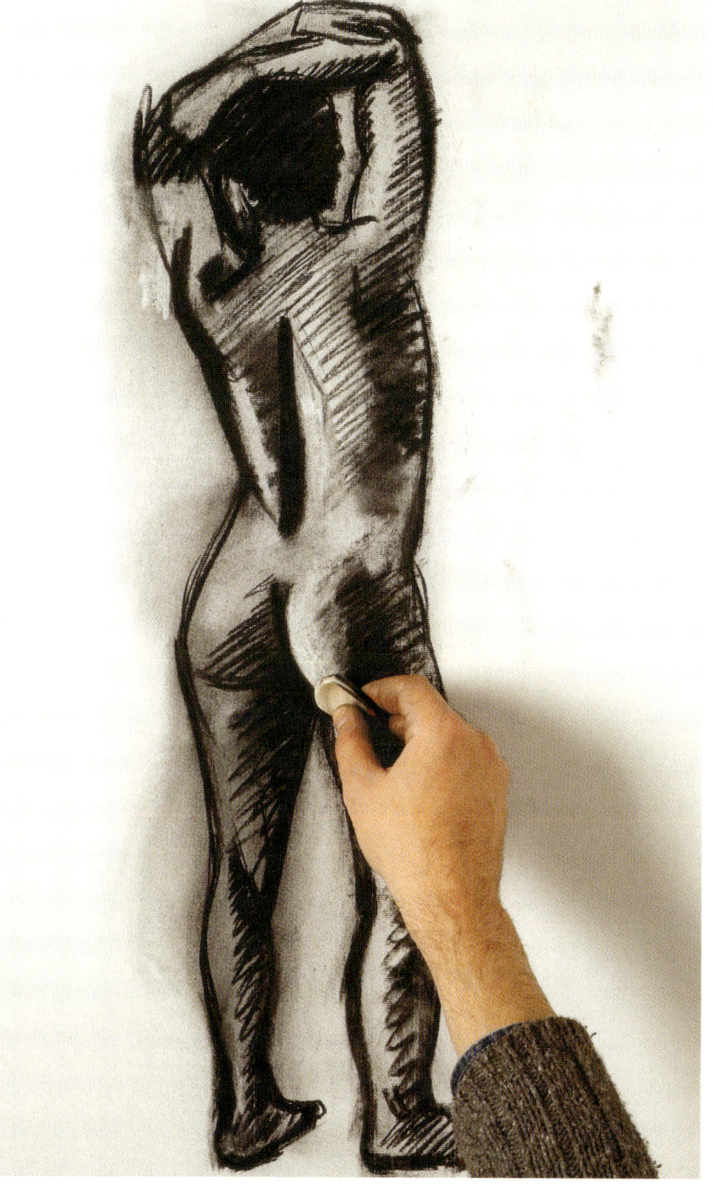

4

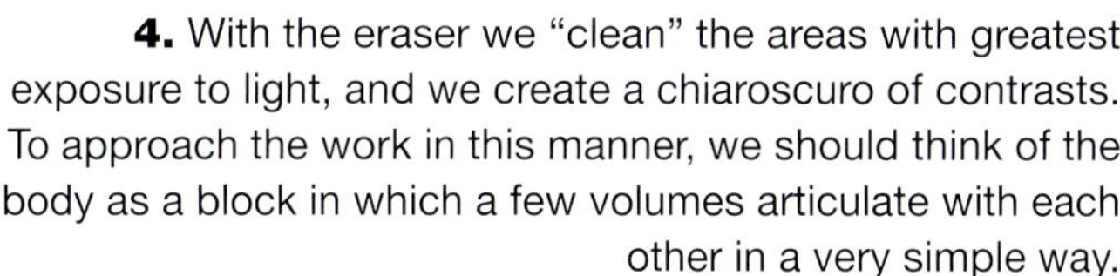

4. With the eraser we "clean" the areas with greatest exposure to light, and we create a chiaroscuro of contrasts. To approach the work in this manner, we should think of the body as a block in which a few volumes articulate with each other in a very simple way.

5

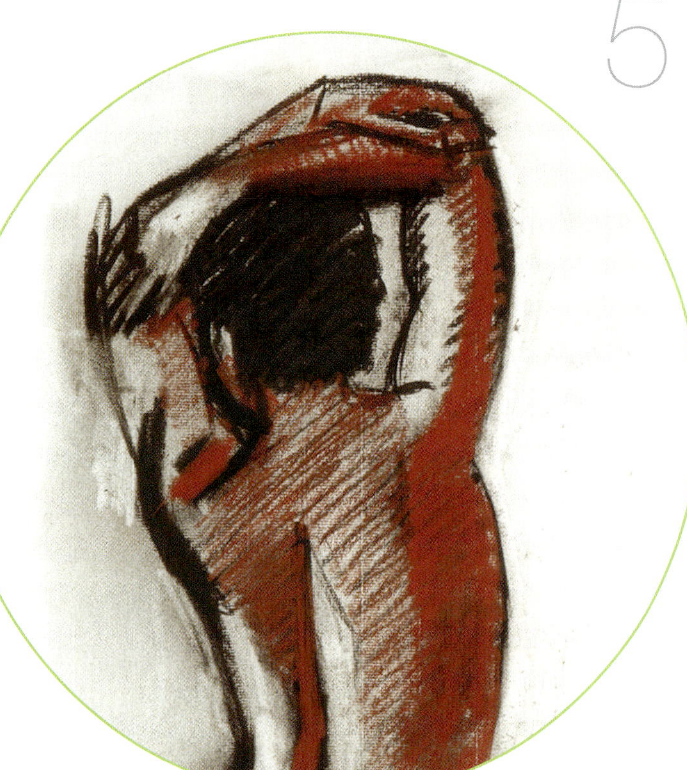

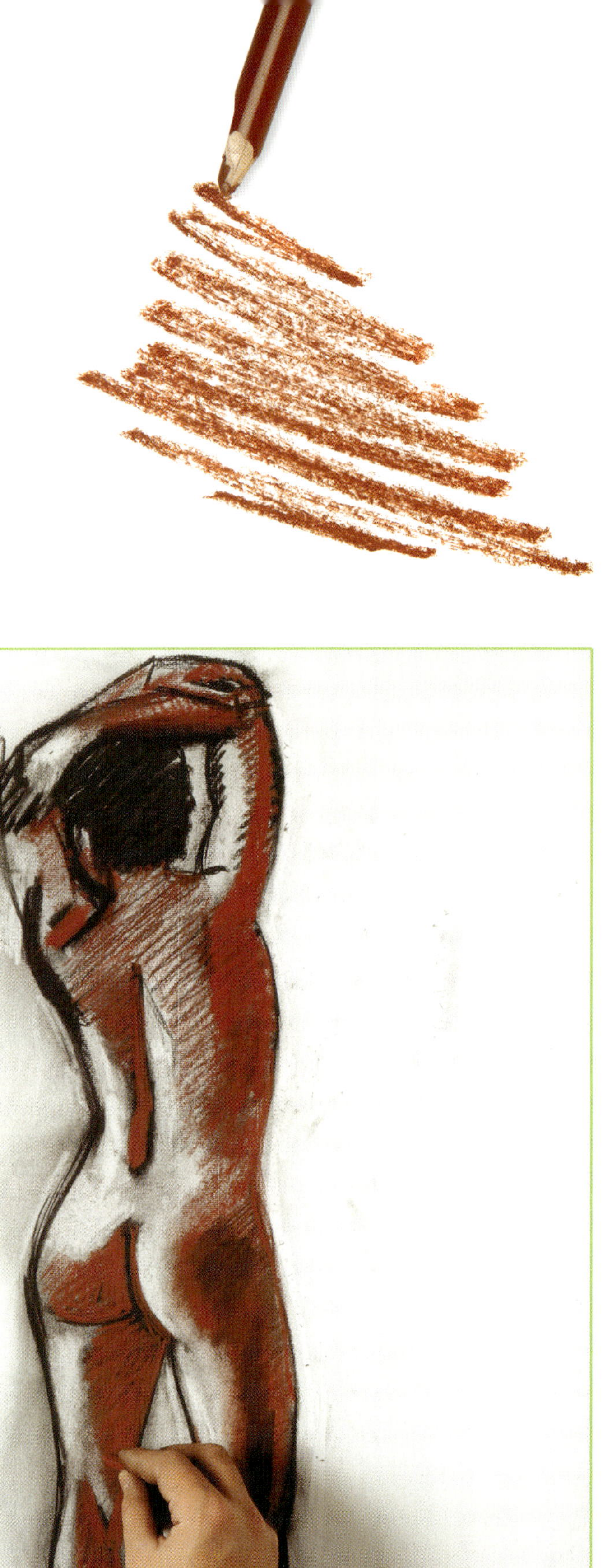

5. The sanguine is applied vigorously, covering all the shaded areas with a solid and compact layer of color that highlights the volume of the figure.

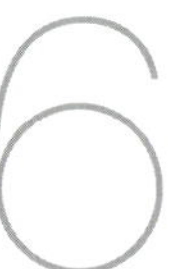

6. In this last phase of the drawing, the sanguine is used to define some blacks that are too dark in contrast with the white of the paper. Sanguine makes the shadows warmer and lighter. The sanguine lines are mixed with the charcoal by blending with the finger.

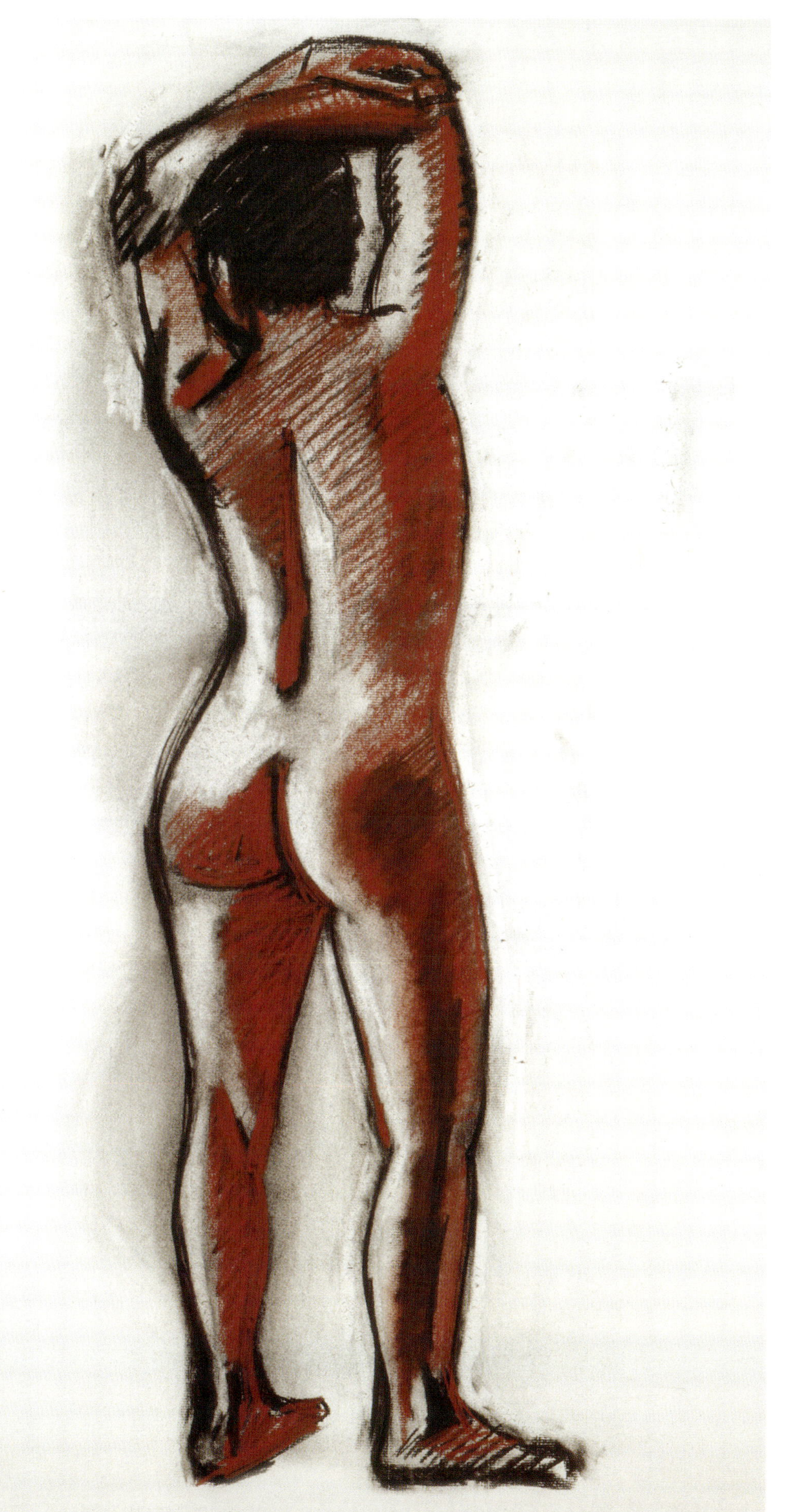

7. The result is a very vibrant and direct drawing, which has hardly any shading but does have strong dimensionality. It is interesting to study certain aspects where one can clearly see the anatomical synthesis that has ruled its execution at all times. The spinal column, for example, has been drawn with a very simple and precise contrast, marking the depression of the column very clearly.

7

Male Figure
with Color Pencils

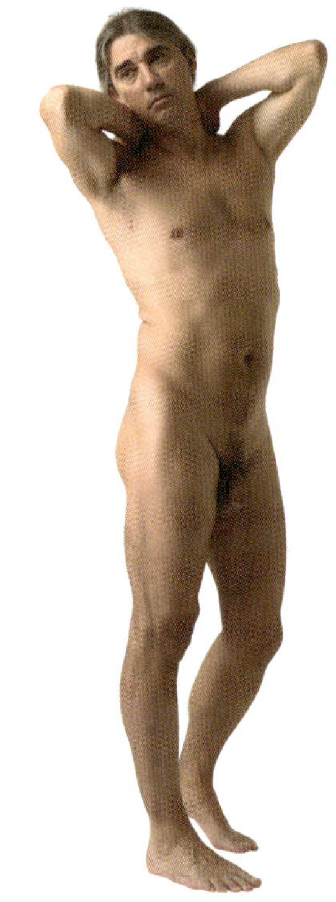

The pose chosen for this exercise drawn by Mercedes Gaspar offers a very complete and harmonious view of the male anatomy. In its apparently static pose, this figure involves multiple articulations: flexion and extension of the arms, elevation of the hips, elevation of the thigh, and flexion of the calf. The pose of the model is relaxed, and therefore there are not many strongly tensed muscles, but we can clearly see many anatomical features that need to be resolved correctly.

1. Evolution of the basic line diagram of the pose. With a hard lead graphite pencil, the artist has drawn the axes of movement and the basic skeleton and has worked the structure of the main anatomical features to completion.

2. It is very interesting to study the variety of compositional resources used: drawing of axes, rectangular diagrams, and oval diagrams. This graphic application has defined a proportionate and anatomically correct figure.

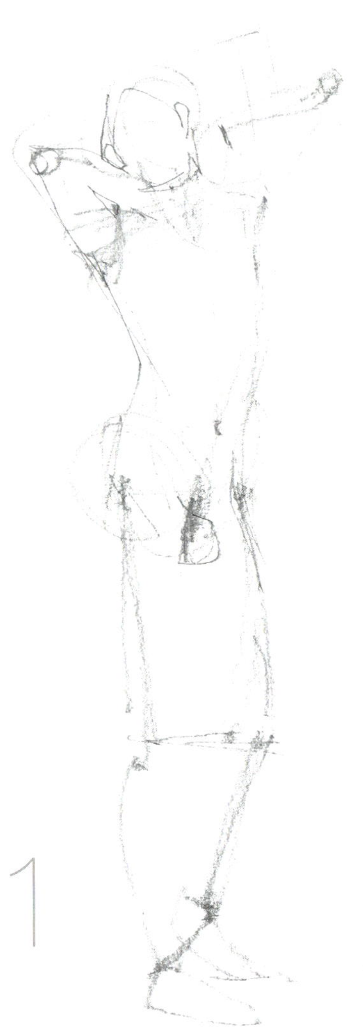

1

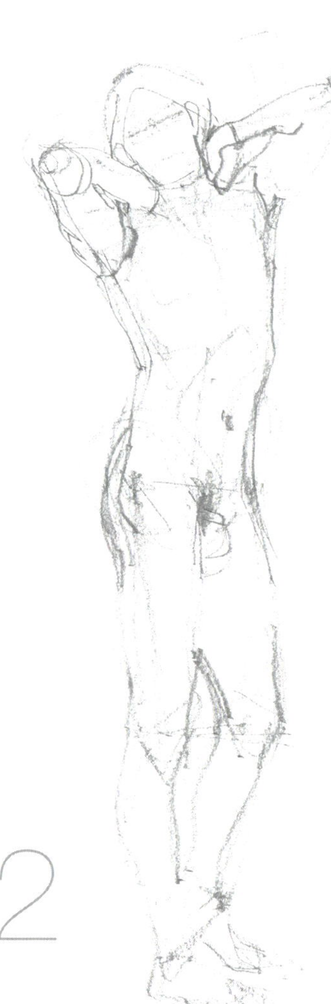

2

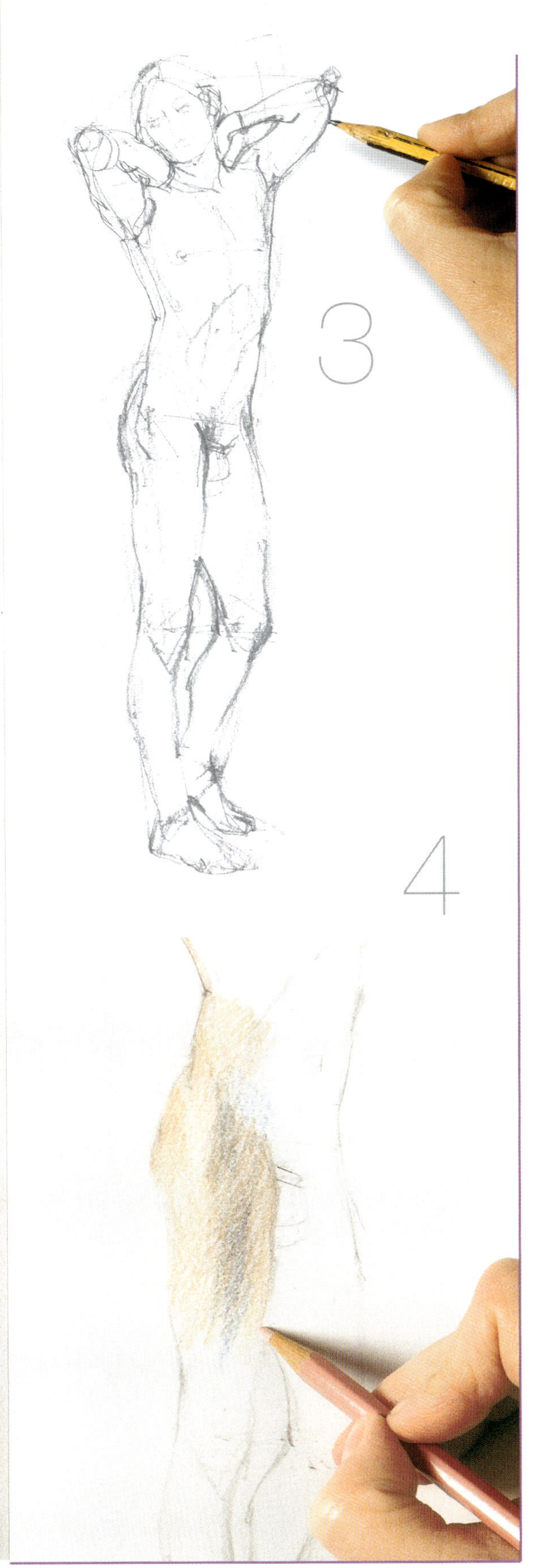

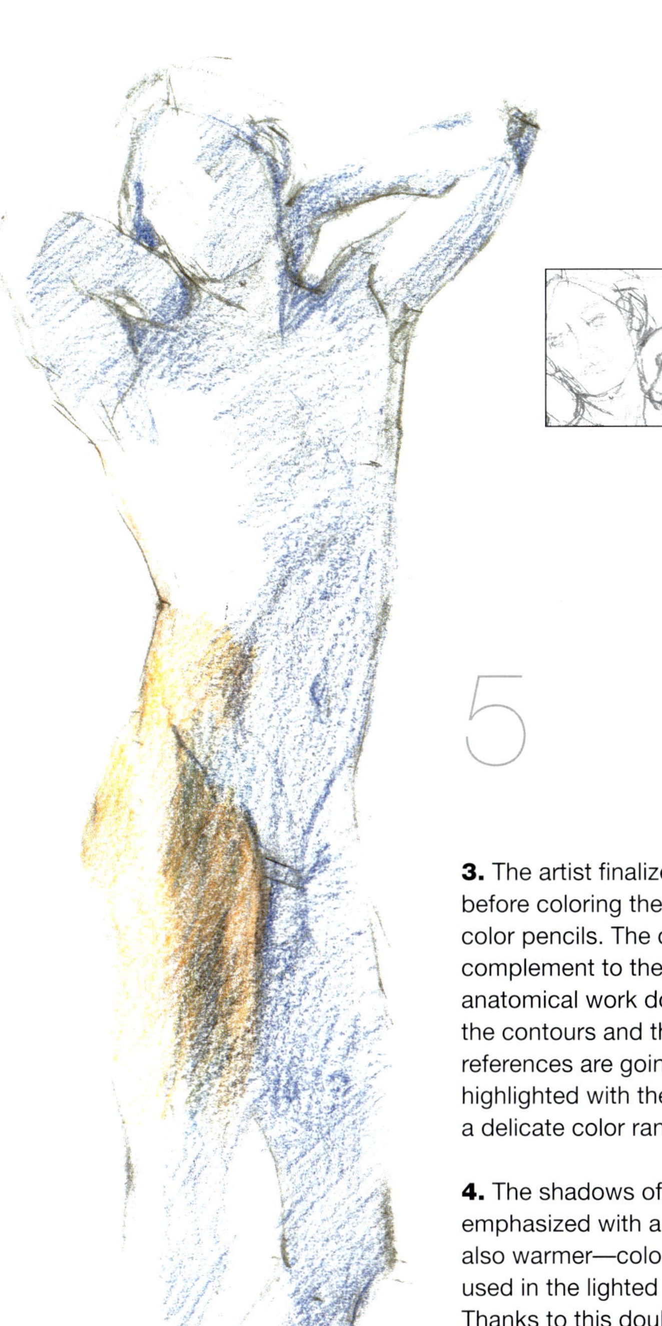

The blue color pencil complements and further develops the basic concept of the sketch made with the graphite pencil.

3. The artist finalizes the details before coloring the drawing with color pencils. The color will be a complement to the basic anatomical work done so far; the contours and the muscle references are going to be highlighted with the application of a delicate color range.

4. The shadows of the legs are emphasized with a darker—and also warmer—color than the one used in the lighted areas. Thanks to this double contrast, the anatomy of this drawing has a harmony and spontaneity lacking in the dry academic exercise.

5. In this illustration we can see very clearly how the delicate shading of the warm modeling is enriched by its contrast with the underlying cool tone.

The relief of the female body, softer and more sinuous than the male counterpart, requires an equally articulated anatomical approach. The most outstanding anatomical feature of this pose is, without a doubt, the pronounced movement of the spinal column. This is always an advantage because the undulation of the spinal column determines the entire movement of the back and makes it easier to define the placement of the axes of the shoulders and hips. In addition, drawing the spinal column correctly ensures the balance of the figure. This drawing with sanguine executed by Óscar Sanchís resolves all these points in a simple and direct manner.

Female Figure with Sanguine

1

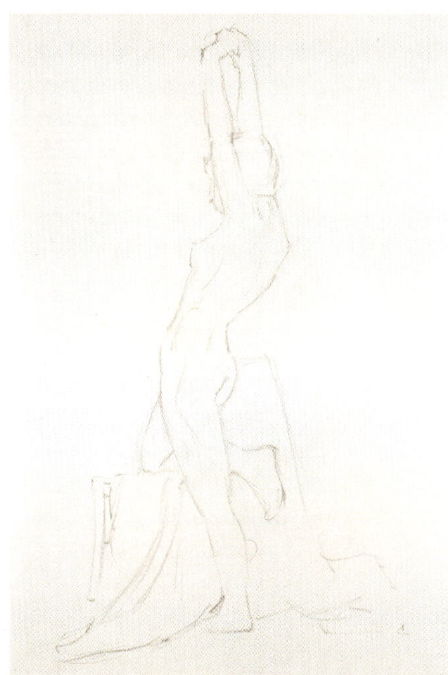

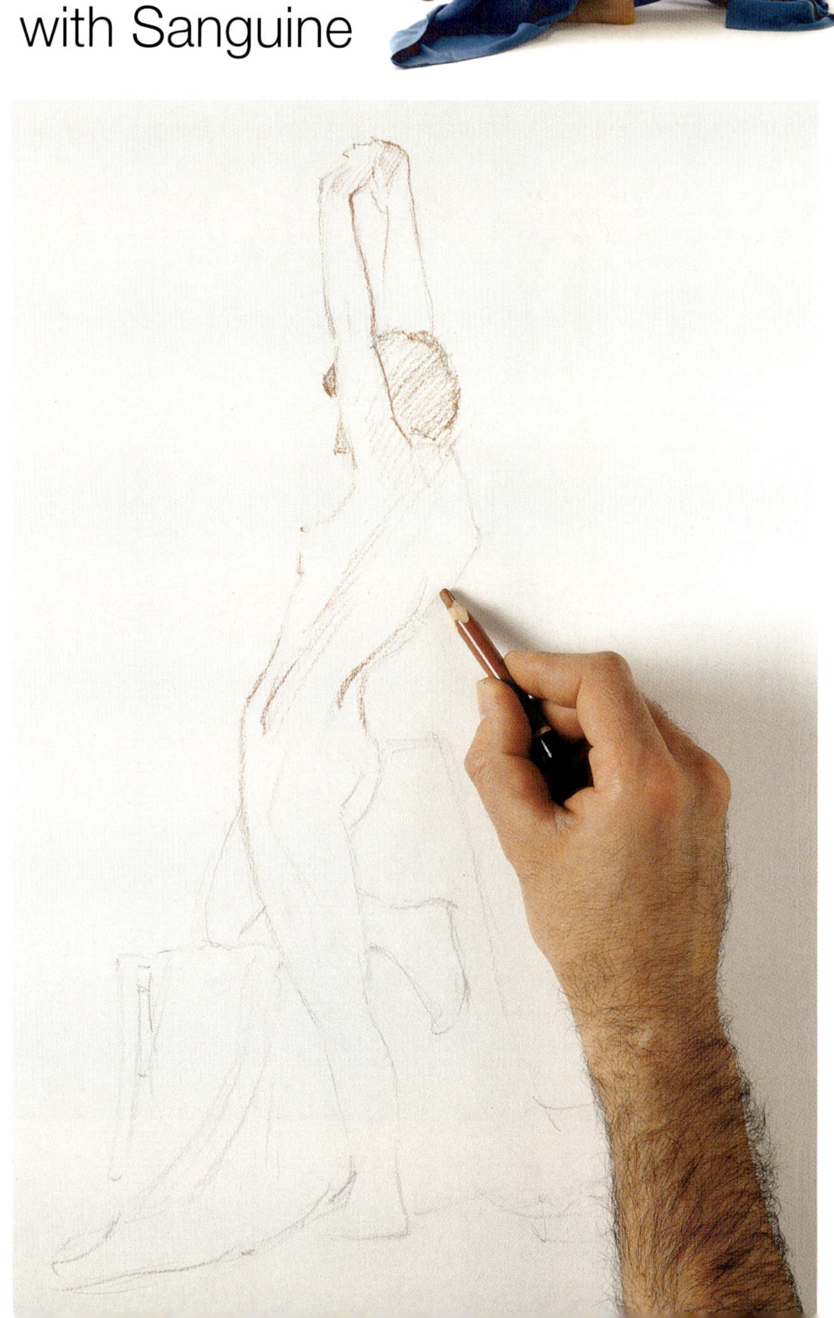

2

1. The artist has drawn a fairly detailed outline of the model using a hard lead pencil.

2. The drawing takes into account all the anatomical features related to the profile of the body, although a few corrections will be needed when shading. Next, the lines are redrawn with a sanguine pencil.

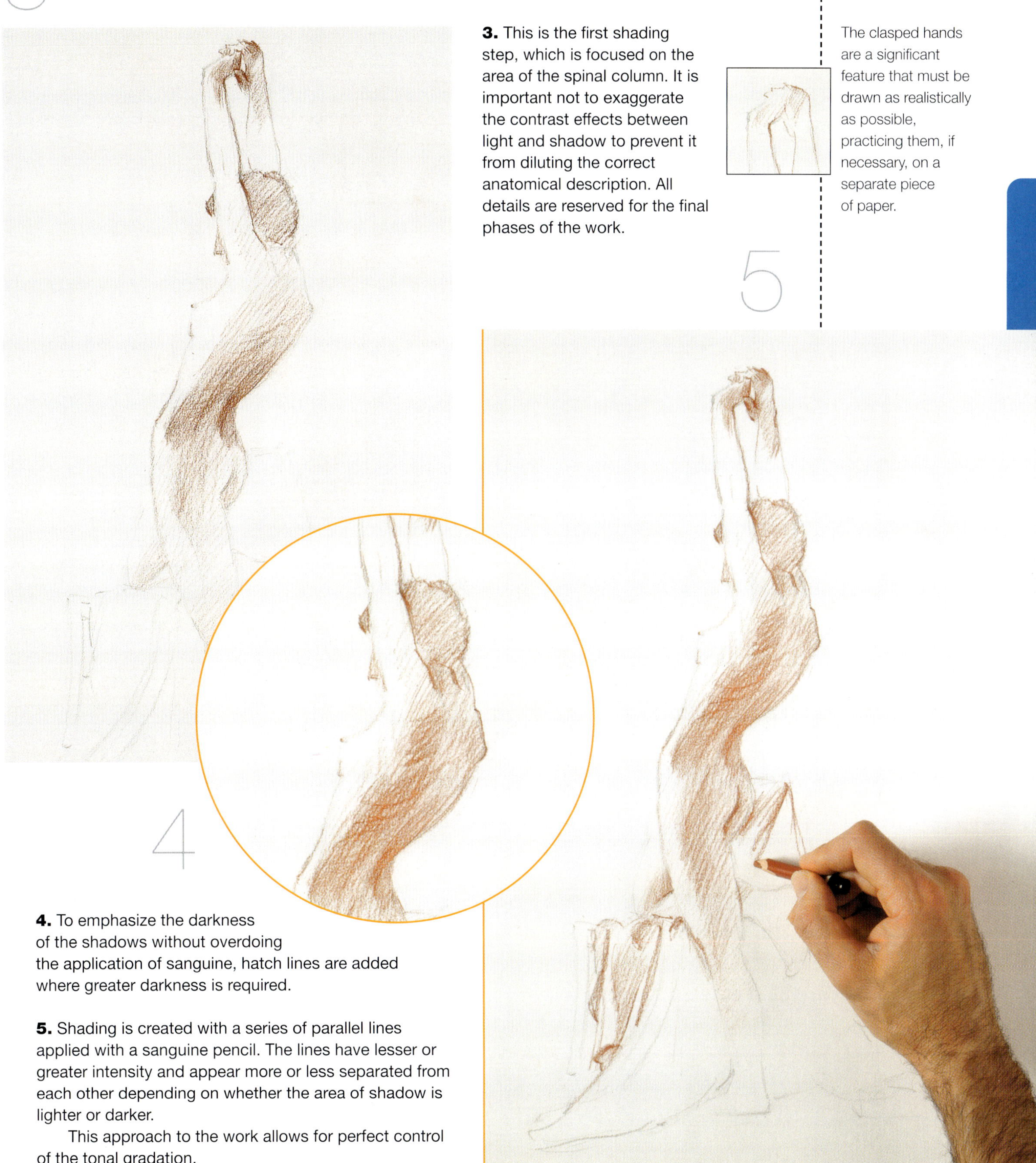

3. This is the first shading step, which is focused on the area of the spinal column. It is important not to exaggerate the contrast effects between light and shadow to prevent it from diluting the correct anatomical description. All details are reserved for the final phases of the work.

The clasped hands are a significant feature that must be drawn as realistically as possible, practicing them, if necessary, on a separate piece of paper.

4. To emphasize the darkness of the shadows without overdoing the application of sanguine, hatch lines are added where greater darkness is required.

5. Shading is created with a series of parallel lines applied with a sanguine pencil. The lines have lesser or greater intensity and appear more or less separated from each other depending on whether the area of shadow is lighter or darker.

This approach to the work allows for perfect control of the tonal gradation.

6. In this third to last step the contrasts can be emphasized to create a livelier and more expressive result. This is achieved by going over the lines with the sanguine pencil or blending with the finger where darker shading is needed. The lines blend together, and the anatomy overall becomes more unified.

7. The softness of the sanguine lines does not create any confusion in the precise shading of the figure's volumes: From this point on, the work is going to consist of emphasizing specific shadows and blending the modeling of the masses.

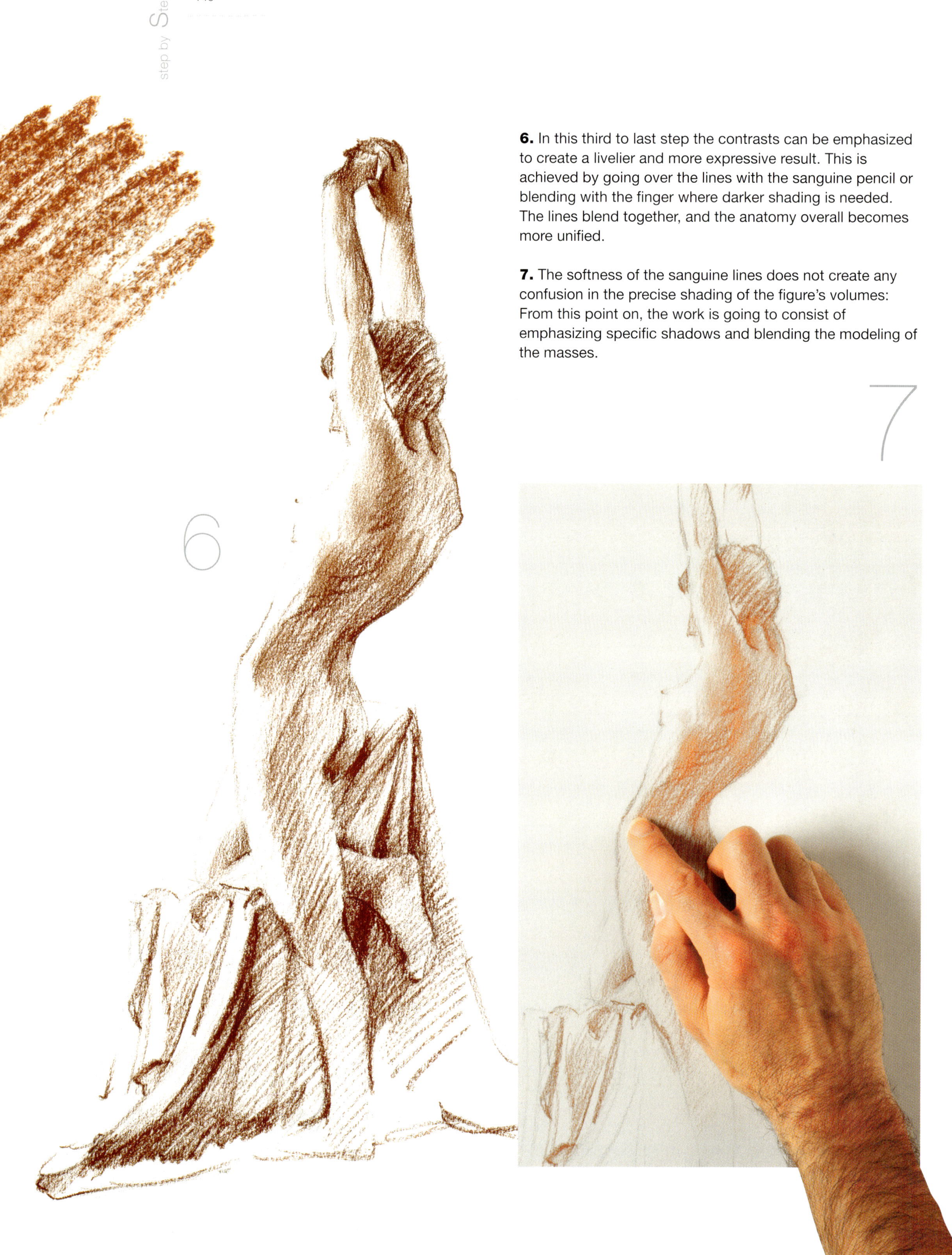

8

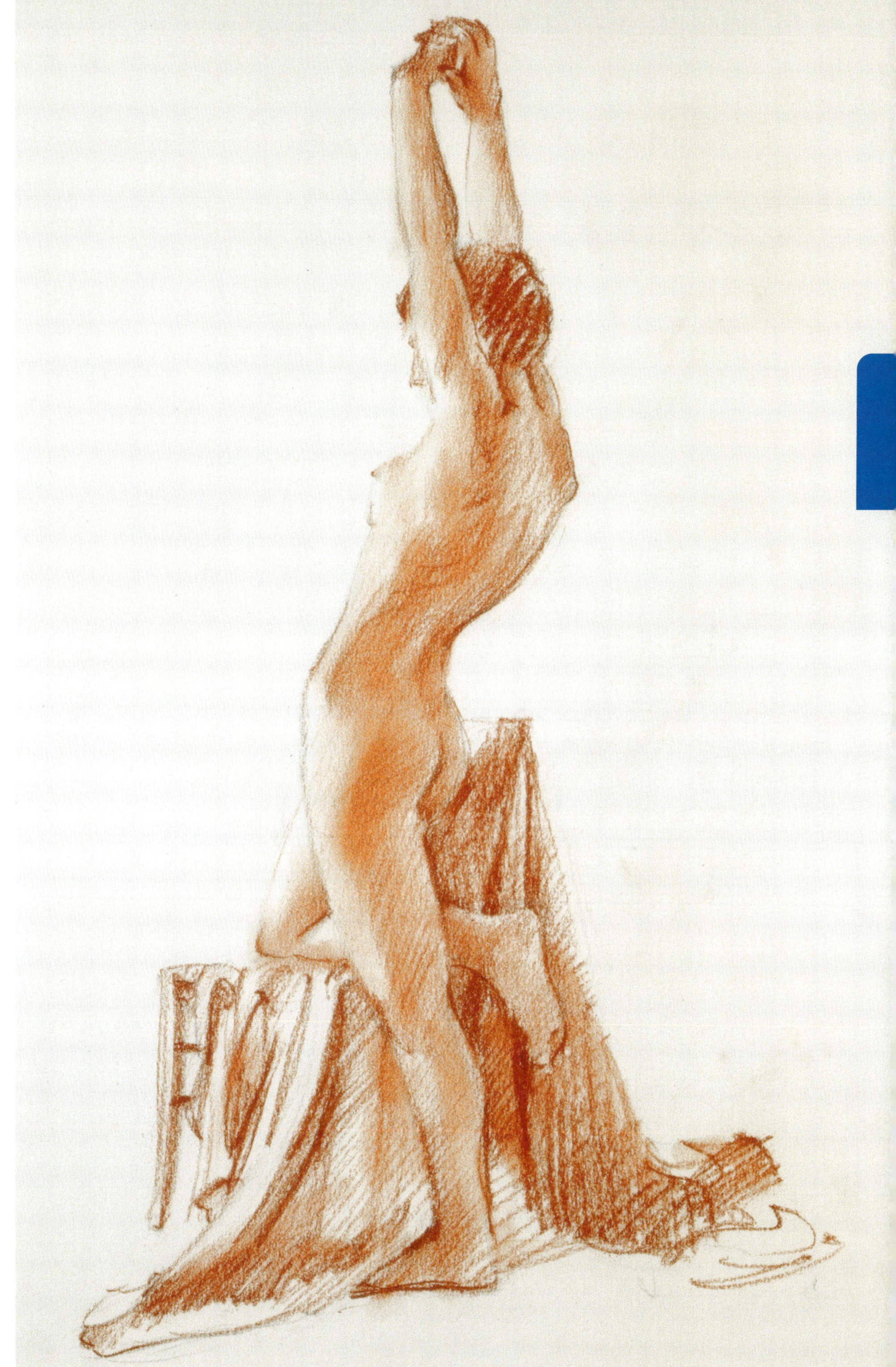

8. The most interesting aspect of this drawing is the delicate work done with the halftones, that is, with the tones of intermediate shading. The deepest shadows are the ones that are immediately adjacent to the most illuminated areas or are the ones that are located in the most hidden areas of the spinal column.

Male Figure

Seen from Behind

The pose chosen for this drawing shows a complete view of a male figure seen from behind. Its execution by Mercedes Gaspar with color pencils requires the correct representation of all the muscular forms of the figure: the legs, the arms, and the torso are fully extended, and the lighting does not cast any important area in shadow. Color pencils make it possible to draw the details that will allow the meticulous study of all the masses once the general drawing of the pose has been firmly balanced and proportioned.

1. We begin by drawing a diagram of the axes that define the pose and that clearly balance the figure. It is interesting to see how the axis of the spinal column clearly defines the areas of the back, which are different for the lumbar and dorsal regions. Drawing the contour from this diagram is much easier.

1

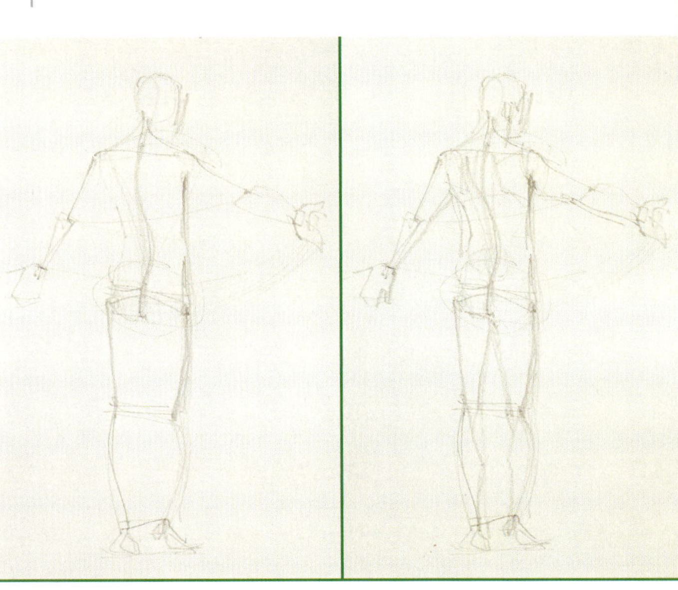

2

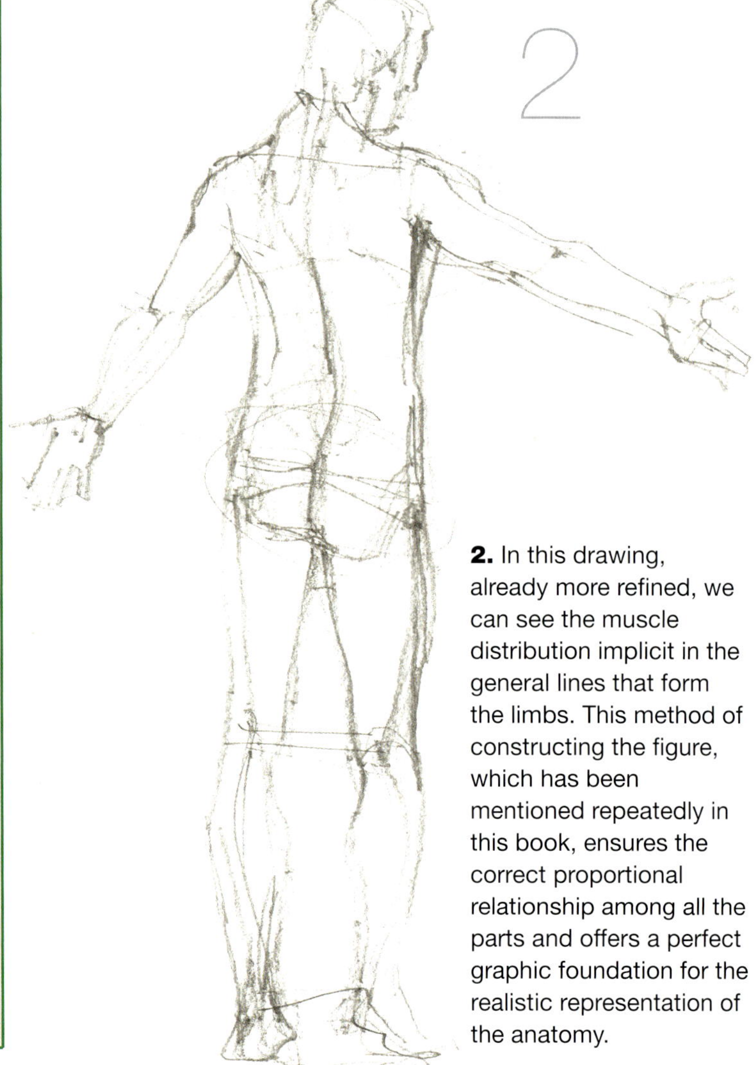

2. In this drawing, already more refined, we can see the muscle distribution implicit in the general lines that form the limbs. This method of constructing the figure, which has been mentioned repeatedly in this book, ensures the correct proportional relationship among all the parts and offers a perfect graphic foundation for the realistic representation of the anatomy.

3. The initial pencil drawing can be touched up until it is complete and accurate. Then it is important to reduce the intensity of the lines by partially erasing them so they do not interfere with the delicate modeling work to be done with the color pencils.

4. The artist has used warm and luminous color pencils to give volume to the muscular features. The areas of greater light intensity are left practically untouched in order to achieve the necessary value contrast where the light affects the figure's body most brightly.

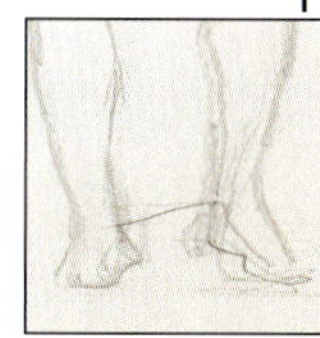

The weight of the figure is placed on one of the legs. This must be reflected not only in the placement of the feet but also in the lines of the entire figure.

3

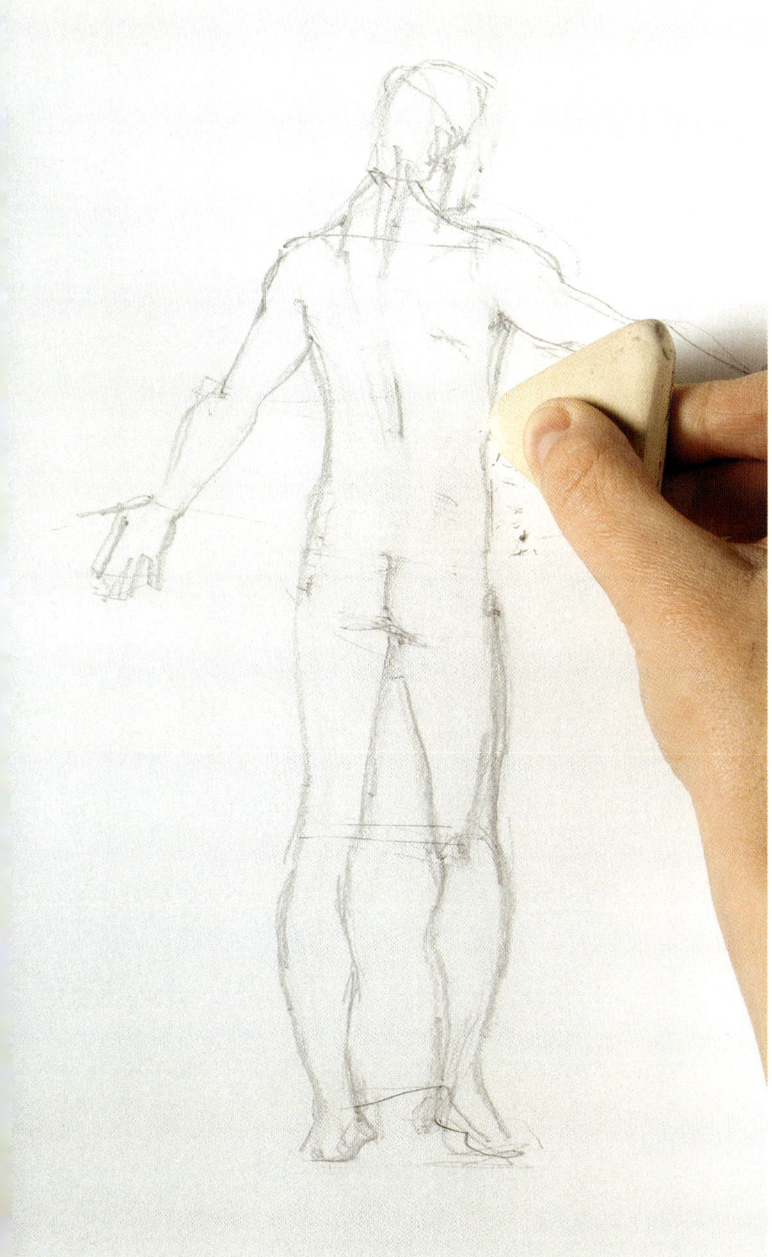

4

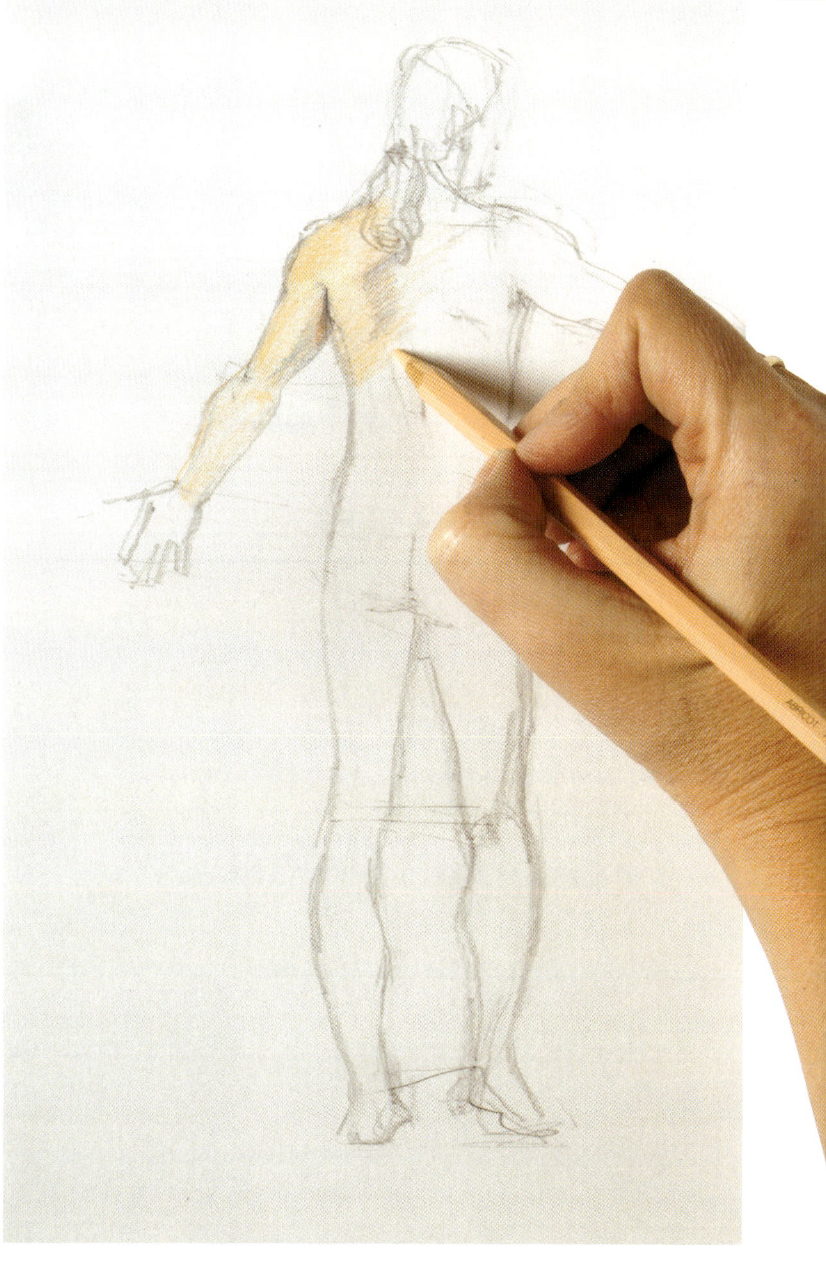

5

6

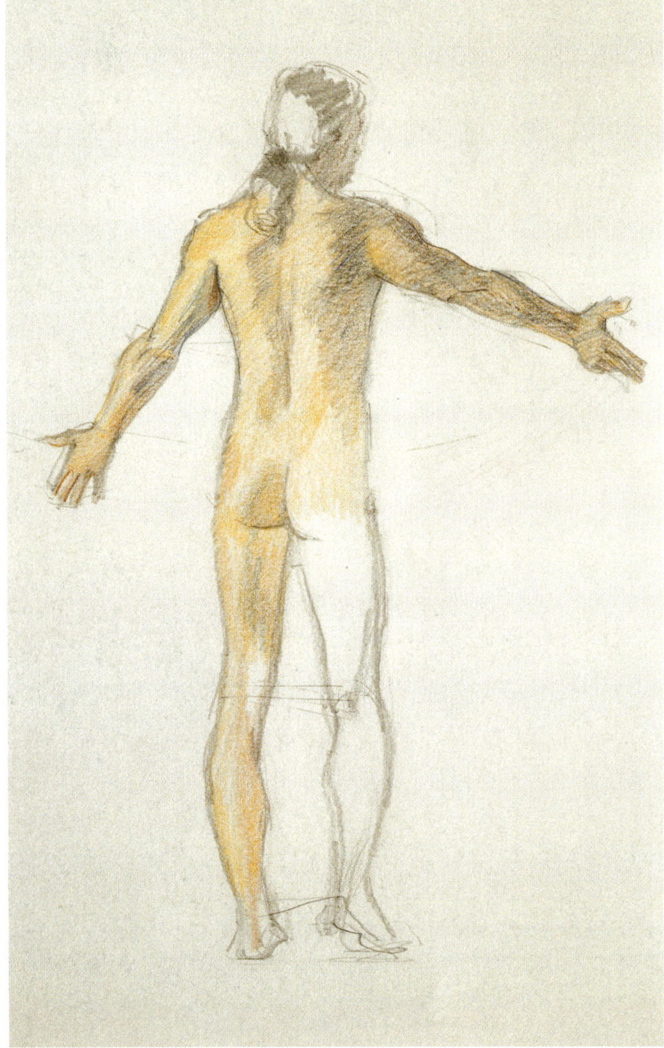

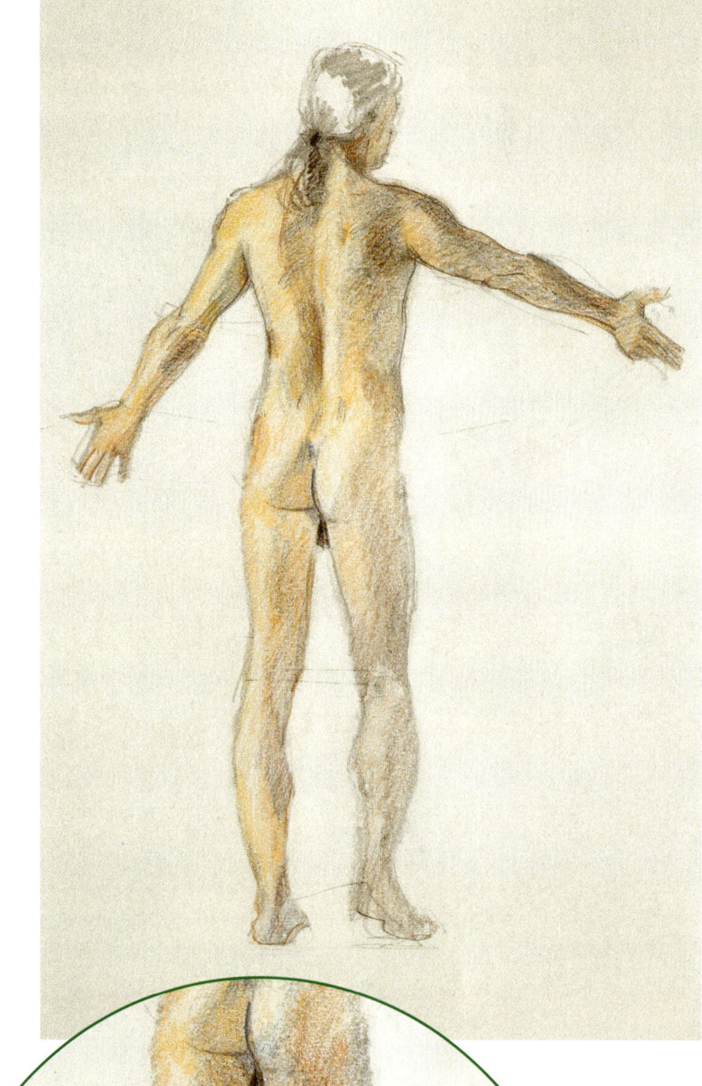

5. The shadows are worked with a blue color that is cool and that contrasts with the warm color of the skin. At no time has the volume been emphasized with harsh shading because the overall effect should be luminous and soft.

6. The modeling of the anatomy is in an advanced stage. All the anatomical features of the back and the legs that stand out and that have relevance in this drawing have been clearly defined.

7. The artist has further developed and refined the volumes of the legs. To do this, she has emphasized the intensity of the colors with the addition of orange lines and shading.

7

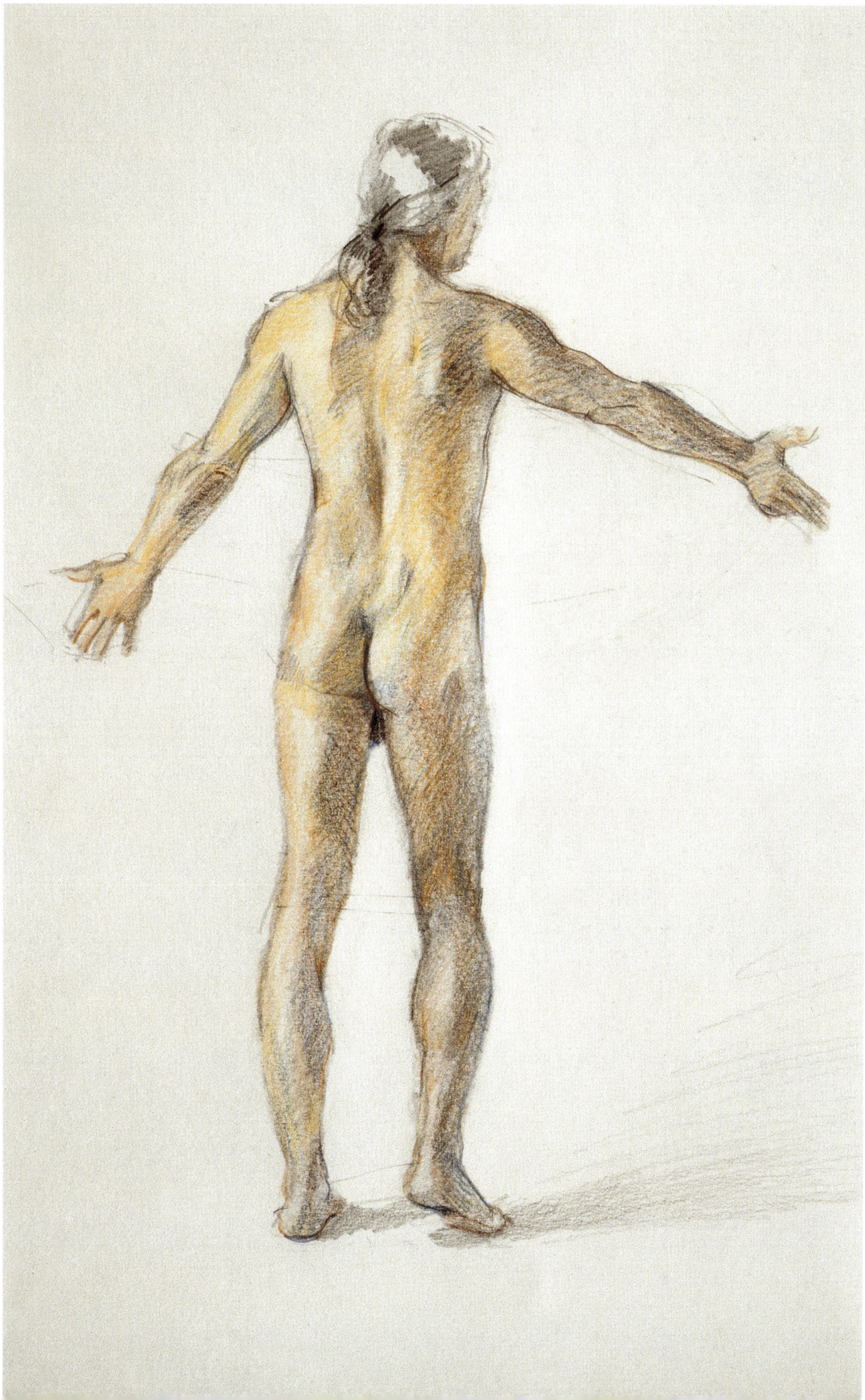

8. Despite the softness of the finish, the most voluminous areas of the anatomy are clearly defined. Therefore, the volume of the glutei has been drawn with clarity and in perfect harmony with the contiguous areas: the lumbar region and the muscles of the backs of the thighs.

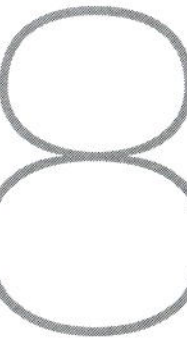

Female Figure
with Charcoal Pencil

Even though this exercise may appear insignificant from the anatomical point of view, it involves many interesting aspects: For example, the transitions are much less abrupt, and it is not easy to pinpoint the beginning and the end of the muscles. In this pose the contour of the figure and the strong combination of light and shadow are more important than the meticulous description of the muscle outline. Óscar Sanchís develops the project without blending and uses a simple and vigorous approach.

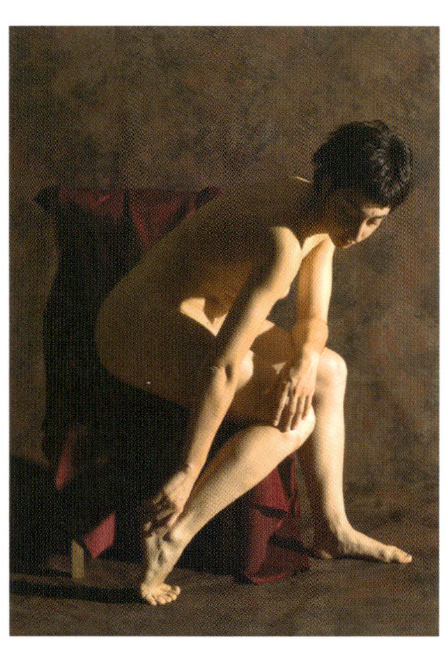

2

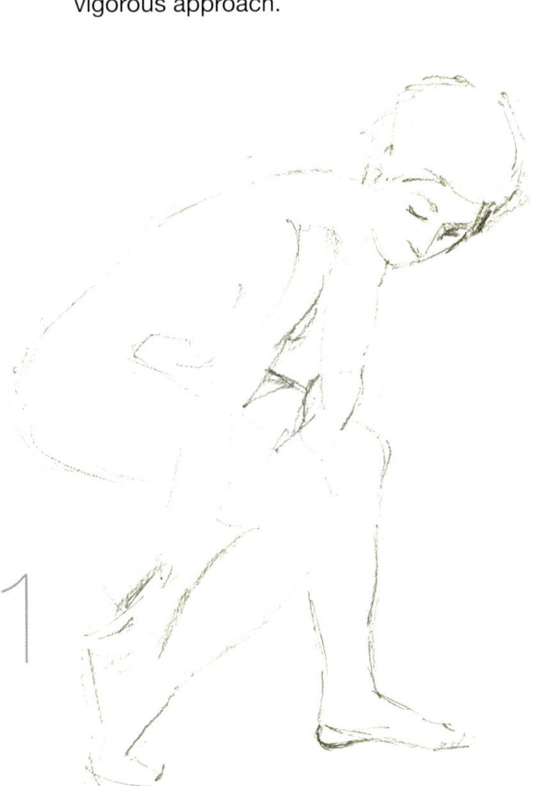

1

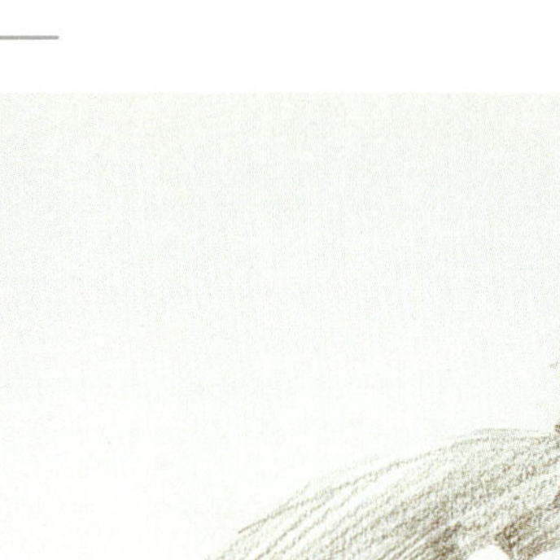

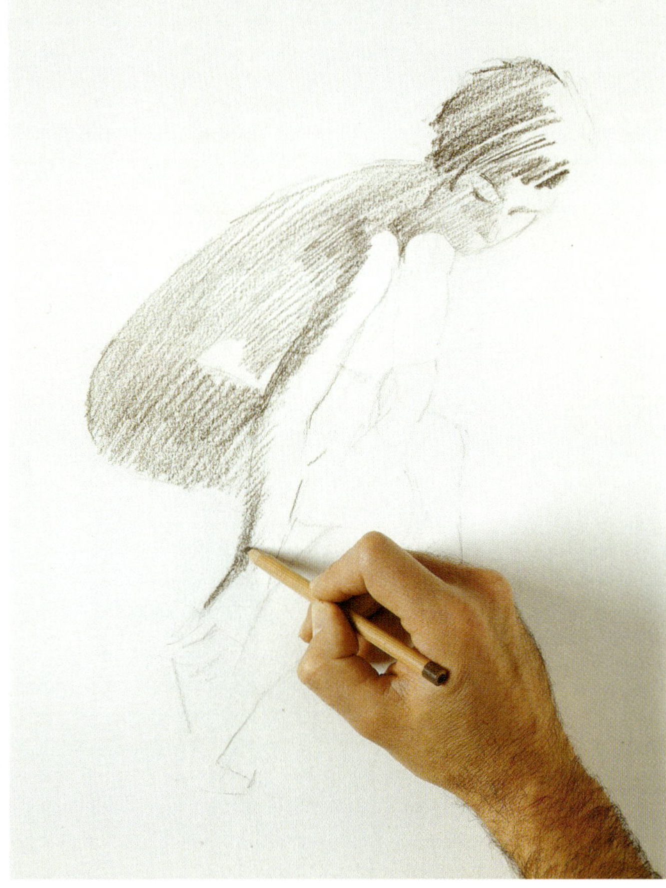

1. The initial drawing consists of a line that defines the figure's general outline, without paying particular attention to specific masses.

2. It is an outline reduced to the basic lines that leaves a lot of room for the subsequent shading applications.

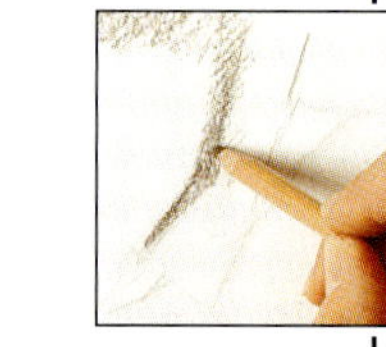
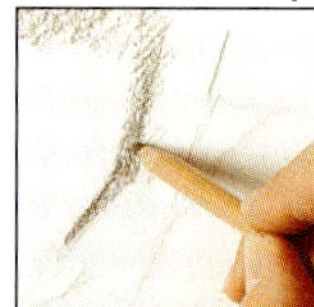

We can hardly see any contour lines in this drawing: The forms are constructed using contrast rather than lines.

3

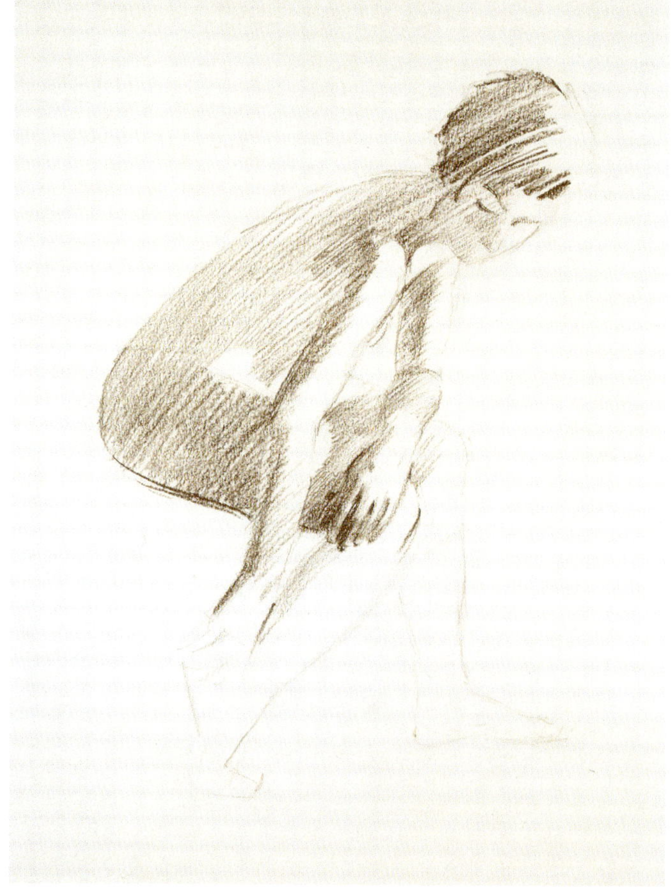

3. The shading is applied by drawing parallel lines that cover almost the entire surface of the body diagonally. The artist follows a procedure that goes from light shading to dark, trying not to focus excessively on any one area to avoid filling up the drawing with too much shading, which could compromise the soft progression of the volumes.

4

4. Parallel lines drawn in the same descending direction provide a sense of unity to the modeling that avoids the harsh transition that is often characteristic of this approach.

5. It is very important to model the different shaded areas correctly because otherwise a good portion of the figure would look as if it were a dark silhouette.

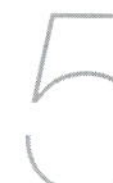

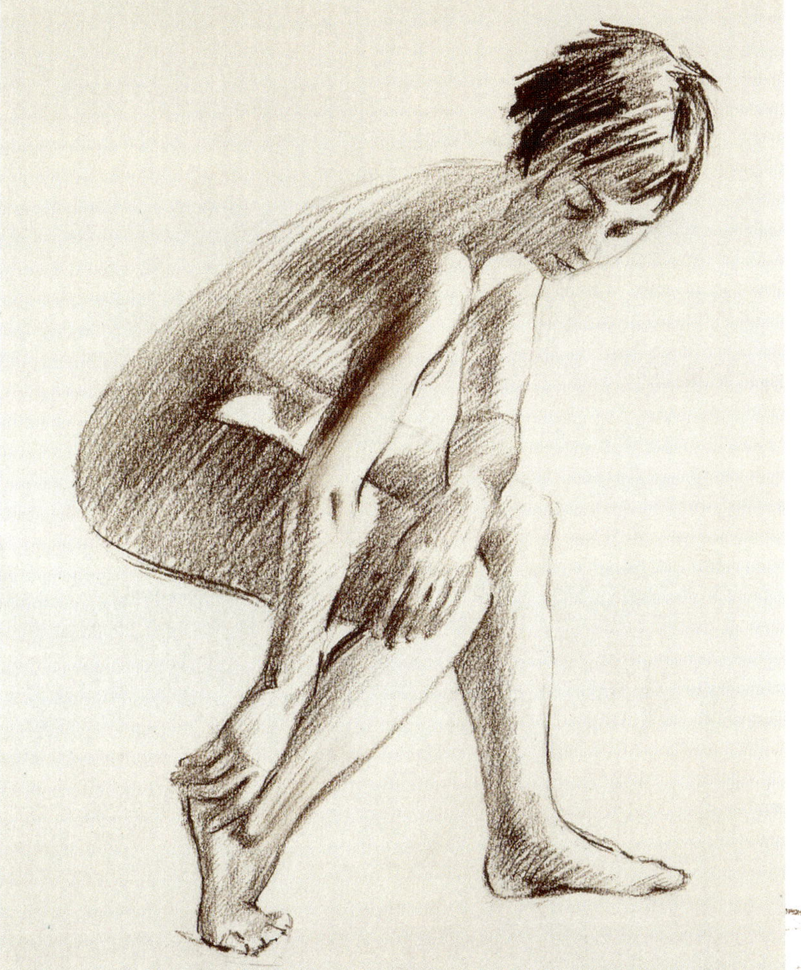

6

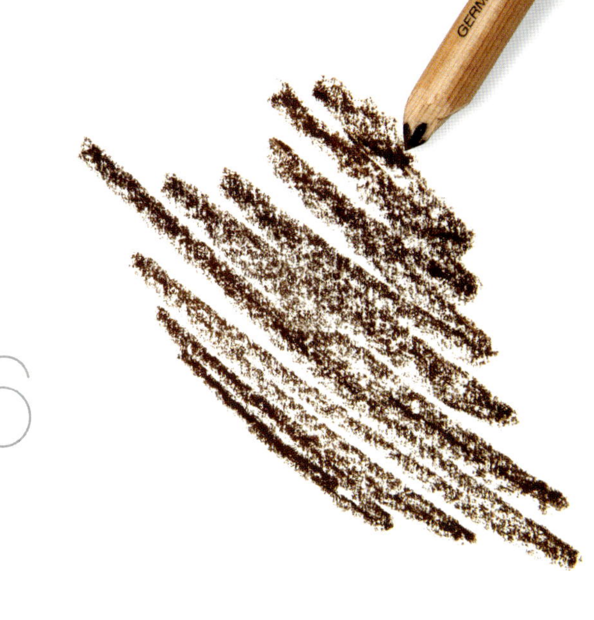

6. Only the hair has been done with heavy lines, which contrast with the highlighted areas. Knowledge of anatomy is apparent in the chiaroscuro contrasts that describe the forms of the arm and the soft transition between light and shadow that can be seen on the thigh and the back.

7

7. The treatment of the drapery that covers the chair is necessary to achieve a darker surface that makes the back stand out. This dark background should be in harmony with the shading of the body, and in some areas there should a transition between the drapery and the values of the anatomy's shading; in other words, we should make sure that the body does not appear completely detached from the surface of the cloth.

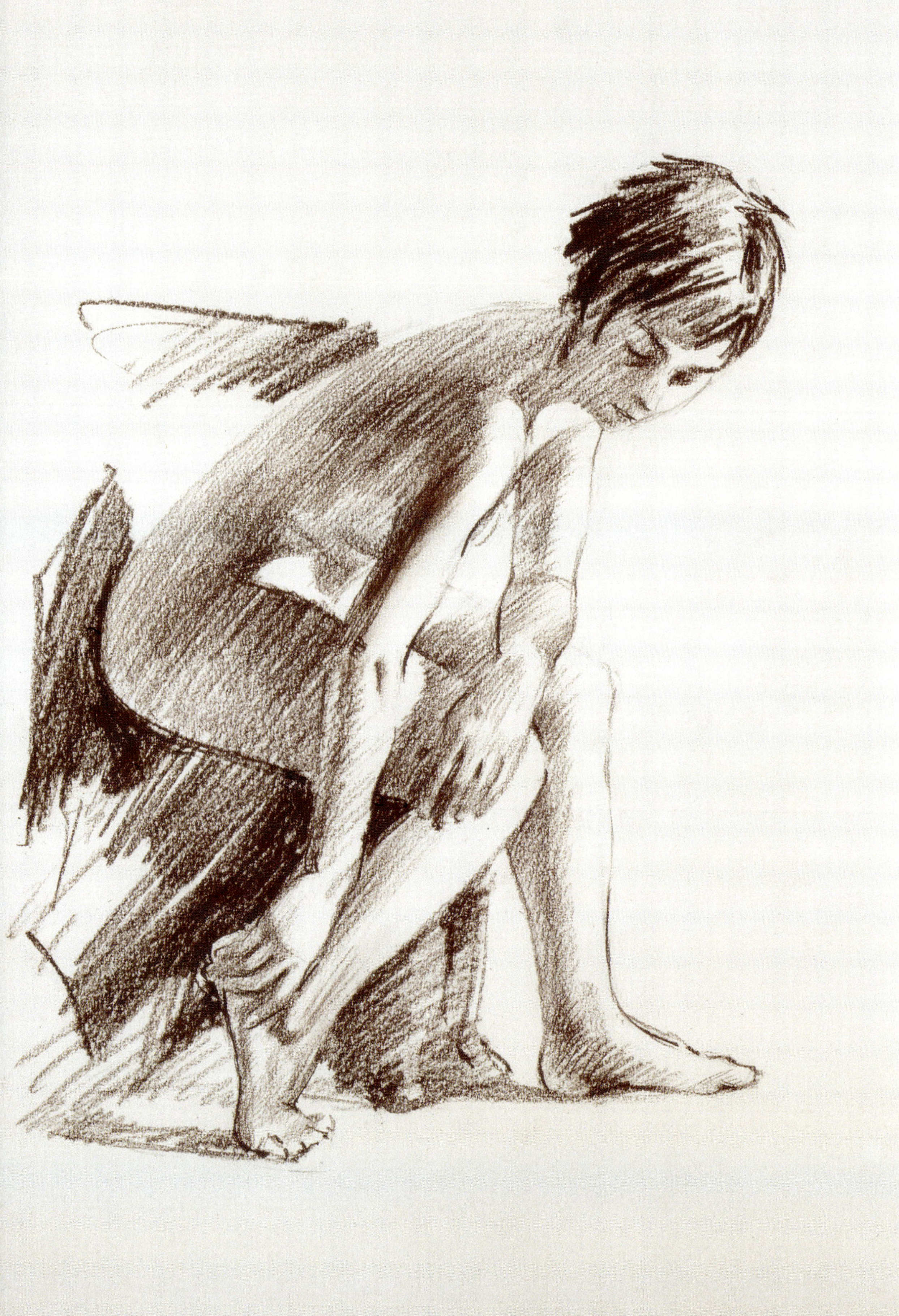

8

8. The chiaroscuro effect always adds a dramatic touch to representations involving the figure. In this instance, the soft transitions between the muscles of the female figure are highlighted by the strong side light. The result of this light is the treatment that the artist has applied to the most notable anatomical features of the pose. On the right arm of the figure, for example, the strong contrast between light and shadow describes its anatomy very effectively and makes it stand out against the rest of the body.

Figure with a Monochromatic Wash

A wash is not exactly a conventional drawing medium but it is an excellent method for modeling forms. When applied to anatomical representations, it describes the body like no other medium, even though it does not allow perfect control of the outlines or the shading as do pencils, charcoal, sanguine, and chalk. In this exercise, Óscar Sanchís uses a watercolor wash to create the drawing of a male figure. The color used is burnt sienna, a very warm color that provides a wide tonal range when diluted.

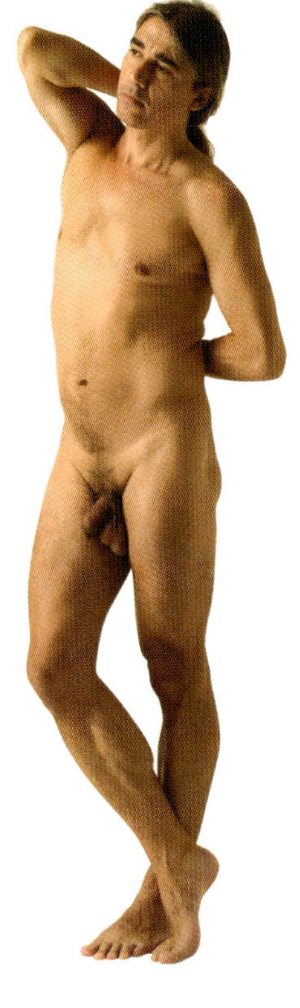

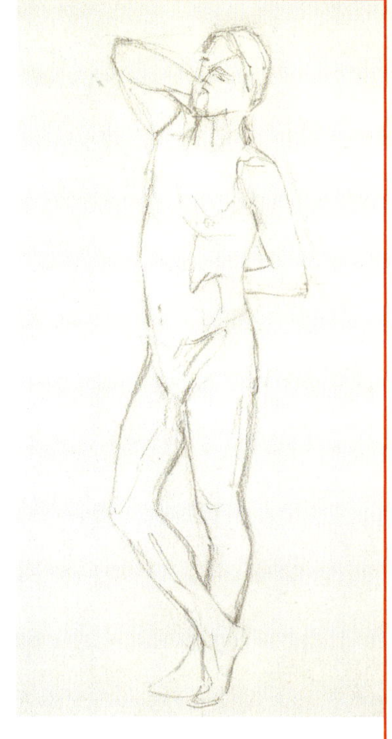

1

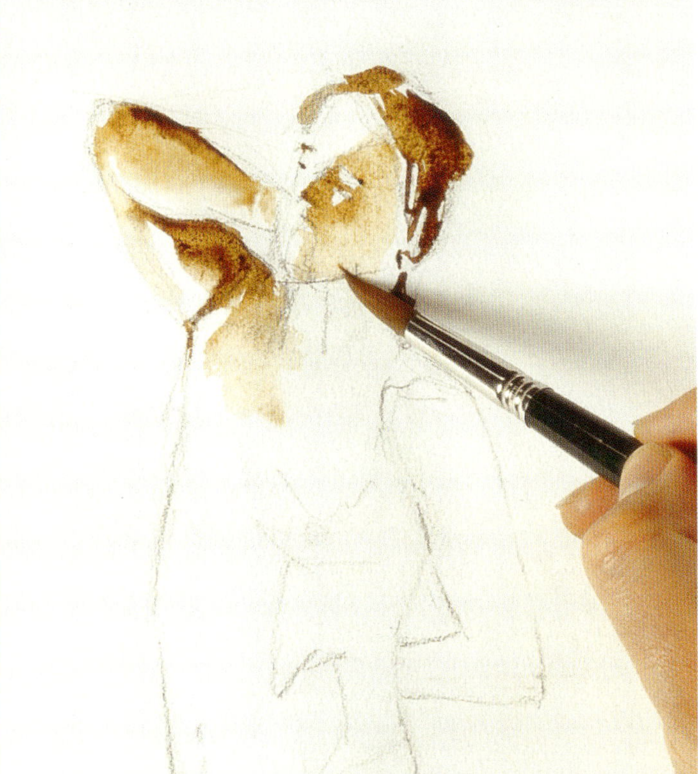

2

1. The initial drawing should be complete and accurate. All the subsequent work with the brush depends on it. This drawing has been executed with a hard lead graphite pencil, without any shading, to a fairly complete finish.

2. The brushwork begins at the upper part of the drawing, as if it were watercolor.

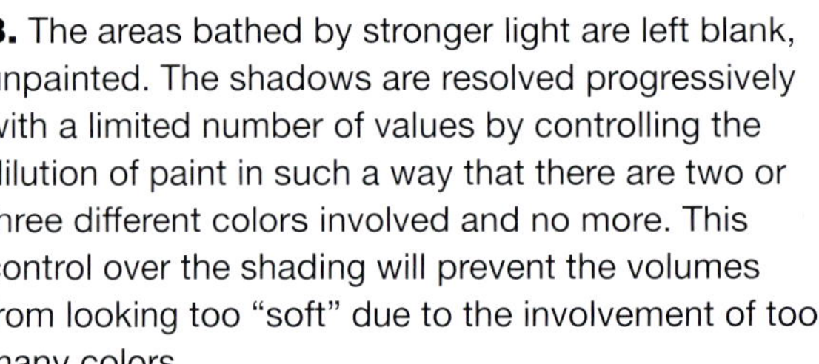

3. The areas bathed by stronger light are left blank, unpainted. The shadows are resolved progressively with a limited number of values by controlling the dilution of paint in such a way that there are two or three different colors involved and no more. This control over the shading will prevent the volumes from looking too "soft" due to the involvement of too many colors.

The lines of the preliminary drawing are usually very soft so they do not stand out under the color of the wash.

3

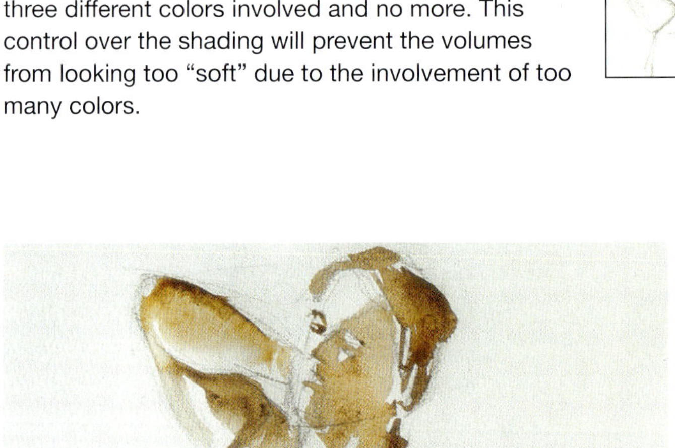

4. The areas left unpainted are as important as the painted ones. This is the secret of washes: the painted parts are the shadows that highlight the areas located next to them.

4

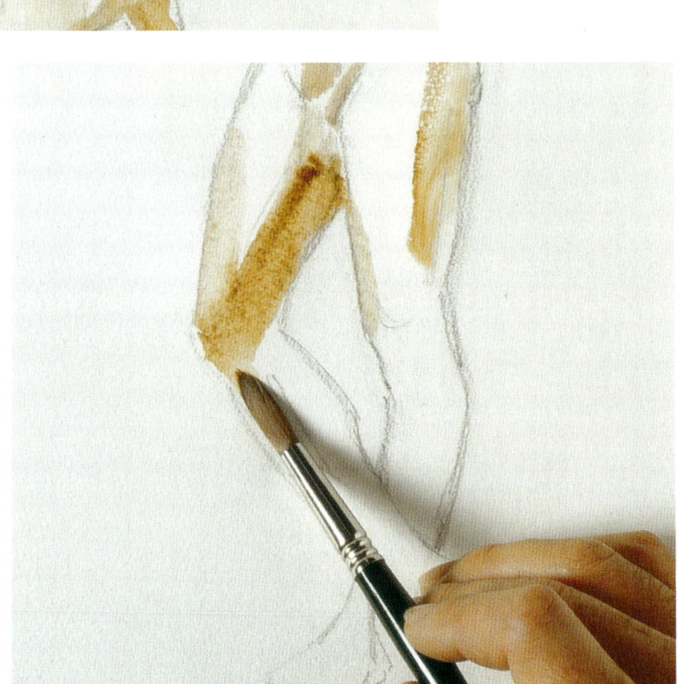

5

5. The process used for the modeling phase is to apply the color first with the tip of the brush and to spread it later, adding more or less water according to the desired tonal intensity. It is always better to create clear contrast rather than a color that is too soft and that requires repainting.

6

7

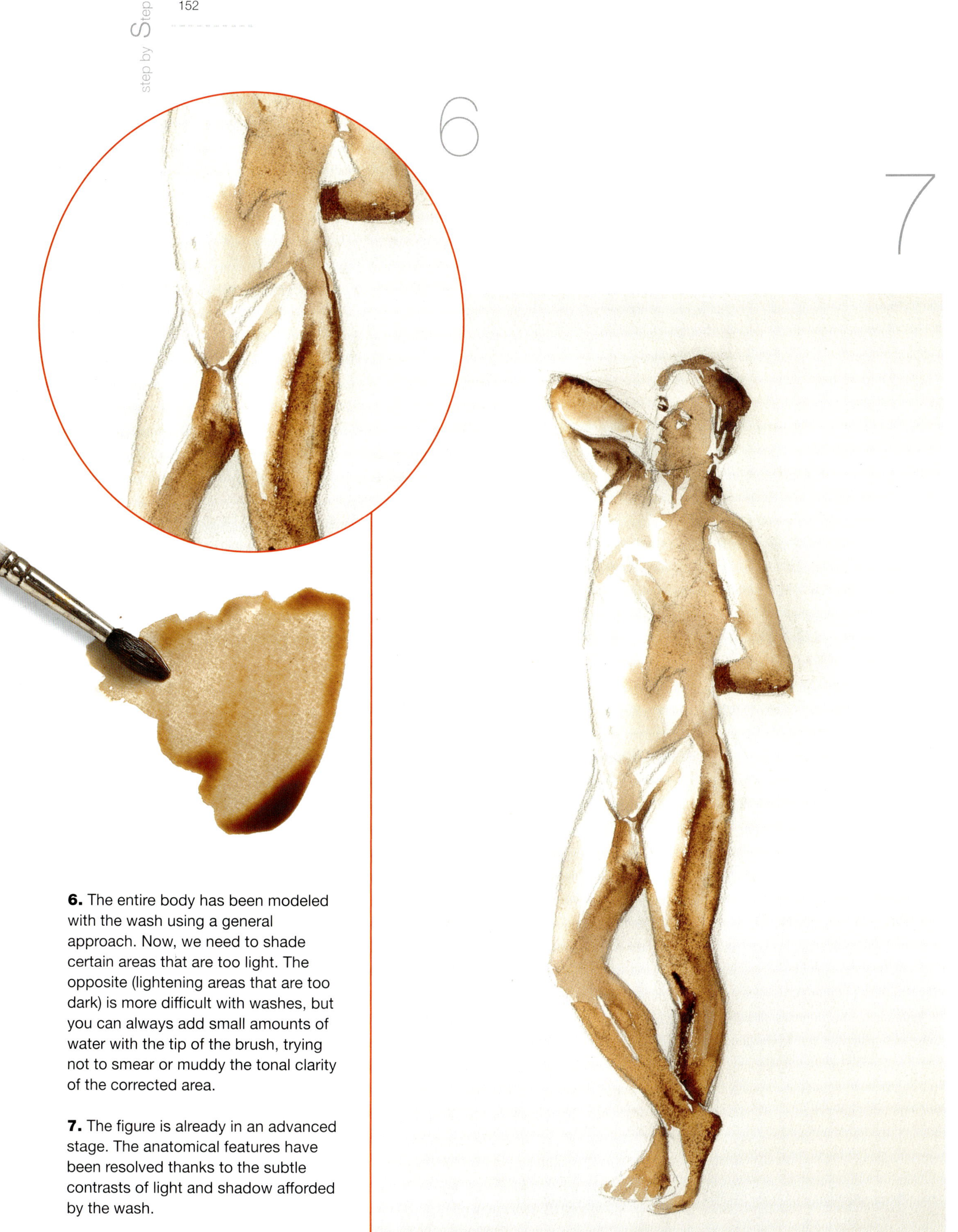

6. The entire body has been modeled with the wash using a general approach. Now, we need to shade certain areas that are too light. The opposite (lightening areas that are too dark) is more difficult with washes, but you can always add small amounts of water with the tip of the brush, trying not to smear or muddy the tonal clarity of the corrected area.

7. The figure is already in an advanced stage. The anatomical features have been resolved thanks to the subtle contrasts of light and shadow afforded by the wash.

8

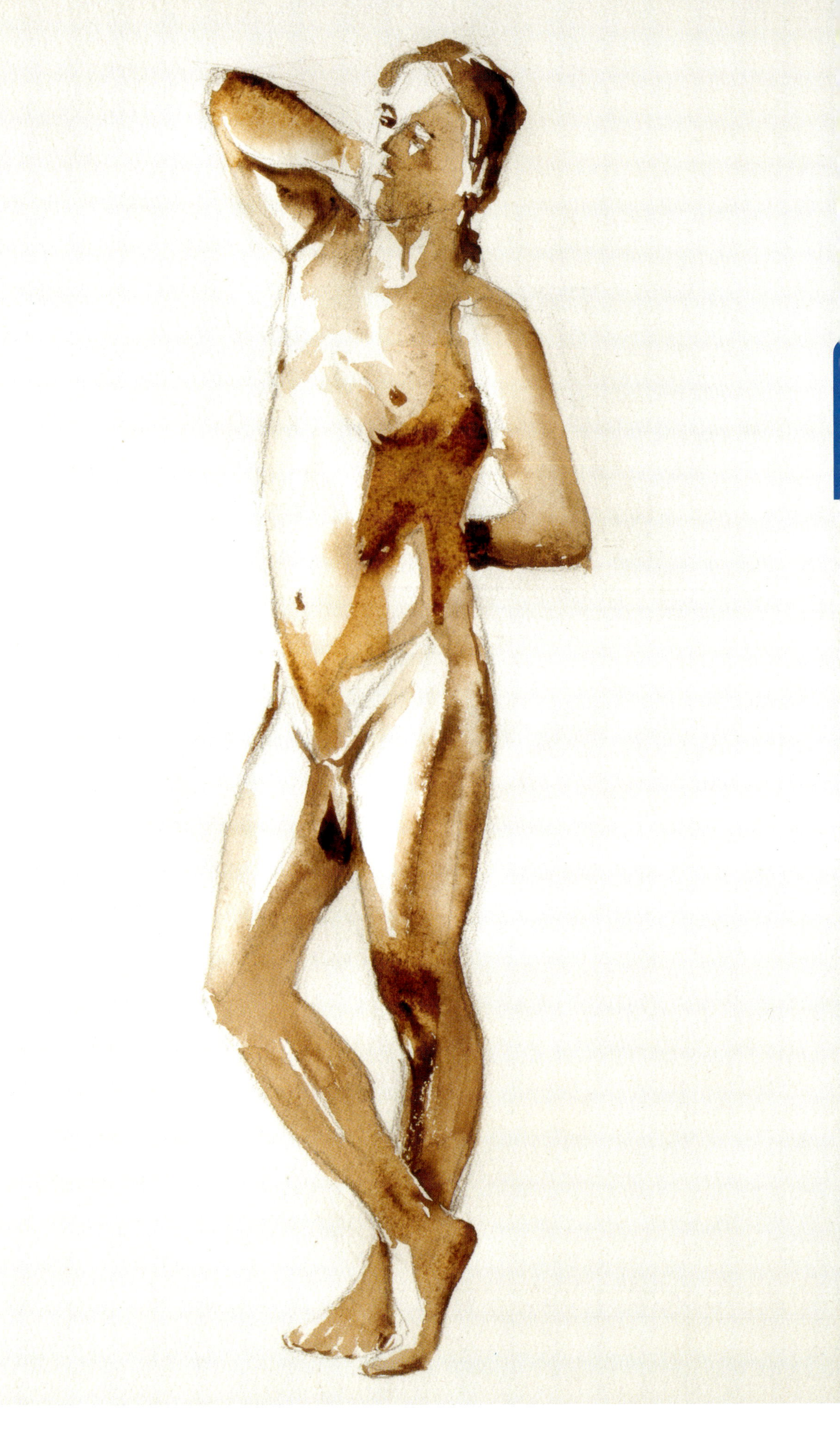

8. The representation of the anatomy with the wash technique tends to be a synthesis between volumes rather than an aggregate of very well-defined and individualized parts. In this piece we can see how the forms are resolved with areas of color that are not strictly confined to the outlines of the muscles like on the right side of the torso.

Male Figure
with Charcoal and Chalk

The back is one of the most difficult parts of the anatomy to draw. It does not have an outline that is as well defined as that of the arms or the legs (which are, after all, like cylinders attached to the body). It does not have the pronounced relief of the torso that facilitates the separation of each part either. To all of this we must tie in the muscles of the arms and legs. This is therefore an exercise that requires a complete envisioning of the anatomy of these areas of the body. To make this drawing, Óscar Sanchís uses charcoal and three different chalks in sanguine, sepia, and white tones. As usual, the initial lines will be blended until a unity has been achieved where all the volumes are presented correctly.

1

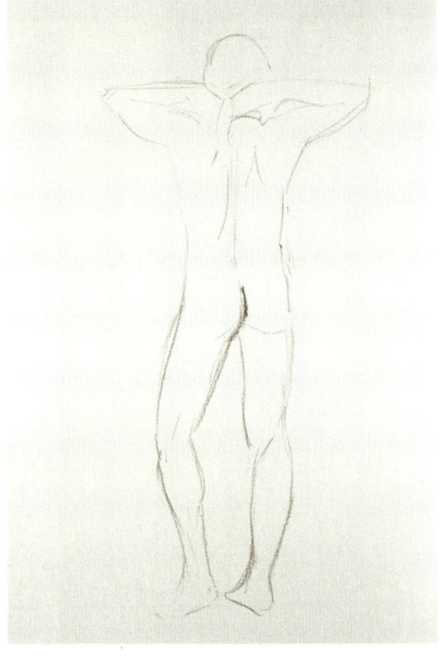

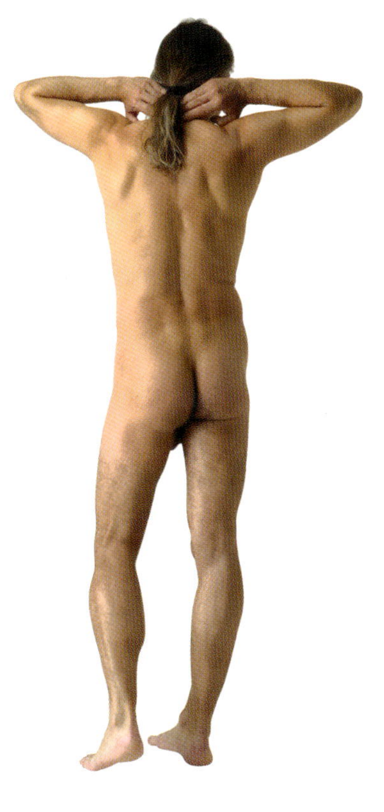

2

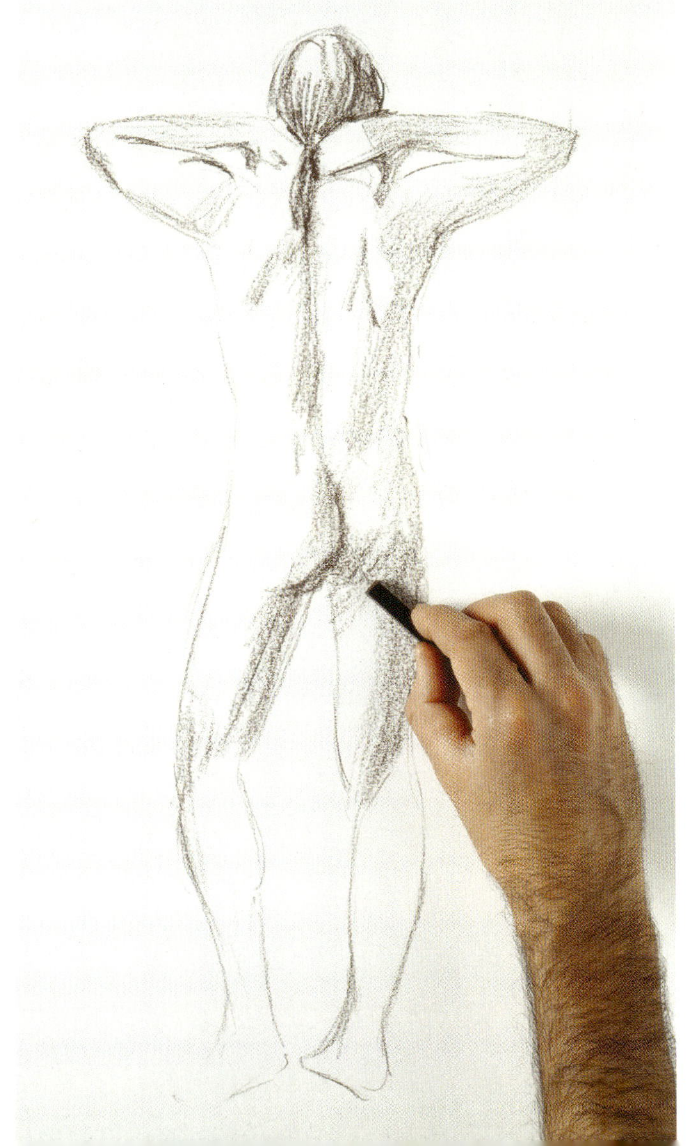

1. Initial rough sketch. The figure has been drawn with very few lines made with a hard lead graphite pencil. Just a few lines define the most significant anatomical features.

2. In this drawing the artist looks for a strong contrast between light and shadow with the subsequent volumetric effect derived from it. Naturally, before highlighting the masses in such a vigorous way, we need to make sure that all the parts of the anatomy involved in the drawing have been defined correctly.

3

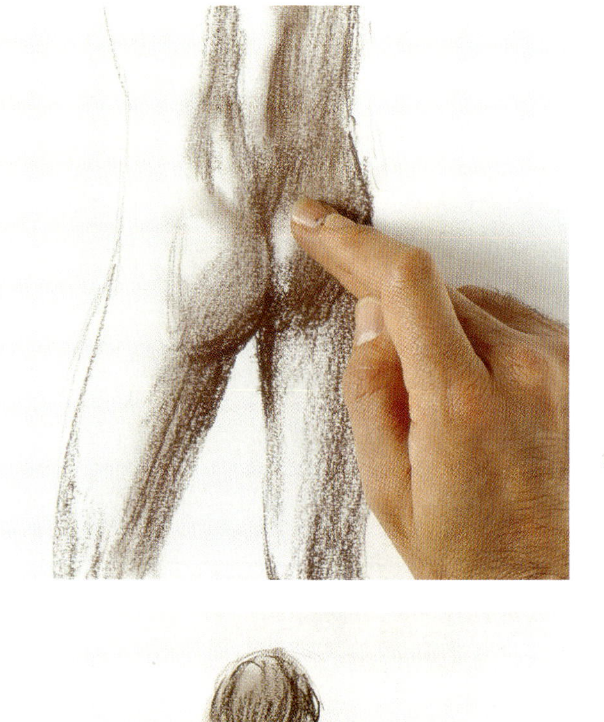

3. Light shading done with charcoal gives way to more precise modeling applied with sepia color.

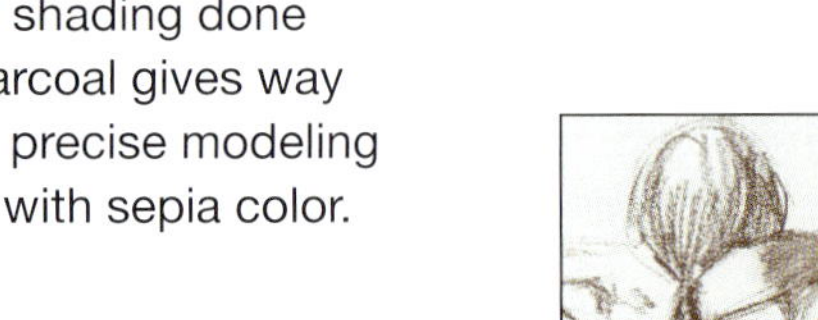

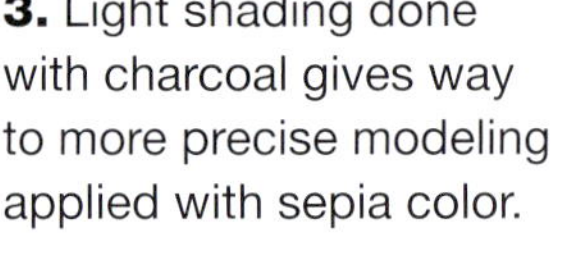

Placing the hands behind the head requires special attention right from the start to avoid the accumulation of too many trial and error lines.

4

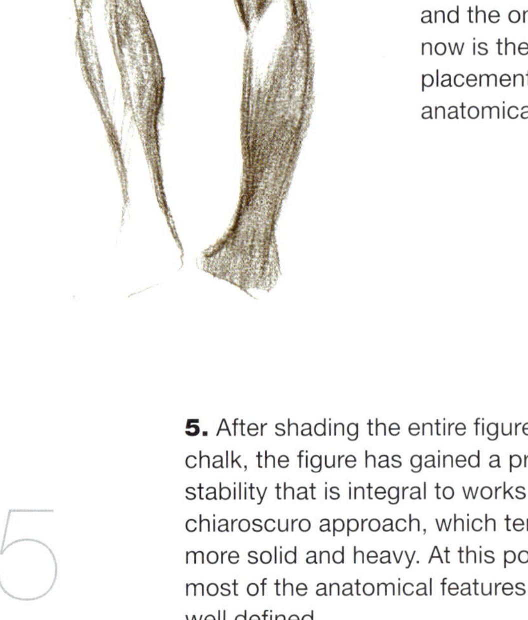

4. The shading has been applied loosely, and the only goal for now is the correct placement of the anatomical features.

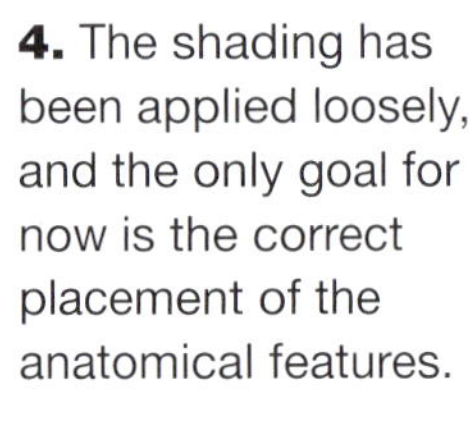

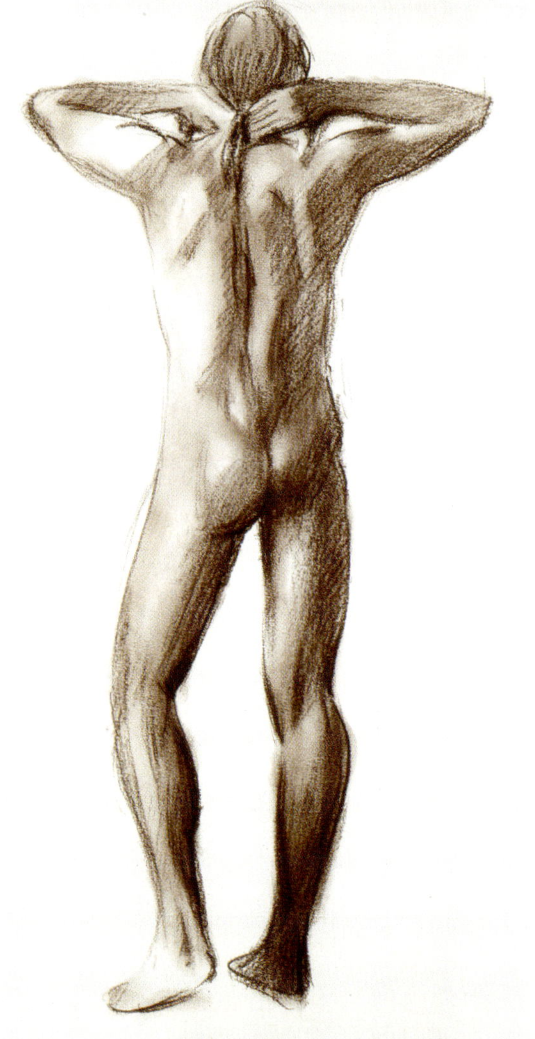

5

5. After shading the entire figure with the sepia chalk, the figure has gained a presence and stability that is integral to works based on the chiaroscuro approach, which tends to make forms more solid and heavy. At this point of the project, most of the anatomical features have been fairly well defined.

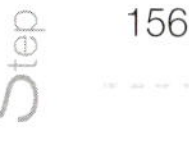

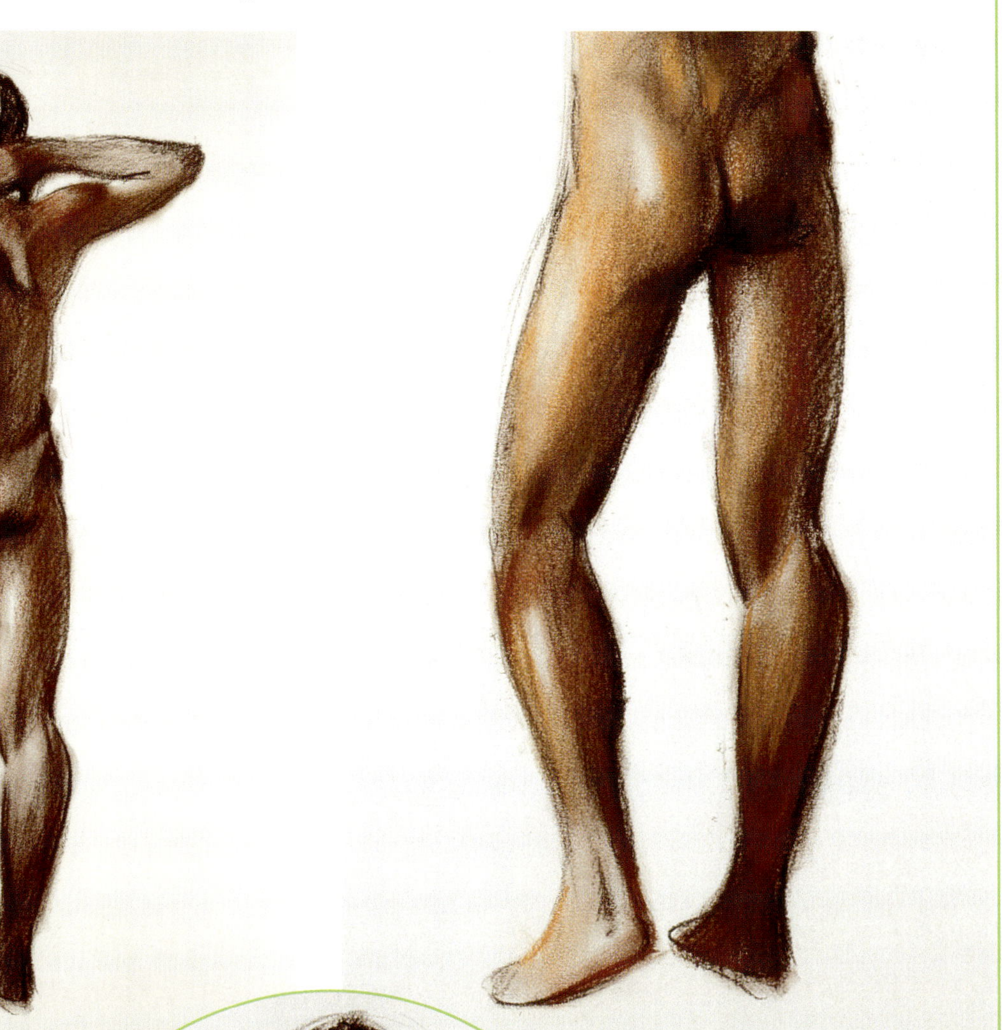

6

7

8

6. Using sanguine does not alter the modeling of the anatomy, but rather it defines it, making it stronger and warmer. The artist has applied sanguine lines and has rubbed them systematically with the finger to blend the two colors together; this has created a rich chiaroscuro where the deeper colors correspond to the chalk and the halftones to the sanguine.

7. This is the area of the body most affected by light; here, the sanguine blends are very soft and create a warm and delicate tone. The strongest lights are still those of the white of the paper, but the artist will go beyond them and apply highlights with white chalk.

8. The dorsal and lumbar areas of the spinal column have been defined with very dark shadows to create the appropriate effect of relief.

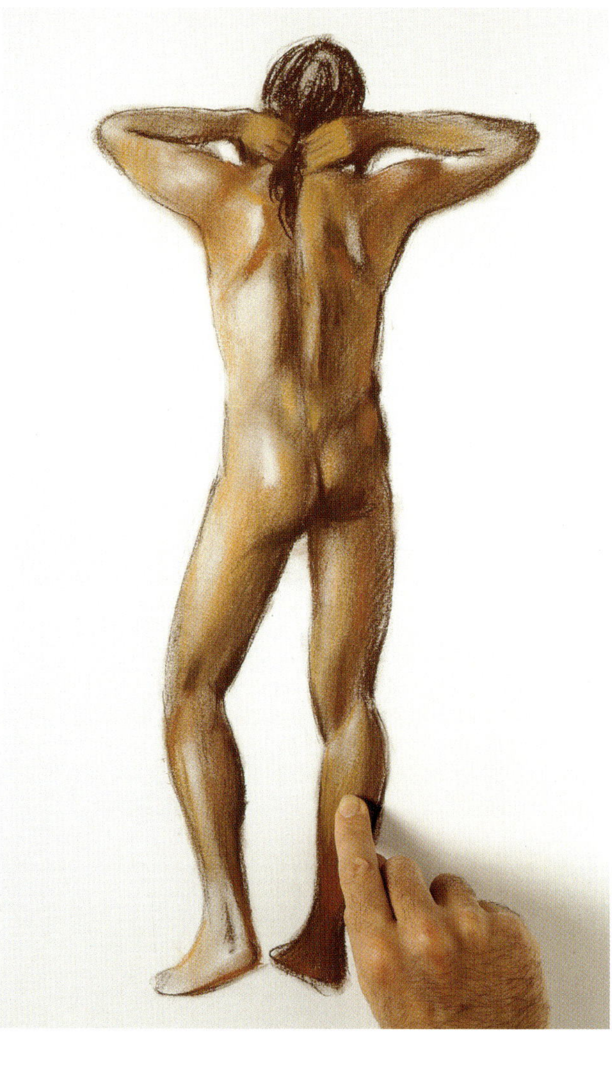

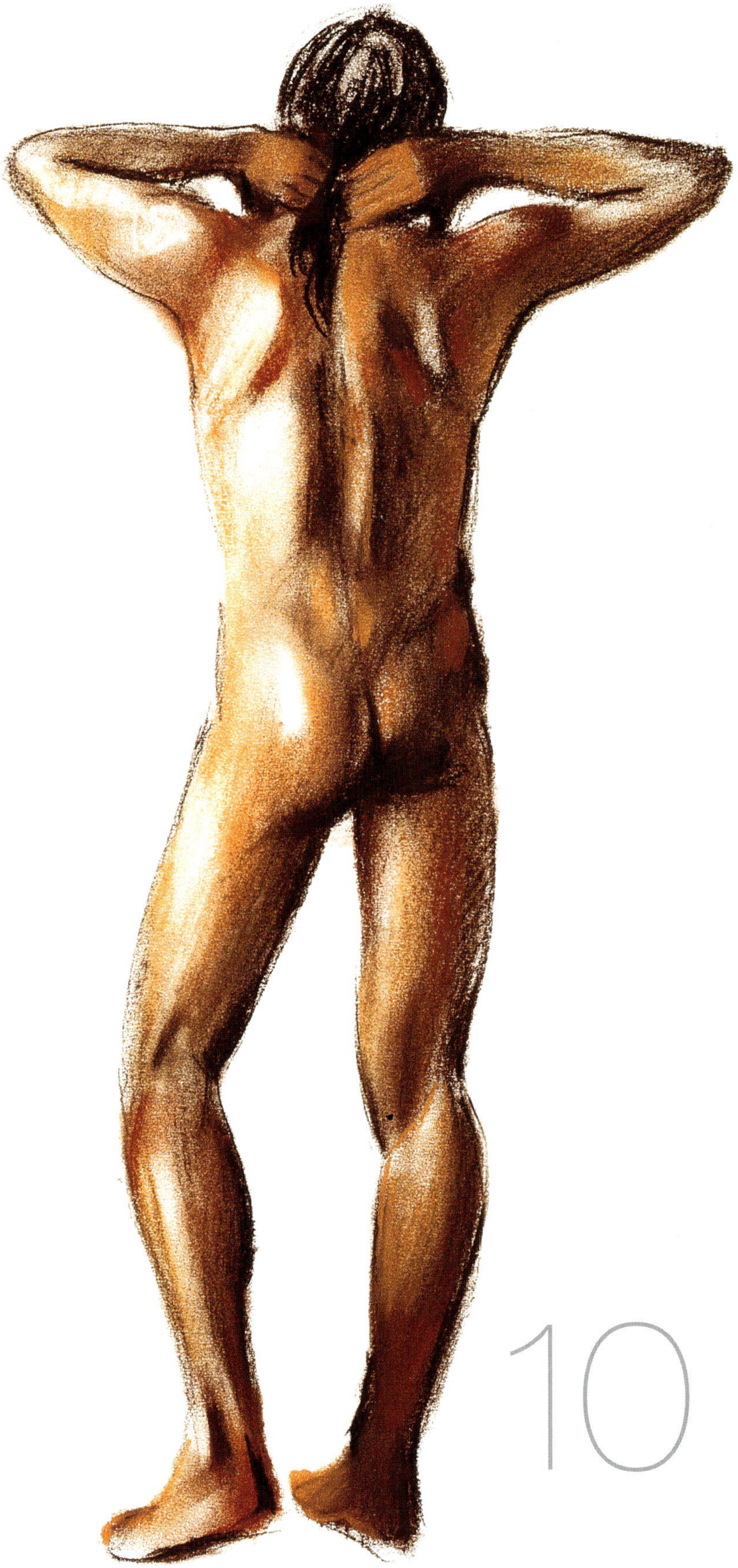

9

9. The systematic blending of the lines gives unity to the modeling of the figure. If it were not for this blending, the use of different colors would create confusion.

10. The white chalk reinforces the contours and gives a rounded effect to the entire modeling of the work. The resulting effect is a series of rich tones achieved by combining sanguine, sepia, and white. In this exercise, the power of chiaroscuro has been the expressive vehicle for the figure's anatomical strength. The spinal column stands out from the rest of the anatomical features.

10

In

ex